GLOBAL TRENDS IN INCOME INEQUALITY

GLOBAL TRENDS IN INCOME INEQUALITY

ALMAS HESHMATI

Nova Science Publishers, Inc.
New York

For permission to use material from this book please contact us:
Telephone 631-231-7269; Fax 631-231-8175
Web Site: http://www.novapublishers.com

NOTICE TO THE READER

LIBRARY OF CONGRESS CATALOGING-IN-PUBLICATION DATA

Global trends in income inequality / Almas Heshmati
    p. cm.
  Includes index.
  ISBN-13: 978-1-60021-012-9
  ISBN-10: 1-60021-012-0
  1. Income distribution. I. Heshmati, Almas.
  HC79.I5G576 2004
  339.2 – dc22

Published by Nova Science Publishers, Inc. ✦ New York

To my daughters:
Emma Shirin, Sara Shilan and Lisa Sharmin

CONTENTS

ABOUT THE AUTHOR

Almas Heshmati
University of Kurdistan Hawler and
Techno-Economics & Policy Program
College of Engineering, Seoul National University
San 56-1, Shinlim-dong, Kwanak-gu
Seoul 151-742, South Korea
Tel: +82-2-880-9141, Fax: +82-2-880-8389
E-mail: heshmati@snu.ac.kr

PREFACE

This book attempts to fill the gap in the existing literature on income inequality and income distribution by focusing on the compilation of economic concepts, statistical and econometric techniques developed and used in the measurement and empirical analysis of inequality at different levels. In particular a number of issues crucial to the studies of global income inequality are addressed. These are the concepts, measurements and decomposition of inequality, the world distribution of income. Inequality is measured at different levels such as at the global, continental, international, intra-national and regional levels. Experiences gained from the analysis of these issues are then reflected in the discussion of the data and their role in the generation of the differences in conclusion drawn regarding the disparity and direction of changes in global income inequality.

In review of recent empirical studies of global income inequality, the focus is on global income inequality with emphasis on inequality among individuals and representative individuals. The volume consists of a number of separate yet stand-alone chapters with the objective to compile a large and major collection of papers published mainly from the beginning of 1990s and onwards. The collection represents new developments in various decomposition of income and poverty measurement to illustrate methods, their usefulness and empirical results. In the evaluation of diverse methodologies their strength and weaknesses are highlighted.

This book provides readers the knowledge on the current state of measurement and decomposition techniques and also benefits when choosing appropriate approaches for specific tasks at different levels of aggregation. The collection of topics here are interrelated and very important to the practitioners. This survey is the most recent and comprehensive survey of literature and it covers the development of poverty and inequality decomposition jointly. It can serve as a bibliographical reference for the specialists. In addition it is aimed at a broad readership including: specialists, researchers, development scholars (intermediate graduate and graduate students of economics, students taking a course in development studies), non-governmental organizations, policy makers, bureaucrats, aid, and international governance agencies, as well as a useful introduction for others.

An earlier version of the manuscript was used as main teaching material for two courses: one on "Globalization, Growth, Poverty and Inequality" and another on "Topics in Applied Economics". The first course was given during February 2005 as an elective part of the three MA programmes: Globalisation, Governance, and Development Evaluation, offered at Institute for Development Policy and Management (UA-IDPM), University of Antwerp,

Antwerp, Belgium. It consists of a series of lectures on different topics in development economics – a cross-cutting theme on poverty, income inequality, growth and globalization. In addition to students enrolled in any of the three MA programmes, it is aimed as an elective course, by PhD students, as well as non-economists. The number of attendants was about 50 persons. The second course consisted of a series of lectures and served as an elective part of any PhD and Master programmes in Economics given during April 2005 at the Dongbei University of Finance and Economics (DUFE), Dalian, China. It consisted of a series of lectures on different topics in economics – a cross-cutting theme on poverty, income inequality, growth, globalization and applied industrial organization. The course was aimed to be followed, as an elective course, by Master and Ph.D. students in economics as well as non-economists and decision makers. The number of attendants was about 60 persons.

An earlier version of this book was completed while I was working at the World Institute for Development Economic Research, UNU/WIDER. I would like to thank Tony Shorrocks, Subu Subramanian, Tony Addison, Matti Pohjola, Guanghua Wan, and Machiko Nissanke for their comments and suggestion on earlier versions of Chapters 4 and 5. Thanks also go to Amit Bhandari, Farideh Ramjerdi, Dany Aoun, Inha Oh and Adam Swallow for their suggestions to improve the text. My special thanks go to Professor Danny Cassimon, Didier van Houts, and Philip Woodhouse from IDPM, Wang Qingshi and Wang Weiguo from DUFE for their kind invitation to teach this book at their universities. In undertaking revision of this book, I benefited from teaching and research at MTT Economic Research, Helsinki, Finland, Techno-Economics and Policy Program (TEPP), College of Engineering, Seoul National University, Seoul, Korea and the RATIO research institute, Stockholm. I would like to thank Kyösti Pietola from MTT, Tai-Yoo Kim from TEPP, Nils Karlson from RATIO and Ms. Hyuna Jeong for their support and encouragement. Responsibilities for errors and omissions are my own.

Chapter 1

INTRODUCTION

BACKGROUND AND MOTIVATION

There is ongoing and increasing interest in measuring and understanding the level, causes and development of global income inequality; increasing interest has been considerable particularly during the 1990s. This period was signified by a shift in research which previously focused on economic growth, the identification of the determinants of economic growth and convergence in GDP per capita across countries[1] to analyse the distribution of income, its development over time and identification of factors determining the world-wide distribution of income.[2] This shift in focus is specifically from the issues of convergence or divergence of per capita income to the long-term equalisation or polarisation of income across regions and countries of the world.

This shift in research orientation is not only a reflection of technological change and raised human capacity to create growth, wealth and in the effective use of resources, but also due to awareness of the importance of redistribution and poverty reduction. Rapid technological changes, heterogeneous economic growth and differences in countries potential to take advantage of those opportunities together with their poor redistributive policies and institutions has however resulted in large and growing disparities in the living standards within and foremost between countries of the world. The growing disparity is the key background that calls for the analysis of possible trends in global income inequality.[3]

There are a number of comprehensive surveys of income inequality and poverty. Subramanian (1997a) presents a number of essays on the measurement of inequality and poverty, with an approach that has introduced readers to the theory and applications in the

---

[1] For a selection of studies of growth and convergence in per capita incomes see: Barro (1991, 1997, 2000), Barro and Sala-i-Martin (1995), Bernard and Durlauf (1995), Bernard and Jones (1996), Caselli, Esquivel and Lefort (1996), Dowrick and Nguyen (1989), Islam (1995), Jones (2002), Lee, Pesaran and Smith (1997), Mankiw, Romer and Weil (1992), Nerlove (2000), and Quah (1993, 1996a, 1996b, 1996c, 1996d, 1997).

[2] For a selection of such recent studies on convergence in income inequality see: Quah (2002), Ravallion (2003b), Sala-i-Martin (2002a, 2002b), and Solimano (2001), and for related research on the distribution of income see: Acemoglu and Ventura (2002), Atkinson (1997, 1999, 2000), Bourguignon and Morrisson (2002), Cornia (1999), Gottschalk and Smeeding (1997), Jones (1997), Epstein and Spiegel (2002), Iacoviella (1998), Milanovic (2002a), Svedberg (2002), and Wade (2001b).

[3] For a selection of studies on trends in income inequality see: Acemoglu (2002), Caminada and Goudswaard (2001), Cornia (1999), Cornia and Kiiski (2001), Gottschalk and Smeeding (2000), Maasoumi and Joeng (1985), Milanovic (2002a), O'Rourke (2001), Park (2001), Sala-i-Martin (2002b) and Schultz (1998).

measurement of inequality and poverty. Both conceptual and technical issues of measurement are addressed and the relevance of these concerns in the context of developing country's experience explored. The chapter by Anand (1997) presents a review of the measurement of income inequality including indices (among others) based directly on the Lorenz diagram, the effect on inequality of changes in income, the ranking of income distribution and the comparison of inequality.

Another edited comprehensive and related volume on different aspects of inequality measurement is by Silber (1999). This volume begins with a foreword by Amartya Sen, discussing some conceptual issues in particular the relationship between economic inequality and non-income influences whose consequences are difficult to transform into practical implications. The contributions consist of survey articles. In the first part of the volume the emphasis is on the theoretical foundations of inequality measurement, and their extensions and applications. The second part is on decomposition of inequality, equivalence scales, multidimensional approaches of welfare analysis, lifetime versus annual income distribution, measurement of horizontal inequality and income mobility, and the interrelation between inequality, welfare and poverty.

In addition there are several surveys covering different aspect of inequality, poverty and welfare. For instance Maasoumi (1997) in his survey of empirical analysis of inequality and welfare finds that the modern theory of income distribution and welfare has experienced radical progress towards a more objective and systematic analysis of welfare and inequality. Statistical and econometric techniques have been developed but their application in empirical research is not as yet widespread. In this survey he brings together a selective body of economic concepts and econometric tools and applications to encourage a statistically sounder development of empirical work in this area. Among applications discussed and partially illustrated by Maasoumi are the measurements of world inequality by several attributes including incomes, dynamic analysis of inequality and mobility. In related research the analysis of inequality (Cowell, 2000) is placed in the context of recent developments in economics and statistics. Inequality is seen as an attempt to give meaning to the methods of characterising and the comparison of income distribution. The basic questions in inequality measurement discussed are related to individual income, income differences, the shape of income distribution and the theoretical reasoning and practical questions in understanding the real world.

THE OBJECTIVES

Biewen (2002b) in his review finds the edited volume by Silber (1999) a useful and satisfying handbook which fulfils the purpose of serving as a bibliographical reference for specialists as well as a useful introduction for others. However, Biewen presents a reservation that it focuses on the theoretical foundations and its extensions, and not other aspects of inequality measurement. This volume attempt to fill the gap in the existing literature by focusing on the compilation of economic concepts, statistical and econometrics techniques developed and used in the measurement and empirical analysis of inequality at different levels.

In particular this monograph addresses a number of issues crucial to the studies of global income inequality. These are the concepts, measurements and decomposition of inequality, the world distribution of income and inequality measured at different levels such as at the global, continental/sub-continental, international, intra-national and regional levels, and in a limited form investigates the relationships between openness, growth, inequality, poverty and globalization. Experiences gained from the analysis of these issues are then reflected in the discussion of the data underlying the literature and their role in the generation of the differences in conclusion drawn regarding the disparity and direction of changes in global income inequality. This introduction sets out the issues to be discussed and reviews briefly a number of recent surveys and collected work on global income inequality.

To survey recent empirical studies of global income inequality, the focus of present volume is on global income inequality emphasising on inequality among individuals, representative individuals and regions. It consists of a number of separate yet stand-alone chapters. It is worth to note that several studies are cited covering several countries. The objective here is to compile a large and major collection of papers published from the beginning of 1990s and onwards. The collection represents new developments in various decomposition of income and poverty measurement to illustrate methods, their usefulness and empirical results. In some cases it has been difficult to yield up a connected picture on what has been happening across the world. Although in the evaluation of diverse methodologies their merits and demerits are highlighted. In reporting research, only the empirical model specification is reported. In order to make the notation throughout the manuscript consistent minor changes are introduced to the notation of the original equations.

This volume provides readers the knowledge on the current state of measurement and decomposition techniques and also benefits when choosing appropriate approaches for specific tasks. The collection of topics here are interrelated and important foremost to the practitioners. Furthermore, this survey is the most recent and comprehensive survey of literature and it covers the development of poverty and inequality decomposition jointly. It can serve as a bibliographical reference for the specialists. The monograph is aimed at a broad readership including: specialists, researchers, development scholars[4] (intermediate graduate and graduate students of economics, students taking a course in development studies), non-governmental organizations, policy makers, bureaucrats, aid, and international governance agencies, as well as a useful introduction for others.

THE SCOPE OF THIS STUDY

Inequality can have several dimensions. We economists are mostly concerned with the income and consumption dimensions of inequality. Several inequality indices can be derived from the Lorenz diagram which is shown and discussed in Chapter 2. The most widely used index of inequality is the Gini coefficient. Subramanian (1997b) and Cowell (2000) provide

---

[4] An earlier version of the manuscript was used as main teaching material for two courses: one on "Globalization, Growth, Poverty and Inequality" and another on "Topics in Applied Economics". The first course was given as an elective part of the Ph.D. and three MA programmes offered at Institute for Development Policy and Management (UA-IDPM), University of Antwerp. The second course consisted of a series of lectures and served as an elective part of any PhD and Master programmes in Economics at the Dongbei University of Finance and Economics.

comprehensive reviews the notion and the measurement of inequality. Non-income inequality, although often income related, includes items like skill, education, opportunity, happiness, health and wealth. The effects of inequality on non-income factors of earnings and health are equally important. For instance joblessness has direct cost to the labour market and to the society. The additional burden of being unemployed upon an individual's wellbeing, the non-pecuniary cost, are an important non-monetary cost of joblessness and probably much larger in impact than the pecuniary effect in the form of the loss of income. These areas although not directly in the scope of this study are briefly discussed as well.

Different methods have been developed to decompose inequality (Pyatt 1976; Shorrocks 1980, 1982 and 1984; Fields 2000; Morduch and Sicular 2002), and changes in poverty (Kakwani and Subbaro 1990; Jian and Tandulkar 1990; Datt and Ravallion 1992; Shorrocks and Kolenikov 2001). A decomposition of changes in poverty into growth and redistribution is important in the evaluation of inequality and its impact on growth and on poverty among regions, sub-groups and sectors. In the above studies inequality is decomposed by sub-groups, income sources, causal factors and by other characteristics of the observation units. Inequality can also be decomposed at different levels of aggregation. At the national level it can be decomposed into within-subgroup and between-subgroup components while at the international level it can be decomposed into within-country and between-country components. Inequality can also at the micro level be decomposed parametrically and into permanent and transitory components of earnings. These issues are discussed in details in Chapter 3. The main benefits of parametric approaches are that the changes are conditional on various attributes and confidence intervals for disaggregated contributions to the inequality index can be constructed.

The relatively extensive literature emerging in recent years that has focused on the study of how the distribution of incomes across countries and globally has developed over time. Availability of household surveys has been improved and several standardized databases have been created. These allow analysis of income distribution at disaggregate per capita household levels. Income distribution is otherwise often analyzed at three levels of aggregation, namely global, international and intra-national. Global or world income inequality refers to inequality differences between all individuals in the world (Milanovic 2002a; Schultz 1998; Quah 1999; Bourguignon and Morrisson 2002; Sala-I-Martin 2002b), while international income inequality refers to the economic disparity between countries (Acemoglu 2002; Cornia and Kiiski 2001; Gottschalk and Smeeding 1997; Milanovic 2001). Global income inequality is discussed in Chapter 4. At the intra-national level inequality refers to the distribution of income among people within individual countries (Cameron 2000b; Cowell, Ferreira and Lichtfield 1998; Gustafsson and Shi 2002; Liebbrandt, Woolard and Woolard 2000; and others). A discussion on the benefit and limitations of each approach in the measurement of world income inequality is important for a number of reasons. This includes the desire to increase awareness of the problem, its measurement and quantification, identification of causal factors and for policy measures which affect global inequality.

Two empirical regularities identified in the distribution of income are the tendency for income per capita to converge, and an increase in inequality in the distribution of personal income in many countries. Different studies have reached different results regarding the direction of changes in world income distribution Sala-I-Martin 2002a; Bourguignon and Morrisson 1999; Maddison 2001; and Milanovic 2002a). Svedberg (2002) and Capéau and Decoster (2003) attempt to explain the reasons for such differences: the disparities largely result from the use of different measurements of income and its distribution, adjustments, the choice of base year, the selection of countries and applied population weights. Svedberg further attempts to explain why convergence in relative per capita income and growth rate across countries can co-exist with divergence in absolute per capita income between countries. The conclusions are that the relative differences between the poorest and the richest countries have increased but the relative distribution of income across all countries has remained unchanged. The use of Gini has limitations when it comes to transitions. Another review of the changes in distribution of incomes but within developing countries and of the proportion of people below the poverty line has been presented by Bigsten and Levin (2003). They do not find any systematic patterns of changes in income distribution during recent decades or any links between rapid growth and increasing inequality. However, the more recent evidence tends to confirm the negative impact of inequality on economic growth.

Income inequality, in addition to the extreme levels of global and international, can be measured at an intermediate level, equivalent to continental and sub-continental areas. This investigation examines both between and within regions consisting of continents or sub-continents. There is evidence that poverty and inequality has developed differently among transition economies (Milanovic and Ytzhaki 2001; Ivaschenko 2002; Ram 1995; Wan 2002a), East Asian countries (Kakwani and Krogkaew 2000; and You 1998); the European Union (Ritakallio 2001; Belbo and Knaus 2001; Gottschalk and Smeeding 2000; Iacoviello 1998; Lindert and Williamson 2001; Mahler 2001), Latin American (LondoNo and Szekely 2000; Wood 1997) and sub-Saharan African (Milanovic and Yitzhaki 2001; Canagarajah, Newman and Bhattamishra 2001; Svedborg 2002) countries. In several of these studies inequality and poverty are related to a number of determinant factors. Due to the availability of data, the empirical results are mainly based on the second half of the twentieth century. Chapter 5 covers a range of measures and methods frequently employed in empirical analysis of global and regional income inequality and distribution. Different determinant factors and quantification of their impacts from different studies are discussed. These results are further contrasted to those obtained based on the World Income Inequality Database (WIID) covering the same period and group of countries.

Income inequality can also be measured at a within-country regional level. Due to the limited space here in Chapter 6 the focus is on inequality in income distribution in a selection of large countries measured in terms of the population size and land area, where regions include states, provinces, federations or geographic locations within a country. Such studies focus on large countries like China (Tsui 1993; Xu and Zou 2000; Lee 2000; Gustafsson and Shi 2002), Russia (Commander, Tolstopiatenko and Yemtsov 1999; Yemtsov 2002; Luttmer 2001; Shorrocks and Kolenikov 2001; Fedorov 2002), India (Mishra and Parikh 1997; Jha 2000; Datt and Ravallion 1992) and the USA (Patridge, Rickman and Levernier 1996; Black and Dowd 1997; Zandvakili 1999; and Moffitt and Gottschalk 2002), as well as a number of smaller developing and transition countries with major impacts on global inequality and poverty. China and India experienced rapid economic growth after economic reform, accompanied by increased inequality and a reduction in poverty. The level and development of inequality has varied by location and sector. This inequality can further be decomposed into components associated with inter- and intra-sector and provincial components and their determinants in turn are identified. Analysis of within-country regional inequality can reveal the differences in the effects of factor mobility and inequality driven by structural differences between regions. Furthermore it is important to consider heterogeneity in income inequality in both level and development over time, as well as different sub-group characteristic dimensions. It is interesting to know how poverty and inequality by sub-groups was altered following structural adjustment programmes.

A number of databases are frequently used in applied growth and income inequality research. Descriptions of such databases are found in Summers and Heston (1991), Barro and Lee (1996), Deininger and Squire (1996) and Atkinson and Brandolini (2001). Despite the differences in objectives, country coverage, sources, units of measurement and income definitions, each plays an important and complementary role in growth and inequality studies. Each set of data of course has benefits and limitations, and the choice of data might affect the conclusions drawn about trends in inequality. Certain properties like consistency, income definition and measurement, changing population, household size and various variable adjustment procedures are among the important data related issues that are discussed in Chapter 7.

THE LIMITATIONS OF THIS STUDY

This volume despite its broad coverage due to space limitation excludes systematic reviews of a number of important areas that was initially aimed to be incorporated. In this context two areas are of particular interest. One is the relationship between inequality, poverty and growth and another is the link between inequality, poverty and globalization.

The Link between Inequality and Macroeconomic Variables

The world economy grows constantly but the growth pattern can differ over time and among countries. Economic downturn, crises, shocks and other factors from time to time result in negative growth in regions and countries. Large disparities and negative growth rates undermine the global integration of economies, social stability and hamper long-term economic growth. The relationship between different combinations of openness, growth, inequality and poverty is investigated by Sachs and Werner (1995), Dollar and Kraay (2001a), Person and Tabellini (1994), Deininger and Squire (1998), Goudie and Ladd (1999), van der Hoeven and Shorrocks (2003). In general, they find a positive relationship between openness and growth but differences between and within countries in the impact of growth on the poor.

In recent years the research and debate has focused on the extent to which the poor benefit from this economic growth (Ravallion 1998, 2001; Ravallion and Chen 2003; Ravallion and Datt 2000; Quah 2001), where one opinion argues that the benefits of economic growth to the poor are undermined or offset by inadequate redistributive policies and the increase in inequality. Another opinion is that despite increased inequality liberal economic policies and open markets raise the income of everyone in a society, reducing the incidence of poverty.

Empirical results from the existing cross country studies suggest that outcomes of policy measures are heterogeneous in their impact. Economic growth benefits the poor but in the absence of effective redistribution policies it may also negatively affect income distribution.

Several country-specific factors play a significant role in targeting policies to make economic growth pro-poor. Due to limited spaces here we do not in a systematic way review the causal relationship between inequality and macroeconomic variables. For a recent comprehensive review see Heshmati (2004a).

The literature investigating the relationship between openness, growth, inequality and poverty is comprehensive. In Heshmati's summary, in general the finding suggests a positive relationship between openness and growth, but its impact on distribution of income is different. There is no indication of a systematic relationship between trade and inequality, but a conflicting viewpoint about the causal effects of inequality on growth. The empirical results indicate the presence of convergence in per capita income, but divergence in income inequality. There is evidence of strong convergence among more homogenous and integrated advanced countries but also divergence among less developed countries or regions. Democratisation in Western countries has led to institutional changes and the changes in taxation and redistribution reducing inequality and poverty. The East Asian countries have been successful in coupling low inequality and high growth, while the sub-Saharan Africa has high inequality and low growth. One major shortcoming of the literature is that the simultaneity and direction of causal relationships between these four key variables has been neglected.

Empirical results on the relationship between growth, inequality and poverty, show that outcomes of policy measures are heterogeneous in their impacts. In general it is rather difficult to measure the effects of inequality and growth on the developing countries' efforts to reduce poverty in the course of economic development. Economic growth benefits the poor but at the absence of effective redistribution policies it might deteriorate the income distribution. Initial conditions, institutions, specific country structures, and time horizons each plays a significant role in targeting policies to make economic growth pro-poor. Globalization, openness and technical change have been biased to skilled labour in industrialized countries widening wage differentials suggesting positive association between openness and wage inequality. For developing countries these changes are expected to reduce wage inequality by narrowing the wage gap between skilled and unskilled workers. Regression results based on the WIID database in Heshmati (2004a) suggest that income inequality is declining over time. Inequality is also declining with the growth of income. There is significant regional heterogeneity in the levels of inequality and its development over time.

The Link between Inequality, Poverty and Globalization

Globalization describes changes in international economy and world politics. It is defined as the free movement of goods, services, labour and capital across borders. The process has made the developed economies strongly interrelated. Parallel to the rapid process of globalization, global inequality has increased, hampering the process of global integration and the growth prospects of many poor countries. Global inequality embodies both inequality between nations, as a result of divergence in their economic performance, as well as inequality within countries as a result of poor institutions, inappropriate redistributive policies, prices, resource ownership and other contributing factors. Evidence suggests that there is a large heterogeneity in the degree of globalization over time and across countries and regions. This heterogeneity causes disparity in development, especially when linked with negative effects like rising inequality within and between countries.

Research on the link between globalization and world inequality and poverty is plentiful (Lindert and Williamson 2001; O'Rourke 2001; O'Rourke and Williamson 2000; Maddison 2001; Williamson 2002; and Solimano 2001), however analysis of the link at the empirical level, with a few exceptions (Heshmati 2003; Mahler 2001; Agenor 2003; and Andersen and Herbertsson 2003) is more scarce. Globalization is generally expected to reduce poverty through faster growth in more integrated economies, but its sources and consequences remain poorly understood. Heshmati (2004b) investigate the usefulness of indices of globalization to compare countries by their integration in the world economy, and also for between and within region comparisons. They are used in regression analysis to study the causal relationship between income inequality, poverty and globalization.

The alternative indices of globalization introduced in Heshmati (2004b) quantify the level and development of globalization to rank countries. The indices are decomposed into four main components: economic integration, personal contact, technology, and political engagements. A breakdown of the indices provides possibilities to identify the sources of globalization and associate it with policy measures to bring about desirable changes. The results show that internal and external conflicts reduce the countries' globalization prospects. A low rank is often associated with political and personal factors, while high ranked countries share similar patterns in various component distributions. The mean globalization by region shows that technology factors play an important role in the ranking of regions. Simple unconditional correlation among the inequality, poverty and globalization indices show that the Gini coefficients negatively correlated with personal, technology and political components, but not correlated with the economic component. The same negative relationship holds between income inequality and the aggregate globalization indices. Increased inequality is mostly disadvantages to the poor. Globalization reduces poverty and increases the poorest's share of income and thereby reducing inequality. The reduction in poverty is mostly associated with technology component of globalization.

Conditional results from a regression analysis of the relationship between inequality, poverty and globalization in Heshmati (2004b) show that the globalization index explains only 7-11 per cent of the variations in income inequality, and 9 per cent of variations in poverty among the countries. The conditioning covariates include different globalization components and regional location of the countries. Personal contacts and technology transfers reduce inequality, while economic integration increases inequality. Political engagement is found to have no significant effects on income inequality. Economic globalization increases poverty, while personal contact reduces poverty. When controlling for regional heterogeneity, we find that the regional variable plays an important role in the explanation of variations in inequality and poverty. Several of the shortcomings of the proposed index are addressed. The index is yet in an early stage of development but the exercise has resulted in the identification of several directions along which future advances can be made. In order to make the regression results on the link between globalization, inequality and poverty more stable and covering different phases of globalization, one should extend the data both in time and country dimensions.

ORGANIZATION OF THE STUDY

Rest of the monograph is organized as follows. Chapter 2 is a review of several inequality indices and their generalizations used in the analysis of income and non-income inequality. Chapter 3 looks at the measurement and decomposition of income inequality by sub-groups and income sources and decomposition of the changes in poverty into growth and redistribution components. The chapter also contains a discussion of the distinction between permanent and transitory components of earnings and statistical inference for inequality measurement. Alternative ways of measuring inequality among individuals and inter- and intra-country inequality and the distribution of income is addressed in Chapter 4, where factors affecting the shape of world distribution of income and redistribution are discussed. A similar decomposition based on continents and sub-continents around the world are reviewed in Chapter 5. Here we examine another dimension of inequality by looking at the inter- and intra-regional inequality in the world. Empirical results found in the literature on inequality at the regional level in a selection of large countries and those based on the WIID material is found in Chapter 6. The data issues are discussed in Chapter 7. Major databases, data quality and consistency, variable definitions and measurements, various adjustment procedures, changing population over time, and other important data issues are covered. The final Chapter 8 contains summary and conclusions.

Chapter 2

INEQUALITIES AND THEIR MEASUREMENT

ABSTRACT

This chapter is a review of the recent advances in the measurement of inequality. Inequality can have several dimensions. Economists are mostly concerned with the income and consumption dimensions of inequality. Several inequality indices including the most widely used index of inequality namely the Gini coefficient is discussed. Non-income inequality includes inequality in skills, education, opportunities, happiness, health, wealth, and others. The direct and indirect effects of inequality in non-income factors on earnings and health are discussed. Results from reviewing the literature suggest presence of a relationship between inequality in income and non-income dimensions. This indicates that one should account for the interrelationship between the different dimensions in the measurement and analyses of inequalities.

Keywords: Income inequality, inequality indices, income distribution

INTRODUCTION

There is ongoing and increasing interest in measuring and understanding the level, causes and the development of inequality during 1990s. This period signified by a shift in research which was previously focused on economic growth, the identification of the determinants of economic growth and convergence in GDP per capita across countries to the analysis of distribution of income, its development over time and the identification of factors determining the distribution of income. This shift is focused specifically from the issues of convergence or divergence of per capita incomes to the long-term equalisation or polarisation of incomes across regions and countries of the world. This shift is not only a reflection of technological change and raised human capacity to create growth, wealth and in the effective use of resources, but also due to the awareness of growing disparity and the importance of redistribution and poverty reduction. The growing disparity calls for the analysis of possible trends in global income inequality.

Inequality can have many dimensions. Economists are concerned specifically with the economic or monetarily dimension related to individual or household income and consumption. However, this is just one perspective and inequality can be linked to the inequality in skills, education, opportunities, happiness, health, life expectancy, welfare, assets and social mobility. This chapter will, in reviewing the literature on inequality, its measurement and determinants, the chapter gives attention to the relationship between income inequality and the non-income inequality dimensions. Inclusion of the material in this chapter is necessary and relevant for the subsequent chapters.

Remaining parts of the chapter are organised as follows. In Section 2 distribution and inequality of income are illustrated in the Lorenz diagram. Section 3 introduces several inequality indices. Generalizations of Gini index is discussed in Section 4. Section 5 is on the link between inequality and mobility. Section 6 and 7 discusses income and non-income inequalities. The final Section concludes.

THE LORENZ CURVE

Income inequality refers to the inequality of the distribution of individuals, household or some per capita measure of income among the population of a country.[1] In illustrations we follow the notation found in Anand (1997). An income distribution is a vector of incomes, $x = (x_1, x_2, ..., x_n)$, where x_i indicate the income of the ith individual in a society consisting of n individuals. The mean of the distribution of x and its dimensionality are written as $\mu(x)$ and $n(x)$. Here income is a continuous random variable bounded within the interval $x_0 (\geq 0)$ and $\bar{x}$. The density, distribution and the first moment functions for a continous random variable are $f(x), F(x)$, and $\Phi(x)$. Where $f(x), F(x) = \int_{x_0}^{\bar{x}} f(y)dy$, and $\Phi(x) = 1/\mu \int_{x_0}^{\bar{x}} yf(y)dy$ are the proportion of the population with income not exceeding x, cumulative proportion of the population with income not exceeding x, and cumulative share in total income respectively. The mean distribution is $\mu = \int_{x_0}^{\bar{x}} yf(y)dy$.

The graph of $\Phi(x)$ against $F(x)$ is the Lorenz (1905) curve representing the inequality of income distribution. The divergence of a Lorenz curve for perfect equality and the Lorenz curve for a given income distribution is measured by some index of inequality. The most widely used index of inequality is the Gini coefficient. The distribution and inequality of income is illustrated in the Lorenz diagram, Figure 2.1.

The Lorenz curve plots the cumulative share of total income against the cumulative proportion of income receiving units. It is used in analysing the size distribution of income and wealth, to estimate the Gini index and other measures of inequality and poverty. However, an important drawback of the traditional models of the Lorenz curve is the lack of satisfactory fit over the entire range of a given income distribution. There are two parametric approaches to estimate the Lorenz curve (Ryu and Slottje, 1999). In the first approach one

---

[1]   For a review of the notion of inequality and alternative ethical theories see Subramanian (1997a). Cowell (2000) provides a comprehensive survey where analysis of inequality is placed in the context of recent developments in economics and statistics. The focus is on inequality measurement to give meaning to comparisons of income distributions. The natural limitations of the subject and answers to a number of questions raised are also discussed.

assumes a hypothetical statistical distribution for income distribution on which to base the estimate of the Lorenz curve (McDonald and Xu, 1995). In the second approach, a specific functional form is fit to the Lorenz curve directly to estimate the empirical Lorenz curves (Ryu and Slottje 1996; and Chotikapanich and Griffiths 2002).

The estimated Lorenz curve is sensitive to the errors in survey data. The robustness properties of inequality and poverty measures assuming contaminated data and using parametric and non-parametric methods with illustrations are considered in Cowell and Victoroa-Feser (1996a and 1996b). Hasegawa and Kozumi (2003) propose an alternative approach to estimate Lorenz curve with contaminated data using Bayesian non-parametric analysis and presents a method for removing the contaminated observations. Results obtained using both simulated and real data suggests that this approach estimates the Lorenz curve and Gini indices adequately.

A further drawback of the traditional models of the Lorenz curve is that they lack satisfactory fit over the entire range of a given income distribution. Ogwang and Rao (2000) propose two hybrid Lorenz curve, namely the additive models and the multiplicative models by the combination of traditional models which are written as:

$$
\begin{aligned}
&y = f(p) = \delta\, f_1(p) + (1-\delta) f_2(p) \quad \text{and} \\
&y = f(p) = f_1(p)^\gamma f_2(p)^\lambda
\end{aligned}
\tag{2.1}
$$

where $0 \le \delta \le 1, \gamma \ge 1, \lambda \ge 1$, and the subscripts 1 and 2 denote the two additive and multiplicative descriptions of a Lorenz curve. A comparison of the performance of the hybrid and traditional curves shows that the hybrid models are flexible and perform better in fitting different portion of the observed income distribution as well. This is illustrated by using US income data for 1977.

INEQUALITY INDICES

Several inequality indices can be derived from the Lorenz diagram. The Lorenz Curve construction also gives us a rough measure of the amount of inequality in income distribution. The measure is called the Gini Coefficient. Computation of the Gini Coefficient is illustrated in Figure 2.1. The Gini coefficient is a standard measure of inequality defined as the area between the Lorenz curve and the line of perfect equality divided by the area below the perfect equality line as expressed in the following formula:

$$
Gini = 1 - \sum_{i=0}^{n-1} (F_{i+1} - F_i)(\Phi_{i+1} + \Phi_i)
\tag{2.2}
$$

where F and Φ are as previously defined (see Figure 2.1). The index lies within the interval 0 (perfect equality) and 1 (perfect inequality). Among other notable measures of inequality are: the range, the variance, the squared coefficient of variation, the variance of log incomes, the absolute and relative mean deviations, and Theil's two inequality indices (see Anand 1997).

The range (RGE) and the variance (VAR) are the two common statistical measures of dispersion for a distribution in general. These are useful measures in the context of income. The range is defined as the absolute difference between the highest and the lowest income levels. The measure is normalized by dividing the range by the mean income:

(2.3) $RGE = (x_{max} - x_{min})/\mu$

where the arithmetic mean income is $\mu = 1/n\sum_{i=1}^{n} y_i$. The method is very sensitive to the extreme observations. The variance of income is written as:

(2.4) $VAR = \text{var}(y) = \dfrac{1}{n}\sum_{i=1}^{n}(y_i - \mu)^2$.

The squared coefficient of variation (SCV) is obtained by dividing the variance with squared mean:

(2.5) $SCV = VAR/\mu^2$.

In similarity with the range, the variance and squared coefficient of variation are also sensitive to the extreme observations. The variance of logarithm of income (VLI) can be written as:

(2.6) $VLI = \text{var}(\log y) = \dfrac{1}{n}\sum_{i=1}^{n}(\log y_i - \log \tilde{\mu})^2$

where

(2.7) $\tilde{\mu} = \dfrac{1}{n}\sum_{i=1}^{n}\log y_i$

is the geometric mean income of the distribution. Finally, the first Theil's entropy index (T) of inequality is defined as:

(2.8) $T1 = \dfrac{1}{n}\sum_{i=1}^{n}\dfrac{y_i}{\mu}\log\dfrac{y_i}{\mu}$.

The second measure can be written as:

(2.9) $T2 = \sum_{i=1}^{n}(1/n)\log\dfrac{(1/n)}{(y_i/Y)} = \dfrac{1}{n}\sum_{i=1}^{n}\log\dfrac{\mu}{y_i}$

where $Y = n\mu$ is the total income. The $T2$ is analogous to $T1$ except that it reverses the role of income shares (y_i/Y) and population shares $(1/n)$. Both Theil's indices measure the divergence between income shares and population shares, but using different distance functions.

Anand (1997) discuss indices based on the Lorenz diagram and also several other indices. The Absolute Mean Difference (AMD) index is among the indices based on the Lorenz diagram as an alternative definition to the Gini coefficient (AGC) is specified as:

(2.10) $AGC = 1/2(AMDiff / \mu)$

where $AMDiff = \int_0^\infty \int_0^\infty |x - y| f(x) f(y) dx dy$ is the absolute mean difference of two income distributions of x and y. The AMD is more widely known as Gini's mean difference. AGC can also be defined as one-half of the relative mean difference:

(2.11) $AGC = 1/2(AMDev / \mu)$

where $AMDev = \int_0^\infty |y - \mu| f(y) dy$ is the absolute mean deviation. These absolute and relative definitions are equivalent. Another measure of inequality based on the Lorenz diagram is the value of the maximum discrepancy (p^*) between the line of perfect equality and the Lorenz curve written as:

(2.12) $MD = \left[p^* - L(p^*) \right] = 1/2(AMDev / \mu) = RMDev / 2$

where $RMDev$ is the relative mean deviation. Another divergence measure proposed is based on the area of the largest triangle between the Lorenz curve and the line of equality and the area below the line of perfect equality. This measure reduces to the value of MD.

We have listed several inequality indices and showed how these are measured. The indices have different properties that can be used in their ranking, relevance and performance evaluation. There are three basic properties that one would expect that the above indices of inequality to satisfy: mean or scale independence, population size independence and the Pigou-Dalton condition. According to the first two properties the index remains invariant if everyone's income or if the number of people at each income level is changed by the same proportion, respectively. The third condition states that the value of an index is reduced if there is a rank preserving transfer of income from a richer to a poorer.

The Gini coefficient and the squared coefficient of variation satisfy all three conditions, while the relative and absolute mean difference and the range measures satisfy only the first two conditions but violate the Pigou-Dalton condition, if formulated in strict sense, by ignoring the distribution inside the range. The variance measure violates the mean independence property. Unlike the variance of income, the variance of log income is a mean independent measure. The two Theil's inequality measures also satisfy each of the three desirable properties.[2]

---

[2]   For more details on the properties of the different indices of inequality see Anand (1997).

GENERALIZATIONS OF THE GINI COEFFICIENT

Generalization of the Gini coefficient in the sense of transfer sensitivity is important. A generalization of the Gini coefficient, called the extended Gini coefficient, was proposed by Kakwani (1980), Donaldson and Weymark (1980) and Yitzhaki (1983). The generalized Gini is further discussed by Barrett and Pendakur (1995), Xu (2000) and Zitikis and Gastwirth (2002). The new index accommodates differing aversions of inequality. Empirical estimation of the extended index has been limited to the covariance formula suggested by Lerman and Yitzhaki (1989):

$$(2.13) \quad \hat{G}_1(v) = -\frac{v}{\bar{x}} \sum_{i=1}^{M} p_i (x_i - \bar{x}) \left[(1 - \hat{\pi}_i)^{v-1} - m \right]$$

where $\hat{\pi}_i = (\pi_i + \pi_{i-1})/2$, $p_i = 1/M$ is the proportion of observation in each of the M income groups, $\pi_i = p_1 + p_2 + ... + p_i$ is the cumulative proportion of observations in the income groups, $m = \sum_i p_i (1 - \hat{\pi}_i)^{v-1}$, and $v > 1$ is an inequality aversion factor. The extended Gini is equal to the original Gini coefficient when the aversion factor $v = 2$. Chotikapanich and Griffiths (2001) suggest an alternative estimator, obtained by approximating the Lorenz curve by a series of linear segments:

$$(2.14) \quad \hat{G}_2(v) = 1 + \sum_{i=1}^{M} \left(\frac{\phi_i}{p_i} \right) \left[(1 - \pi_i)^v - (1 - \pi_{i-1})^v \right]$$

where $\pi_i = p_1 + p_2 + ... + p_i$ is the cumulative proportion of observations, and $\phi_i = p_i x_i / \sum_j p_j x_j$ is the proportion of income. The covariance and the linear segment estimators are identical for the original Gini coefficient ($\hat{G}_1(v) = \hat{G}_2(v)$ if $v = 2$) but differ for the extended Gini coefficient where $v > 1$. In a Monte Carlo experiment designed to assess the relative bias and efficiency (relative variance and mean-squared-error) of the two estimators, Chotikapanich and Griffiths shows that the two estimators have similar properties when calculated from individual observations or from grouped data where the number of the group is 30 or more. The dimensions over which sensitivity was assessed were: (I) the distribution function, (ii) value of aversion parameter ($v = 1.33, 1.67, 2, 3, 5$), (iii) number of income groups ($M = 10, 20, 30$), and (iv) drawing 5,000 samples each of size 2,000. However, when calculated from grouped data with 20 or fewer groups, the linear segment estimator outperforms the covariance estimator in terms of both bias and mean-squared-error. The log-normal where $\log(x)$ is normally distributed with mean $\mu = 5$ and standard deviation $\sigma = 1.5$, and Singh and Maddala (1976) distributions:

$$(2.15) \quad \pi = F(x) = 1 - \frac{1}{\left(1 + a_1 x^{a_2}\right)^{a_3}}$$

are used as hypothetical income distributions, where $a_1 = 1/b$, $a_2 = a\alpha$, $a_3 = 1/a$, and $b = 1/e^{c_1}$, where c_1 is a constant integration in the three parameters of the distribution. Empirical results in Singh and Maddala (1976) based on US income data shows that the function suggested above gives a better fit than the log-normal and gamma distributions of income.

INEQUALITY AND MOBILITY

This section provides a very brief review of the link between inequality and mobility. A more detailed review of mobility indices will be given in Chapter 3. Static analysis of distributions does not provide information about changes in the relative positions of different units over time. Measures of mobility are constructed when data are provided in the form of a transition matrix illustrating the dynamic movements of different units over time. Shorrocks (1978a) explores some of the issues involved in the construction of mobility measures, presenting a number of properties required for an index of mobility, a proposed set of axioms and discussion of the problems of comparing matrices defined over different time intervals. Shorrocks discusses an index that is incompatible with the objective notion of perfect mobility but able to compensate for differing time periods important for the observed mobility.

King (1983) discusses horizontal equity and social mobility, proposing an alternative index of overall inequality which is possible to be decomposed into vertical and horizontal equity components. King derives a functional form for the social welfare function and presents results from an application of the index to UK households to a model of optimum lump-sum taxation. The proposed index is expected to supplement the analysis of the effect of tax reform on the level and distribution of welfare by explicitly accounting for horizontal equity or social mobility. Maasoumi (1996) surveys the two main welfare theoretic approaches to the measurement of mobility. One is based on transition matrices (Shorrocks, 1978b) and their reduction to a scalar measure, and the other is a generalization of the index initiated by Shorrocks (1978a) labelled the Maasoumi–Shorrocks–Zandvakili 'inequality reducing' measure applied to long-run incomes and describes statistical methods for their implementations. Some popular mobility indices are also analyzed.

INCOME INEQUALITY

Traditional measures of inequality, such as the Gini coefficient computed for a single year, do not capture much about what is happening over time and/or within the income distribution of a particular society. Two societies with exactly the same Gini coefficient, could be extremely different in terms of mobility, individual opportunity and vulnerability and their intergenerational differences over time (see Graham, 2002).

In reviewing the literature on income inequality it is important to distinguish between inequalities measured at different levels, its decomposition into different components and to identify their determinants. Pyatt (1976) introduced a decomposition where the overall Gini is broken into three components

$$(2.16) \quad Gini = (m' p)^{-1} p' E p$$

where p and m are the k-element column vectors of population proportions (p_i) and average income of individuals in population group i (m_i), and E is a $k \times k$ matrix with (i, j) elements. An empirical illustration of the disaggregation based on a 1973 household survey of income distribution in Sri Lanka in which the total population of income receiver is classified geographically by location in urban, rural or estate areas. The Gini is the sum of three non-negative parts. The components are between-groups due to differences in mean incomes between groups, the within-group due to variations in income within groups, and overlapping component due to overlaps between the income ranges in different groups. It is also suggested that the method may have relevance for the study of migration from one group to another and their discrimination.

The above decomposition is applicable to the aggregate levels of data where inequality is decomposed into three components. At the country level these are within country, between country and overlapping components. The first component reflects inequality due to the differences in income between the recipients in individual countries. The second component accounts for the differences in mean incomes among the countries, while the third component reflects the homogeneity of the population (Yitzhaki, 1994) and appears because the Gini coefficient is not exactly decomposable by recipients. Using a similar Pyatt-type decomposition technique the index of world inequality can be decomposed into international, national and overlapping or residual inequality components. At the disaggregate level the overall inequality is decomposed into within-subgroup, between-subgroup, and overlapping components. Here the subgroup refers to the sub-groups of a population.

International inequality refers to the inequality across countries due to the differences in per capita income among them. Here the unit of analysis is country and the intra-country income differences among its citizens are ignored. Among the important methodological considerations in studies of inter-national inequality are the uses of exchange, the source of income data, the reference unit, data coverage and how to weight countries by their population. In the measurement of world inequality the unit of analysis is preferably the citizens of the world rather than countries (Milanovic, 2002a). Here the distribution of income is the outcome of all three (within country, between country and overlapping) components. The decomposition formula is:

$$
\begin{aligned}
Gini &= \sum_{i}^{n} G_i p_i \pi_i + \sum_{i}^{n} \sum_{j>i}^{n} \left(\frac{y_j - y_i}{y_i} \right) \pi_i p_j + L \\
&= \sum_{i}^{n} G_i p_i \pi_i + \frac{1}{\mu} \sum_{i}^{n} \sum_{j>i}^{n} (y_j - y_i) p_i p_j + L
\end{aligned}
$$

(2.17)

where y_i is mean income of country i, G_i is Gini coefficient of country i, π_i is income share of country I in total income of the region, p_i is country's population share, μ is the mean income of the region, and L is the overlapping component. The national inequality component refers to the disparity of the distribution of income within a country. It serves as an informative complement to the two extreme cases of inter-national and aggregate world income inequalities.

NON-INCOME INEQUALITY

Income inequality is just one dimension of inequality. Other dimensions include inequality in skills, education, opportunities, happiness, health, life-years, welfare, assets and social mobility. It should be noted that this monograph is concerned primarily with the income dimension, but in both principle and practice, income inequality could both influence and be influenced by non-income inequality. A selection of studies analyzing different non-income inequalities, their interrelationship and their relations with income inequality found in the economic and sociology literatures are briefly given below.

Relationship between Inequality in Income and Education

Education has positive effects on earnings. Differences in opportunities to invest in human capital, its levels and quality, together with poor redistributive policies may result in increased inequality. Higher educational attainment and more equal distribution of education should enhance economic growth and more equal income distribution in a society. Due to limited number of relevant studies that are not country specific but general, no distinction is made between studies of inequality in education or skills and studies analysing the link between inequality in income and that in education or skills.

Castello and Domenech (2002) provide new measures of human capital inequality for a panel of countries. Taking school attainment levels they compute Gini coefficients and the distribution of education by quintiles for 108 countries over five-year intervals from 1960 to 2000. The human capital Gini coefficient is computed as:

$$(2.18) \quad Gini^h = \frac{1}{2\overline{H}}\sum_{i=0}^{3}\sum_{j=1}^{3}\left|\hat{x}_i - \hat{x}_j\right|n_i n_j = n_0 + \frac{n_1 x_2(n_2 + n_3) + n_3 x_3(n_1 + n_2)}{n_1 x_2 + n_2(x_1 + x_2) + n_3(x_1 + x_2 + x_3)}$$

where $\overline{H}$ is the average schooling years of the population aged above 15 years, i and j denote different levels of education (no schooling (0), primary (1), secondary (2), and higher education (3)), n_i and n_j are the shares of population with a given level of education, x_i and x_j are average schooling years of each educational level and $\hat{x}_i$ and $\hat{x}_j$ are their cumulative averages, $\hat{x}_0 \equiv x_0 = 0$, $\hat{x}_1 \equiv x_1$, $\hat{x}_2 \equiv x_1 + x_2$, and $\hat{x}_3 \equiv x_1 + x_2 + x_3$. Here

(18) is an empirical version of (10) for 3 groups. The results show that most countries have tended to reduce the inequality in human capital distribution. Moreover, human capital inequality measures provide more robust results than income inequality in the estimation of growth and investment equations. Yemen and the US are found to be at the extremes of the distribution. In a regression of human capital inequality accounting for country specific effects Castello and Domenech estimate the following simple linear trend model:

$$(2.19) \quad Gini_{it}^h = \alpha_i + \beta\, Trend_t + v_{it}$$

where they test for stability of within country and between country variability. The test results show that differences in the distribution of education across countries $(\alpha_i \neq \alpha, \forall i)$ are substantial, and countries have tended to reduce the inequality in human capital over time $(\beta < 0)$. A process of convergence in human capital equality has taken place. Inequality in education is associated with lower investment rate and lower income growth rates. They conclude that, it is desirable that policies aimed to promote growth taking both the level and distribution of education into account.

The effects of inequality in skills on inequality in earnings across advanced major English-speaking and a number of continental European Union countries was investigated by Devroye and Freeman (2001). Using standard adult literacy test scores the results indicate that skill inequality explains only about 7 per cent of the cross-country differences in earnings inequality. Aghion (2002) argues that wage inequality between educational groups in developed economies has increased. The within educational groups inequality is larger, but unlike the between group it affects the temporary component of income. The persistence of increased inequality in transition countries is expected by Aghion and Commander (1999) to depend on the pace at which the acquisition of skills takes place and on the evolution of the educational system in the transition economies. Proper education policies can dampen the increase in wage inequality.

The relationship between inequality in education and inequality in income is investigated by Cornia and Kiiski (2001) using aggregated country level data. Empirically, inequality in education (see references cited therein) rises until the average number of years of schooling reaches 6.3 and declines thereafter. However, the threshold increases with economic development and adoption of skill-intensive technologies. Differences in educational achievement in Latin America and sub-Saharan Africa are identified to be important sources of income inequality in the two regions. Empirical evidence shows that increased educational attainment increased inequality in other geographical regions as well (see Cameron, 2000b). At the international level De Gregorio and Lee (2002) using cross-section and time-series of countries present evidences on how higher educational attainment and more equal distribution of education make income distribution more equal.

Eicher and Garcia-Penalosa (2001) examine how human capital accumulation influences both economic growth and income inequality. They argue that the stock of educated workers determines both the rate of growth and income inequality. Parameters of the demand and supply of labour are crucial determinants of direction and changes in inequality as an economy accumulates human capital. Empirical evidence from Latin America shows that educational attainment in addition to its impacts on inequality affects the future prospects of mobility, opportunity and vulnerability by increasing the probability of moving out of poverty or reducing the probability of not falling into poverty (Graham, 2002). At the micro-level based on data from Holland, Hartog and Oosterbeek (1998) show that the group with non-vocational intermediate level of education score highest on health, wealth and happiness. Clark and Oswald (1996) tested the hypothesis that utility depend on income relative to a comparison or reference level. Results based on British workers data presented in Clark and Oswald suggest that the satisfaction levels are inversely related to their respective wage rates, and that satisfactions are declining with the levels of education.

Relationship between Income Inequality, (Un)employment and (Un)happiness

Employment is not only a source of income; it also provides individuals with social relationships and identity. Unemployment thus has both economic and social costs to the individuals and societies; it affects income, inequality and happiness. Joblessness is expected to be negatively correlated with individual wellbeing and health.

The extent of joblessness in advanced countries has caused concern about the direct monetary costs to both the employers and employees, social costs and the costs of an economy operating below its production potential among others. Concerning the social cost, it is suspected that unemployment imposes additional burdens on the individual, a burden referred to as the non-pecuniary cost[3] of unemployment. Winkelmann and Winkelmann (1998) test for the importance of non-pecuniary costs of unemployment using the longitudinal German Socio-economic Panel Study data-set on life-satisfaction of about 10,000 working age men in Germany for 1984-89. The results from a logit analysis show that unemployment has a larger detrimental effect on satisfaction. The non-pecuniary effect is much larger than the pecuniary direct effect that stems from the loss of income; for instance, adverse psychological wellbeing affects job search strategies and lowers productivity.

The relationships between unemployment and unhappiness is investigated by Clark and Oswald (1994) using mental wellbeing scores.[4] The British Household Panel Study for the 1991 touched upon various questions like presence of differences in concerns about being unemployed by different characteristics. These characteristics include age, location, unemployment rate, duration of unemployment, gender, and level of education. Results from an ordered probit regression of individual wellbeing on a set of personal characteristics, as expected, show that the effect of being jobless is negatively correlated with wellbeing.[5] Clark and Oswald reject the hypothesis that unemployment is voluntary. There is a U-shape in mental wellbeing with respect to age. On an average happiness is lowest in a person's mid-thirties. The high-educated individuals show more distress while married people have the lowest degree of mental distress. Wellbeing is higher among healthy persons. Hartog and

---

[3] Among the non-pecuniary effects of employment are direct costs of decreased psychological wellbeing and its adverse individual outcomes are increased mortality, suicide risk, crime rates, decreased marital stability, etc.

[4] For a recent update of the subjective measures of happiness and the link between inequality in income and happiness see van Praag and Ferrer-i-Carbonell (2004),

[5] Wellbeing is measured based on the General Health Questionnaire (GHQ) survey containing several indicators of psychological distress or 'disutility'. Here 'Caseness scores' are calculated based on the answers of 12 indicators. The highest level of wellbeing (0) corresponds to a caseness level of 'feeling (fairly or highly) stressed', to the lowest level category of 12. The former would benefit from psychiatric treatment.

Oosterbeek (1998) shows that the Dutch group with a non-vocational intermediate level of education score highest on health, wealth and happiness. Fathers working and women, regardless of their employment situation ,are healthier and happier.

The relationship between inequality and happiness[6] is analysed by Alesina, DiTella and MacCulloch (2001). The issue is whether Europeans and Americans are different with respect to inequality and happiness. Inequality is measured as a Gini coefficient of gross family income in the US but is calculated using expenditure, gross or net income for the European countries. Using a large random sample survey of 128,106 answers they find a large, negative and significant effect of inequality on happiness in Europe but not in the US. The period of study covers 1972-94 for the US and 1975-92 for Europe. In an ordered logit model happiness is regressed against inequality, macro and micro variables and personal and subgroup characteristics. The differences in happiness are potentially explained by the European preference for more equal societies and higher social mobility in the US. They test these hypotheses by partitioning the sample across income and ideological lines. Low social mobility in Europe is found to be a source of unhappiness among the subgroups of poor and socialist with preference for more equal societies.

Relationship between Income Inequality and (ill) Health

The connection between income inequality and health is explored by Deaton (2001).[7] The empirical analysis is based on both rich and poor countries. Here ill health is defined as the rate of mortality. In exploring the theoretical basis for such a relationship Deaton discusses a range of mechanisms including education, economic growth, land-holdings, politics, crime, non-linear income effects, credit restrictions, nutritional traps, public goods provision and relative deprivation. Given the poor data quality underlying inequality, the conclusion is that there is no direct link from income inequality to ill health. However, in the design of redistributive policies the importance of income and other inequalities, and the social environment, should not be neglected. Income inequality is an indicator of the quality of social arrangements, of stress in rich countries, and of mortality in poor countries. Deaton and Lubotsky (2002) argued that the correlation between mortality rates and income inequality across the cities and states of the US is confounded by the effects of racial composition. For instance, conditional on the percentage of blacks neither city nor state mortality rates are correlated with income inequality. Mortality and incomes of whites are lower in places where the fraction of black is higher. This result is present within geographical regions of the country and for all age groups and for both sexes (except boys aged 1-9) and it is robust to the

---

[6] For reviews of research on the index measures of happiness and mental health see Fordyce (1998), and Ng (1996).

[7] The literature on the relationship between health and economic development begin with the Preston curve (Preston, 1975), that shows the cross-country relationship between life-expectancy and income per head. Life-expectancy increase with income for poor countries, but at a decreasing rate, and it is weaker or absent for rich countries. For a selection of other (cross-country) studies on economic and social correlates of suicide rates see Chuang and Huang (1997) and Rodriguez-Andres (2003), on income distribution and life expectancy see Wilkinson (2005) and Mellor and Milyo (2001), and on income inequality and population health see Judge, Mulligan and Benzeval (1998). An excellent example of the relationship between inequality in health and economic development based on individual data including income information using Swedish data is by Gerdham and Johannesson (2000). In examining the existence of a negative association between income and mortality they find that inequalities in health favour higher income groups.

conditioning on income, education and unobserved state fixed effects. However, it remains unclear why white mortality is related to racial composition.

Pradhan, Sahn and Younger (2003) explore global inequality in health status and decompose it into within- and between-country inequality components. The data used in their analysis are representative from the demographic and health surveys on child health, fertility, contraceptive use and related demographic characteristics. It covers 55 developing countries and OECD countries since 1989. Health is an important indicator of wellbeing; there is extensive literature on the measurement of health differences across socioeconomic dimensions and linking inequality in health to income and socioeconomic status. Morbidity, mortality and life expectancy are traditionally used as health indicators and income and expenditure as welfare indicators. However Pradhan, Sahn and Younger used standardized height of pre-school children to examine health inequality; an abundance of medical and public health research shows that height is a good objective indicator of the general health status of children determined by nutrient intake, disease and deprivation. Results indicate that in contrast with income inequality research, within-country variation is the source of most inequality, rather than between-country differences. The relationship between income and health when measured by nutrition indicators, is a strongly concave function.

Kakwani, Wagstaff and van Doorslaer (1997) clarify the relationship between two widely used indices of socioeconomic inequality in health, namely the relative index of inequality and the concentration index, and explain their superiority to other indices. On individual-level data the concentration index C is calculated as:

$$(2.20) \quad C = \frac{2}{n\mu} \sum_{i=1}^{n} x_i R_i - 1$$

where x_i is ill health score of the ith individual, n is the number of individuals, $\mu = 1/n \sum_{i=1}^{n} x_i$ is the mean level of ill health, and R_i is the relative rank of the ith person. As indicators of ill health the authors used chronic illness (dummy variable) and a self-assessed health variable (categorical). They also developed distribution-free asymptotic estimators of the standard errors of both the relative index of inequality and concentration index. The role that demographic standardization by gender and age interval plays in the analysis of socioeconomic inequality in health is clarified. Health interview survey data from Holland covering 10,232 individuals for 1980 and 1981 is used in the empirical illustration. The result of their study suggests that extra precision allowed for by individual-level data is to be retained but the gain may not always be that large.

Income-related inequality in self-assessed health in nine industrialized countries[8] was estimated by van Doorslaer et al. (1997). Here the concentration index is used as a measure of inequality, and the results show that inequality in heath significantly favoured the higher income groups in all countries. Gerdtham and Johannesson (2000) find the concentration index to be an incomplete measure of health since it ignores the length of life. They investigate income-related inequalities with respect to life years and quality-adjusted life-years. In the health literature there is evidence of the existence of a negative association

---

[8] East Germany, Finland, Spain, Sweden, Switzerland, the Netherlands, UK, USA, and West Germany.

between income and mortality. Results based on 40,000 Swedish individuals followed up for 10-16 years, shows that inequalities in health favour higher income groups. A Dutch study (Hartog and Oosterbeek, 1998) also indicates the presence of gender effects in the wealth–health–happiness relationship. Women in comparison with men are less wealthy, equally healthy but are happier.

Relationship between Inequality in Wealth and Growth

The growth and inequality literature has recognized that it may be the distribution of assets, rather than income, that underlies effects of inequality on growth by restricting access to credit markets (Stiglitz and Weiss, 1981). In testing the robustness of the inequality–growth relationship using country level data for 108 countries during 1960-1992 on income and land distribution Deininger and Squire (1998) shows that there is a strong negative relationship between initial inequality in asset distribution and long-term growth. Inequality reduces income growth for the poor, but not for the rich. Growth and inequality are affected by the redistribution of assets and increased aggregate investment. Distribution of land is characterized by more cross-country variation than that of income. Distribution of income, assets and government redistributive policies are among important factors determining the level of income inequality.

Available evidence on the distribution of personal wealth,[9] referring to material assets that can be sold in the market and its evolution over time for a number of countries is summarized by Davies and Shorrocks (2000). The results, despite deficiencies of survey data on wealth, reconfirm the known fact that wealth is more unequally distributed than income and points to a downward trend in wealth inequality in several European countries over most of the twentieth century. In addition to lifecycle accumulation and inheritance which plays a major role in the explanation of wealth differences, they also give attention to several factors including: the reasons for holding wealth, individual differences in wealth holdings, examination of the causes of these differences, the link between wealth status across generations, and motives for leaving bequests. Inheritance is found to account for about 35-40 per cent of aggregate wealth in the US. Contributions from demographic trends, and changes in assets and housing prices are found to affect the distribution of wealth.

SUMMARY

This chapter reviewed various tools used in income inequality analysis and looked at the link between income inequality and inequality in education, employment, happiness, health, wealth and growth.

Inequality can have different dimensions. Economists are mostly concerned with the income and consumption dimensions of inequality. Among other non-income inequality

---

[9] Total wealth consists of human plus non-human capital. Here the human capital component is excluded and the focus is on material assets in the form of real property and financial claims. Less attention is paid to private pensions, social security wealth and its link to demographic factors.

dimensions we can include inequality in skills, education, opportunities, happiness, health, life-years, welfare and assets.

Several inequality indices can be derived from the Lorenz diagram. The divergence of a Lorenz curve for perfect equality and the Lorenz curve for a given distribution is measured by some indices of inequality. Among the most notable measures of inequality are: Gini coefficient, the range, the variance, the squared coefficient of variation, the variance of log incomes, the absolute and relative mean deviations, and Theil's two inequality indices. Several inequality indices follow some basic properties that one would expect the indices to satisfy. These properties are to be used in their ranking, relevance and performance evaluation. The most widely used index of inequality is the Gini coefficient. Gini is generalized to accommodate differing aversions of inequality.

Income inequality can be decomposed at different levels of aggregation. At the national level it can be decomposed into within-subgroup, between subgroup, and overlapping components. In a similar way at the international level it can be decomposed into within-country, between-country, and overlapping components. In the measurement of world income inequality it is desirable that the unit of analysis is the citizens of the world rather than countries. Representative individual based micro data is preferable.

The effects of inequality in non-income factors on earnings can be summarized variously. Inequality in education explains a minor fraction of differences in cross-country earnings inequality. The impact decreases by the level of education and depends on the economic development and skill-intensive nature of production technologies. It also negatively affects the investment rate and growth rate of income. There is no direct link from income inequality to ill health measured as mortality, but a range of mechanism ands social arrangements indicate the presence of an indirect link. Unlike in the case of income inequality, within country health inequality is a dominating source of inequality. Regions differ with respect to the effects of inequality on happiness; the differences in happiness are associated with preferences for equal societies and higher social mobility.

Employment in addition to the source of income is also a provider of social relationships and individual social identity. Joblessness has a direct cost effect to the employee and employers, social costs and a cost in in-optimal operation of an economy. The additional burden of unemployment on individual wellbeing, the non-pecuniary cost, is an important non-monetary cost of joblessness and much larger than the pecuniary effect that stems from the loss of income, though the negative effect varies by personal characteristics. Inequality in the distribution of assets is found to affect long-term growth. In sum the results suggests that one should account for the interrelationship between the different dimensions in the measurement and analyses of inequalities.

Chapter 3

A REVIEW OF DECOMPOSITION OF INCOME INEQUALITY AND CHANGES IN POVERTY

ABSTRACT

This chapter is a review of recent developments of parametric and non-parametric approaches to decompose inequality by subgroups, income sources, causal factors and other unit characteristics. Different methods of decomposing changes in poverty into growth, redistribution, poverty standard and residual components are described. In parametric approaches the dynamics of income accounting for transitory and permanent changes in individual and household earnings conditional of various covariates are also reviewed. Statistical inferences for inequality measurement including delta and bootstrapping and other methods to provide estimates of the sampling distribution are presented. These issues are important in the design of policy measures and expectations about their impacts on earnings inequality and poverty reductions.

Keywords: Income inequality, poverty, decomposition, parametric, non-parametric, Gini index

INTRODUCTION

There is an ongoing and increasing interest in measuring and understanding the level, causes and the development of income inequality. The 1990s signified by a shift in research which was previously focused on economic growth, the identification of the determinants of economic growth and convergence in GDP per capita across countries to the analysis of distribution of income, its development over time and identification of factors determining the distribution of income. This shift in focus is specifically from the issues of convergence or divergence of per capita incomes to the long-term equalisation or polarisation of incomes across regions and countries.[1] This shift is not only a reflection of technological change and

---

[1] For a selection of studies of growth and convergence in per capita incomes see: Barro (1991), Barro and Sala-i-Martin (1995), Islam (1995), Lee, Pesaran and Smith (1997), Mankiw, Romer and Weil (1992), and Quah (1996c). Quah (2002), Ravallion (2003b), Sala-i-Martin (2002a, 2002b), and Solimano (2001) analysed

raised human capacity to create growth and wealth, but also due to awareness of the growing disparity and the importance of redistribution and poverty reduction. The growing disparity calls for analysis of various aspects of income inequality including its measurement, decomposition and causal factors.

Income inequality refers to the inequality of the distribution of individuals, household or some per capita measure of income. Lorenz Curve is used for analysing the size distribution of income and wealth and also the measurement of inequality and poverty. It plots the cumulative share of total income against the cumulative proportion of income receiving units (see Chapter 2). The divergence of a Lorenz curve for perfect equality and the Lorenz curve for a given income distribution is measured by some indices of inequality. The most widely used index of inequality is the Gini coefficient (for reviews of the notion and analysis of inequality see Subramanian 1997a and Cowell 2000). There are two parametric approaches to estimate the Lorenz curve (Ryu and Slottje, 1999). In the first approach one assumes a hypothetical statistical distribution for income distribution and in the second approach, a specific functional form is fit to the Lorenz curve directly (Chotikapanich and Griffiths 2002). The selection of parametric Lorenz curves is fairly arbitrary (see Sarabina et al. 1999 for an attmpt at unification). An important drawback of the traditional models of the Lorenz curve is the lack of satisfactory fit over the entire range of a given income distribution. Ogwang and Rao (2000) proposed two hybrid Lorenz curves by combining traditional models. The estimated Lorenz curve is sensitive to the errors in survey data. The robustness properties of inequality and poverty measures assuming contaminated data with illustrations are considered in Cowell and Victoroa-Feser (1996a and 1996b). Hasegawa and Kozumi (2003) propose using Bayesian non-parametric analysis and present a method for removing the contaminated observations.

Several inequality indices can be derived from the Lorenz diagram. The Lorenz Curve construction also gives us a rough but standard measure (Gini coefficient) of the amount of inequality in income distribution. The index lies in the interval 0 (perfect equality) and 1 (perfect inequality). Among the other notable measures of inequality are: the range, the variance, the squared coefficient of variation, the variance of log incomes, the absolute and relative mean deviations, and the Theil's two inequality indices (See Chapter 2). The indices have different properties that can be used in their ranking, relevance and performance evaluation. There are three basic properties that one would expect the above indices of inequality to satisfy: mean or scale independence, population size independence and the Pigou-Dalton condition. The Gini coefficient, the squared coefficient of variation and the two Theil's measures satisfy each of the three properties, while the relative and absolute mean difference and the range measures satisfy only the first two conditions in the strict sense. The variance measure violates the mean independence property. For more details on the properties of different indices of inequality see Anand (1997). A generalization of the Gini coefficient, called the extended Gini coefficient, was proposed by Kakwani (1980), Donaldson and Weymark (1980) and Yitzhaki (1983). The new index accommodates differing aversions to inequality. Empirical estimation of the extended index has been limited to the covariance

convergence in income inequality, while Acemoglu and Ventura (2002), Atkinson (1997, 1999), Bourguignon and Morrisson (2002), Cornia (1999), Gottschalk and Smeeding (1997) and Milanovic (2002a) focus on the distribution of income. More recently Acemoglu (2002), Caminada and Goudswaard (2001), Cornia and Kiiski (2001), Gotthschalk and Smeeding (2000), Milanovic (2002a), O'Rourke (2001), Park (2001), Sala-i-Martin (2002b) and Schultz (1998) studied trends in income inequality.

formula suggested by Lerman and Yitzhaki (1989). Chotikapanich and Griffiths (2001) suggest an alternative estimator, obtained by approximating the Lorenz curve by a series of linear segments.

Inequality can have many dimensions. Economists are concerned specifically with the economic or monetary measurable dimension related to individual or household income and consumption. However, this is just one perspective and inequality can be linked to inequality in skills, education, opportunities, happiness, health, life expectancy, welfare, assets and social mobility. The effects of inequality in non-income factors of earnings can be summarised variously. Inequality in education explains a minor fraction of differences in cross-country earning inequality. The impact decreases by the level of education and depends on the economic development and skill-intensive nature of production technologies. It also negatively affects the investment rate and the growth rate of income. There is no direct link from income inequality to ill health measured as mortality, but a range of mechanism and social arrangements indicate the presence of an indirect link. Unlike in the case of income inequality, within country health inequality is a dominating source of inequality. The non-income dimension of inequality is beyond the scope of this paper. In Chapter 2 we reviewed the recent advances in the measurement of inequality and gives attention to the interrelationship between income inequality and the non-income inequality dimensions.

Different methods have been developed to decompose inequality (Pyatt 1976; Shorrocks 1980, 1982 and 1984; Fields 2000; Morduch and Sicular 2002), and changes in poverty (Kakwani and Subbaro 1990; Jian and Tandulkar 1990; Datt and Ravallion 1992; and Shorrocks and Kolenikov 2001). Inequality is decomposed by sub-groups, income sources, causal factors and by other sociodemographic characteristics. Inequality can also be decomposed at different levels of aggregation. At the national level it can be decomposed into within-subgroup and between-subgroup components. In a similar way at the international level it can be decomposed into within-country and between-country components. A decomposition of inequality and the changes in poverty are important in the design of policy measures, their expected effects and in evaluation of the impacts of inequality and redistributive policies on welfare among regions, sub-groups and sectors. Inequality can also at the micro level be decomposed parametrically into permanent and transitory components of earnings (e.g. Geweke and Keane 2000; Zandvakili 2002; and Moffitt and Gottschalk 2002). The main benefits of parametric approaches are that changes are conditional on various heterogeneity attributes not all captured by the growth and redistribution components. Furthermore confidence intervals for disaggregated contributions to the inequality index can also be constructed.

Having discussed in Chapter 2 the different dimensions and measurement of inequality and listed the indices of income inequality derived from the Lorenz curve this chapter has a major contribution to the inequality literature. First, it provides the current state of knowledge on recent developments in inequality decomposition by population subgroups, income sources, inequality causal factors and other sociodemographic characteristics. Second, different methods of decomposing the changes in poverty into growth, redistribution, poverty standard and residual components are discussed as well. Third, in parametric decomposition approaches the dynamics of income accounting for transitory and permanent changes in individual and household earnings conditional of various covariates are also reviewed. Finally, statistical inferences for inequality measurement including delta and bootstrapping methods to provide estimates of the sampling distribution and jackknife, as well as regression methods to report Gini standard errors and normalised stochastic dominance to rank inequality in case when the distribution of income has different means are discussed.

It should be noted that several studies are cited covering several countries. The objective here is by compiling a large and major collection of papers published in recent years that represent new developments in various decomposition of income and poverty measurement to illustrate methods, their usefulness and empirical results obtained rather than to yield a connected picture on what has been happening across the world. In its evaluation of diverse methodologies this chapter highlights their merits and demerits. It provides the readers knowledge on the current state of decomposition techniques and also benefits when choosing appropriate approaches for their tasks. The collection of topics here is thus important to practitioners and highly relevant for future chapters. In addition to the above advantages, this survey is the most recent and comprehensive survey of the literature, it also covers the development of poverty and inequality decomposition jointly.

Rest of the chapter is organised as follows. The next Section introduces the readers to the origin of the modern income inequality decomposition. Section 3 is a review of the development of decomposition of the changes in poverty into growth, redistribution and standard poverty components. In Section 4 changes in the distribution of income is decomposed and related to the sociodemographic characteristics of the population. Section 5 and 6 are on decomposition of inequality by causal factors and by sub-groups of the population. The adjustment process towards equilibrium income is also discussed. The regression-based inequality decomposition by income sources and confidence intervals for disaggregated contributions to the inequality index are discussed in Section 7. The transitory and permanent components of shocks to the earnings are distinguished in Section 8. Here the focus is on the dynamics in individual earnings, sub-group heterogeneity and their policy implications. Section 9 and 10 are on the statistical inference for inequality measurement and inferences about the Gini index. The final Section summarises.

INEQUALITY DECOMPOSITION

The origin of the modern inequality decomposition literature is to be found in Shorrocks (1980, 1982 and 1984),[2] where he examined decomposition of inequality by income sources such as earnings, investment income and transfer payments; by population subgroups like single persons, married couples, and families with children; or by subaggregates of observations which share common characteristics like age, household size, region, occupation, or some other attributes. He shows that a broad class of inequality measures can be decomposed into components reflecting only the size, mean and inequality value of each population subgroup or income source.

---

[2] The current state of knowledge regarding the theory and the application of inequality decomposition techniques in a spatial and regional context is reviewed by Shorrocks and Wan (2004). They emphasis that the time profile of the within and between-group components of inequality will add a dynamic dimension to the studies of spatial inequality decomposition. An examination of the linkage of between-group inequality to growth is more informative compared to the analysis of sigma convergence. Attention should be paid to the factors contributing to spatial inequality, persistency in spatial differences and the influence of migration.

In decomposing income inequality Shorrocks (1983) examines the relative influence of income components and evaluates the performance of different decomposition rules using US data. The method based on the Gini coefficient can be written as:

$$(3.1) \quad I(Y) = \frac{2}{n^2\mu} \sum_{i=1}^{n} \left(i - \frac{n+1}{2} \right) Y_i$$

where $Y_i = \sum_{k=1}^{K} Y_i^k$ is the sum of these income components k for individual i. The inequality decomposition rules for factor components can be generated for inequality measures of the form:

$$(3.2) \quad I(Y) = \sum_{k=1}^{K} \sum_{i=1}^{N} a_i(Y) Y_i^k = \sum_{k=1}^{K} S_k$$

where S_k is a contribution of factor k to the overall income inequality, a_i is the weight attached to individual i income component k, Y_i^k. The proportional factor contribution on aggregate income is expressed as:

$$(3.3) \quad s_k = S_k / I(Y) = \text{cov}(Y_k, Y) / \sigma^2(Y)$$

with $\sum_k s_k = 1$. Empirical results are based on panel data consisting of 2,755 households observed for 1967-76 obtained from the PSID. Analysis of the distribution of net family incomes results in the identification of ten factor components.[3] There is a fair but far from identical degree of correspondence between the contribution of inequality and income share of each factor component. Labour income of the head (of household) and direct taxes on the head and spouse are the main positive and negative factors respectively, contributing to the inequality of total net family incomes in the US. Cowell and Jenkins (1995) apply different decomposition techniques and investigate the quantitative importance of principal population (sex, race and age of head) and labour market (employment status) characteristics in explaining inequality using PSID data. Results are robust under alternative methods of decomposition and the within-group component dominates. Jenkins (1995) applied inequality decomposition method to the UK data, and the results indicate that these decompositions generate different results when used with different inequality indices, and when the indices are sensitive to the extreme income observations. This, together with the increased interest for and the importance of inequality decomposition, has resulted in development of alternative decomposition approaches.

---

[3] Factors contributing to inequality of total net family incomes are: taxable income of head of household and spouse ((i) labour income of head (ii) spouse and (iii) income from capital), transfer income of head and spouse ((iv) welfare benefits, (v) pensions and (vi) other transfer income), income of other family members ((vii) taxable income, (viii) transfer income), direct taxes ((ix) head and spouse, (x) other family members).

DECOMPOSITION OF CHANGES IN POVERTY

The effects of growth on income poverty have been studied by accounting for the changes in the distribution of income. Income poverty $P(z,\mu,L)$ is expressed in terms of poverty line (z), mean income level (μ) and the relative distribution of income (L). The Lorenz curve represents the structure of relative income inequalities. Assuming the poverty line is fixed at a given level, income poverty is given by $P(\mu,L)$. The total change in poverty (Δp) is then decomposed into two components. The first component is the growth component due to changes in the mean income while holding the Lorenz curve constant at some reference level, and the second a redistribution component due to changes in the Lorenz curve while keeping the mean income constant at some reference level. For detailed description of the mechanics in terms of which it is plausible to expect poverty to be influenced by the level of mean income rises (every person's income were to be scaled up by the same factor) and the level of inequality (improvement in the distribution of income of fixed size) see the reference below.

There are a number of ways to decompose the total change in poverty. Kakwani and Subbaro's (1990) decomposition approach for given poverty line is:

$$
(3.4) \quad
\begin{aligned}
\Delta p = p_1 - p_0 &= P(\mu_1, L_1) - (\mu_0, L_0) \\
&= \{P(\mu_1, L_0) - P(\mu_0, L_0)\} + \{P(\mu_1, L_1) - P(\mu_1, L_0)\} = G + R
\end{aligned}
$$

where μ and L are mean income and the Lorenz curve characterizing the distribution of income respectively. The subscripts 0 and 1 denote the two (consecutive or non-consecutive) initial and final periods of observation, and G and R are contributions from the growth and redistributive components. In analyzing the impact of economic growth on poverty in India, Kakwani and Subbaro measures separately the impacts of the changes in average income and income inequality on poverty. They examine trends in the distribution and the growth of consumption and assess their relative impacts on the poor and ultra poor, over the period 1972-83 and across the 15 major states of India.[4] Results suggest that the beneficial effect of growth on the incidence of poverty during 1973-77 was outweighed by the adverse movements in the inequality of consumption. However, during 1977-83 average consumption grew slowly and the inequality in consumption fell in many states mainly reducing the incidence of ultra poor poverty. States differ in needs, capacities, social policy, intervention programmes and performance.

For the same decomposition purpose Jain and Tendulkar (1990) proposed:

$$
(3.5) \quad
\begin{aligned}
\Delta p = p_1 - p_0 &= P(\mu_1, L_1) - (\mu_0, L_0) \\
&= \{P(\mu_1, L_1) - P(\mu_0, L_1)\} + \{P(\mu_0, L_1) - P(\mu_0, L_0)\}
\end{aligned}
$$

---

[4] The poverty line defined by the Indian Planning Commission in 1979. It corresponds to the per capita total expenditure required to attain some basic nutritional norm: daily intake of 2400 calories in rural area, 1973-74 prices. Ultra poor is defined as based on a poverty line equivalent of 80 per cent of the poor poverty line.

The two decompositions differ by the way of two growths and redistribution components; differences in the reference point: base year versus final year. In the choice of base year in multiple time period comparisons, one might take the quality of the data point and its relevance into consideration. Datt and Ravallion (1992) found the above decompositions of poverty changes as being time path dependent, arising through and dependent on the choice of reference levels. To make the changes path independent they proposed:

$$
(3.6) \quad
\begin{aligned}
\Delta p = p_1 - p_0 &= P(\mu_1, L_1) - (\mu_0, L_0) \\
&= \{P(\mu_1, L_0) - P(\mu_0, L_0)\} + \{P(\mu_0, L_1) - P(\mu_0, L_0)\} + E
\end{aligned}
$$

where E is an extra residual component appended to the (8). The residual exists whenever the poverty measure is not additively separable between μ and L. It is the difference between the growth (redistribution) components evaluated at the terminal and initial Lorenz curves (mean incomes) respectively. The residual does not vanish unless μ and L remain unchanged over the decomposition period, nor apportioned between the two components. The two growth and redistribution components differ by the base year or reference level chosen as a benchmark. This decomposition can be applied to multiple periods where a fixed reference point, like the first period, is required for satisfying additivity of the sub-period.

In their application of the decomposition method Datt and Ravallion used three measures of poverty (headcount, poverty gap and Foster-Greer-Thorbecke – FGT) where the Lorenz curve is parametrized as beta and general quadratic functional form. The poverty measure and their decompositions are estimated for rural and urban India during 1977-78, 1983, 1986-87, and 1988 and for Brazil in 1981-88. In addition to the data problem, the method is found to have a number of limitations. Results indicate the presence of heterogeneity both over time and across the two countries: the method allows quantification of the relative importance to the poor of the differences in mean income and inequality. However it can not identify alternative growth processes with better distributional implications to reduce poverty more effectively, nor whether a shift in the distribution or mean is politically or economically attainable. The method was used by Assadzadeh and Paul (2003) to show how growth and redistribution policies affected poverty measured as headcount, poverty gap and FGT(2) in Iran during 1983, 1988 and 1993. Results show that the growth component affected negatively the rural but positively the urban sector while the redistribution component was positive implying that deterioration of inequality had contributed to the worsening of poverty in Iran.

Dhongde (2002) rewrites the total change in poverty described above decomposed into its two growth and redistribution components as:

$$
(3.7) \quad
\begin{aligned}
\Delta p = p_1 - p_0 &= P(\mu_1, L_1) - (\mu_0, L_0) \\
&= \left[\{P(\mu_1, L_0) - P(\mu_0, L_0)\} + \{P(\mu_1, L_1) - P(\mu_0, L_1)\} \right]/2 \\
&\quad + \left[\{P(\mu_1, L_1) - P(\mu_1, L_0)\} + \{P(\mu_0, L_1) - P(\mu_0, L_0)\} \right]/2
\end{aligned}
$$

where the two growth and distribution components are averaged. The advantage of this method is that with the presence of time dependency the averaging procedure achieves path independence in the decomposition. Another advantage is that there is no residual or unexplained part of the total change. This of course is dependent on the assumption that the total change in poverty can be decomposed into growth and redistribution components. If all income poverty changes can not be explained by these two components the resulting residuals are allocated to the two components biasing the changes but leaving the total unchanged. The method is applied to data from 15 Indian states comparing changes in poverty from 1983/84 to 1993/94 and from 1993/94 to 1999/2000. The poverty lines correspond to the per capita total expenditure required to attain some basic nutritional norm: daily intake of 2,400 calories in rural and 2,100 calories in urban areas, at 1973-74 prices (Kakwani and Subbaro, 1990). The results show that new sets of policies boost the growth of per capita income leading to a decline in poverty. However, as previously observed by Kakwani and Subbaro the growth was accompanied by negative changes in the distribution of income and not in favour of the poor. The adverse impact was stronger in urban areas.

In a similar decomposition approach, but relaxing the assumption of fixed poverty line, Shorrocks and Kolenikov (2001) investigate how changes in mean income, inequality and the poverty standard have affected the level of poverty in Russia. The total change in poverty is defined as:

(3.8)
$$\Delta p = p_1 - p_0 = P(\mu_1, L_1, z_1) - (\mu_0, L_0, z_0) = G + R + S + E$$
$$= \{P(\mu_1, L_0, z_0) - P(\mu_0, L_0, z_0)\} + \{P(\mu_0, L_1, z_0) - P(\mu_0, L_0, z_0)\}$$
$$+ \{P(\mu_0, L_0, z_1) - P(\mu_0, L_0, z_0)\} + E$$

where μ, L and z are mean income, the Lorenz curve and the poverty rate characterizing the distribution of income. The subscripts 0 and 1 denote two periods of observation, and G, R, S and E are contributions from the growth, redistribution, poverty standard effects and the extra residual or overlapping components. Shorrocks and Kolenikov quantify the contributions of these factors to the year-by-year changes in the poverty rate and its development in Russia since 1985. Based on household data for 1985-99 rising inequality is identified as the principal cause of the high poverty rate in Russia. A decomposition analysis based on consecutive year-by-year changes has the advantages that it is not sensitive to random transitory shocks and less to the measurement error in the data.

The recent development of inequality decomposition techniques is summarized as follows. It is possible to decompose inequality by income sources and population subgroups. The results are however sensitive to the choice of different inequality indices resulting in the development of alternative decomposition approaches. Regression-based methods are used to estimate the relative contribution of different variables on aggregate inequality. Personal, family, human capital, regional and political variables explain emerging inequality. Another method is to construct the distribution of earnings or changes in poverty rate by assuming distributional characteristics with different time periods as a benchmark. The changes are then decomposed into various components and related to various determinants.

CHANGES IN DISTRIBUTION OF INCOME

This section reviews a selection of studies on changes in the distribution of income. In addition it presents the estimated relation. For more details on each model the readers are referred to the respective original contribution.

For the purpose of evaluation (of policy), changes in the distribution of income over time is of significant importance. Cameron (2000b) modified DiNardo *et al.* (1996) where the changes in the cumulative distribution functions, Lorenz curves and generalized Lorenz curves (GL) are decomposed. She examines the changes in the distribution of per capita income between 1984 and 1990 in Java and relates it to the ageing of the population, higher educational attainment, movement out of agriculture and changes in average income (y) within industries and age/education categories as:

$$(3.9) \quad \begin{aligned} \Delta y = y_1 - y_0 &= f_{84}(y) - f_{90}(y) \\ &= \left[f_{84}(y; t_y, t_a, t_e, t_m, d_t, s_t) - f_{90}(y; t_y, t_a, t_e, t_m, d_t, s_t) \right] + E \end{aligned}$$

where a, e and m, are the age of the household head, education and main source of income attributes, and d, s, t and E are distributional characteristics, the mean of per capita income in age/education categories, period and residuals. The advantage of this method is that it presents decompositions in terms of probability density function rather than summary statistics such as the Gini coefficient. Ranking income distribution by the means of the GL ordering is a commonly used procedure in welfare economics. However, this approach ignores the needs identified by the non-income demographic characteristics of individuals like marital status, family size, etc. Atkinson and Bourguignon (1987) introduced an approach called the sequential GL rank ordering to more realistic cases with heterogeneous income distribution where the population is partitioned into subgroups on the basis of needs. This ordering has a strong utilitarian support. Ok and Lambert (1999) in their evaluation of social welfare by sequential GL dominance outline an extension of the Atkinson–Bourguignon analysis, and show that the sequential GL ordering is supported by all increasing social welfare functions which record an increase in the overall welfare when a welfare transfer is made from less needy to the more needy subgroups.

Bourguignon, Fournier and Gurgand (2001) proposed a decomposition method where they parametrically construct a distribution at the terminal year with the initial year's characteristics and compare the resulting distribution with the distribution of initial year:

$$(3.10) \quad \begin{aligned} y_{it} &= Y(x_{it}, \varepsilon_{it}; \beta_t; \lambda_t) \\ D_t &= H(\{x_{it}, \varepsilon_{it}\}, \beta_t, \lambda_t) \\ Z_{tt'} &= H(\{x_{it'}, \varepsilon_{it'}\}, \beta_{t'}, \lambda_{t'}) - (\{x_{it}, \varepsilon_{it}\}, \beta_t, \lambda_t) \end{aligned}$$

where y_{it} is the income of individual (household) i in period t, D_t is the overall distribution of household incomes, x_{it} are observable sociodemographic characteristics, ε_{it} are unobservable characteristics, β_t are a vector of prices and labour remuneration rates, λ_t is a vector of behavioural parameters of occupational choice, $Z_{tt'}(B_{tt'}, L_{tt'}, P_{tt'})$ represent a vector of price effects $(B_{tt'})$, participation effect $(L_{tt'})$ and population effect $(P_{tt'})$ computed as the difference between two dates t and t'. This approach accounts for several sources of bias including: endogeneity, heterogeneity and selection bias. It is to be noted that the wage model allows for parameter heterogeneity over time and across gender and in the estimation of the wage equation assuming fixed effects is accounted for selection bias.

Bourguignon, Fournier and Gurgand (2001) applied the above decomposition method to examine the changes in the Taiwanese distribution of individual and household earnings between 1979 and 1994, to isolate the respective impacts of the changes in the earnings structure, labour-force participation behaviour and sociodemographic (age, education, household size, etc.) structure of the population. Results indicate that various structural forces offset each other, and four phenomena were found to be important to the evolution of the distribution of individual earnings. These are: (i) changes in the wage structure due to increased returns to schooling and supply of educated workers which contributed to increased inequality, (ii) a drop in the variance of the effect of unobserved earnings, (iii) changes in participation and occupational choice behaviour that increased the share of middle-income earners, and (iv) changes in the sociodemographic structure of the population. The same phenomena affected the distribution of earnings of household units but somewhat different than that of individual units indicating significance of within household distribution of earnings.

The pro-poor nature of changes in income inequality has received great attention. To evaluate the pro-poor nature of the changes in income inequality Jenkins and Van Kerm (2003) proposed a decomposition that links changes in income inequality over time in the US (1981-93) and Germany (1985-99) to the extent to which income growth is pro-poor and to the extent of income re-ranking. Changes in the Lorenz curve is broken down into two parts: a re-ranking index measuring the relative-income-weighted average of changes in social weights and an index measuring the progressiveness of income growth. Results show that in both countries income growth is pro-poor, reducing inequality; however the effect is offset by the disequalizing impact of the changes in income ranking, and this is stronger in the US.

DECOMPOSITION OF INEQUALITY BY CAUSAL FACTORS

In earlier sections we briefly mentioned inequality decomposition by income sources and by population sub-groups. Here we address the contributions of labour market factors to income inequality. A decomposition of the Theil index of inequality into the unweighted sum of the inequality indices due to: productivity per employee worker (y), employment rate (e), active over-working age population rate (a), and active total population rate (w) is presented by Duro and Esteban (1998):

$$(3.11) \quad T(x,p) = \sum_i p_i \log\left(\frac{\mu}{x^i}\right) = \sum_i p_i \left\{ \log\left(\frac{y}{y_i}\right) + \log\left(\frac{e}{e_i}\right) \log\left(\frac{a}{a_i}\right) + \log\left(\frac{w}{w_i}\right) \right\}$$

where p_i denotes the share of country i in the world population and $\mu = \sum_i p_i x_i$ is the world average per capita income. Duro and Esteban measure the contribution of each individual factor to the overall inequality. The factorial decomposition is applied to a set of 120 countries during 1960-89. However, a complete decomposition has been possible only using OECD country data. The results suggest that there is a rise in international inequality between 1960 and 1970 and a decline thereafter until 1989. The differences in activity rates account for 5 per cent of total income inequality and it has been increasing over time. Since 1975 inequality in productivity has been declining, while inequality in activity rates has been rising steadily. Overall cross-country inequality is less within the 23 OECD countries than worldwide. Both activity rate and working age population jointly play an important and increasing role throughout the period. By 1990, a total of 20 per cent of the joint productivity and employment inequality is associated with unemployment. The above decomposition (3.11) is extended to another Theil index of inequality by Georlich-Gisbert (2001) where instead of the country shares of aggregate population (p_i), the country shares of aggregate income (q_i) are used as weights:

$$(3.12)\quad T(x,q) = \sum_i q_i \log\left(\frac{\mu}{x_i}\right) = \sum_i q_i \left\{ \log\left(\frac{y_i}{y}\right) + \log\left(\frac{e_i}{e}\right) \log\left(\frac{a_i}{a}\right) + \log\left(\frac{w_i}{w}\right) \right\}$$

where $q_i = (x_i / x)$ is the share of country i in the aggregate income. Results based on data from 24 OECD countries for 1962-93 show that the same quantitative general results as Duro and Esteban (1998) are obtained.

Economic theory typically focuses on predicting equilibrium outcomes but ignores the adjustment process towards equilibrium. This is important when market parameters are subject to frequent changes. Knowledge about the properties and determinants of such an adjustment process like the time it takes to converge, factors affecting the speed of adjustment and inefficiency during the adjustment period are important for the success and social cost of welfare policy measures. The issues of the dynamics of market volatility and inequality in earnings are discussed by Huck, Norman and Oechssler (2001) in the context of an experimental oligopoly market where inequality is measured by the Gini coefficient of profits. Knowledge about the dynamics of the adjustment process is also emphasized by Sylwester (2000) who searched for transmission mechanisms to determine how changes in government policies can lower any negative impact that income inequality has upon economic growth. The inequality impact of growth in the context of poverty reduction policies is important.

In sum income distributions are heterogeneous, reflecting differences in the needs of subgroups of the population. In cross-country inequality decomposition where countries differ by the level of development the choice of population or income weights might be important. Taking into account the adjustment process towards equilibrium income the frequent changes in market parameters are also required. Knowledge of the determinants, speed and social cost of policy measures can be of great interest.

SUB-GROUP DECOMPOSITION

Yitzhaki (2002) decomposed the Gini coefficient to evaluate the impact of policy instruments on income inequality and the components of the Gini index. Society is divided into two groups: the poor with income below the poverty line z, $y \leq z$, and the rich with income above the poverty line, $y > z$. The overall Gini coefficient of income is thus composed:

$$(3.13) \quad G_y^o = P^p S_y^p G_y^p + P^r S_y^r G_y^r + G^b$$

where P and S are population and income shares, and the superscripts $o, p, r,$ and b denote the overall, poor, rich and between-groups. The inequality index is decomposed into inequality within poor and rich groups, and between the two groups. The latter can be further decomposed into a poverty gap, an affluence gap, and a poverty–affluence-lines gap component. The analysis is performed with family expenditure data from Romania for 1993. Results suggest that the dominant consideration in any poverty alleviation programme should be devoted to the between group transfer, namely how much is transferred from the less needy to the poor, rather than how subsidies are allocated among the poor.

Income inequality measured for more disaggregated subgroups like single mothers, retired, disabled or by race, sex, age and marital status is important for redistributive policy analysis. Income inequality among female heads of household investigated by Zandvakili (1999) focuses on the factors that might have influenced earnings inequality using generalized entropy measures of inequality in both short- and long-term incomes over 1978-86 with PSID data. Income is measured as total family income adjusted for household size using equal weights given to each household member. Inequality decomposed by short- and long-term and income stability for overall sample and also for sample decomposed by various household characteristics is reported by Zandvakili. The stability (mobility) index is calculated as:

$$(3.14) \quad R_M = \frac{I_\gamma(S)}{\sum_t \mu_t I_\gamma(Y_t)} = \frac{\sum_i N^{-1} \log(1/NS_i^*)}{\sum_t \mu_t I_\gamma(Y_t)}$$

where i and t denote household and periods, $\gamma = \{\neq 1, 0, -1\}$ determine the sensitivity to different portions of the distribution of income, $I_\gamma(S)$ and $\sum_t \mu_t I_\gamma(Y_t)$ are long-term and weighted average of short-term inequalities, $S_i^* = (S_i / \sum_j S_{ij})$ is income share, $S_i = S_i(Y_{i1}, Y_{i2}, \ldots, Y_{iM})$ and $Y_t = (Y_{1t}, Y_{2t}, \ldots, Y_{Nt})$ and income vectors at time t. The stability index, $0 \leq R_M \leq 1$, can be decomposed into between-group and a weighted average of the within-group components, $R_M = R_B + R_W$, by replacing S and Y with S^W, S^B, Y^W and Y^B respectively. The results show that short-term inequality has increased due to the existence of transitory components, while long-term inequality decreased in the early years. Race, in conjunction with education, is found to be the most influential factor explaining more than 30 per cent of the inequality. Age and marital status were also examined as possible contributors. Most movement occurs within each race group and cross group equalization is minimal.

Zandvakili and Mills (2001) used PSID data for 1981-91 to investigate the distributional consequences of changes in tax laws and transfer payments in the US. Income inequality is measured for both pre-tax/transfer and post-tax/transfer definitions of household income. Using bootstrap methods confidence intervals are constructed for various Generalized Entropy measures of inequality and hypotheses are tested. Using decomposable (within and between Theil 1 and Theil 2) measures of inequality the implications of the type of tax scale are investigated. Results suggest that social security income and income taxes reduce income inequality, while income transfers have had minimum reduction impact. Taxes are shown to have lost some of their progressivity after transfers are made. The consequences of changes in the US labour market on female wages, income and earnings inequality over time is investigated by Zandvakili (2000). Analysis of earnings stability profiles reveals the existence of permanent and chronic inequality. Individual characteristics like gender, race and education account for a third of observed earnings inequality in the US.

US income inequality by subgroups like gender, marital status, full-time/part-time employment, over time, and contribution of growing wage disparities and changing family composition on the overall income inequality between 1979 and 1996 is estimated by Burtless (1999). He examines the trend in overall inequality using the concept of adjusted equivalent personal income. The Gini coefficient of family income inequality rose by 16 per cent from 0.36 to 0.43. While growing pay disparities especially among men is the direct contributor to the trend in overall inequality, much of the rise is due to the shifts in family composition and other causes. The impact of growing correlation of husband and wife earned income and the increasing percentage of persons living in single-adult families and with more unequal incomes, on overall inequality are significant. The higher gender earnings disparity, the growing positive correlation of income within families, and growing proportion of families with single adults explains 33-44 per cent, 13 per cent and 21-25 per cent of the increase in overall inequality, respectively.

In sum the Gini coefficient can be decomposed into sub-groups to evaluate the impact of redistributive policy instruments on inequality and its underlying components. The focus is on the within and between-group components of inequality. The subgroups are distinguished by household's characteristics or by various income classes. Studies based on micro data show the importance of initial income, unobserved heterogeneous and some observable individual characteristics causing state dependence. Growing correlation of income within families and changing family composition are important factors causing increased inequality. The main benefits of parametric approaches are that changes are conditional on various attributes and confidence intervals for the effects are estimated. For instance, the changes in poverty may not be limited to the two growth and redistribution components, but also to the initial conditions and the characteristics of the underlying population. The main disadvantage is the assumption of functional forms of the relationship and specification of the relationship.

REGRESSION-BASED INEQUALITY DECOMPOSITION

Fields (2000) and Morduch and Sicular (2002) have proposed regression-based methods of decomposition of inequality by income sources. These methods involve the estimation of standard income generating equations written in terms of covariances. The contribution of the explanatory variables to the distributional changes is determined by the size of the coefficient and changes in the respective variables: elasticities. Compared with the unconditional approach outlined above, the regression-based approach provides an efficient and flexible way to quantify the conditional roles of the variables like race, marital status, education and age in a multivariate context. The proportional contribution of source k to overall inequality is simply (see Morduch and Sicular, 2002):

$$(3.15) \quad s^k = \hat{\beta}_k \left(\sum_{i=1}^n a_i(Y) Y_i^k \bigg/ I(Y) \right)$$

where a_i is the weight attached to individual i income component k, Y_i^k. In the regression-based approach it is assumed that $\hat{Y}^k = X_k \hat{\beta}_k$, X is a vector of sources of income flows, $\hat{\beta}_k$ is estimated coefficient. The average income shares and income shares for each quartile q are calculated as $\hat{\beta}_k (\overline{X}_k / \overline{Y})$ and $\hat{\beta}_k \sum_{i \in q} X_i^k / \hat{\beta} \sum_{\forall i} X_i^k$. This approach also has the benefit, but at the cost of strong assumptions, that confidence intervals for disaggregated contributions to the inequality index can be constructed. Standard errors for the estimated contributions of different variables to the aggregate inequality index and variance are obtained from:

$$(3.16) \quad \sigma(s^k) = \sigma(\hat{\beta}_k) \left[\sum_{i=1}^n a_i(Y) x_i^k \bigg/ I(Y) \right]$$

and

$$(3.17) \quad \sigma(s^\varepsilon) = \left\{ \sigma_\varepsilon^2 \sum_{i=1}^n \left[a_i(Y) / I(Y) \right]^2 \right\}^{1/2}.$$

Morduch and Sicular (2002) illustrate the method using a small survey of 259 farm-household data from rural China for 1990-93. They find that the relative contributions of three frequent explanations for emerging inequality (regional segmentations, human capital accumulation and political variable) are highly sensitive to the decomposition rule used. Earlier Chiu (1998) showed that greater initial income equality implies a higher human capital accumulation and economic performance of that generation, but also an improvement in an overlapping-generations model with heterogeneity in income and talent. However, Chiu does not provide any empirical illustration on the relationships.

PERMANENT AND TRANSITORY COMPONENTS OF EARNINGS

It is important to distinguish between the transitory and permanent components of earnings. In the long-term the effects of transitory shocks average out, while the permanent component persists. Transition and its variations over various individual, household and subgroup characteristics and unobservable permanent characteristics are important issues in the earnings models. Economic policy aimed at the introduction of changes in earnings and related inequality should distinguish shocks that households are able to smooth out from those they are not. It should target those that do not smooth out without intervention; the permanent component and variance of earnings by accounting for subgroup heterogeneity and earning instability factors. In the following several recently introduced dynamic earnings models with various degrees of complexity are presented, and the review contains a summary of their findings based on household surveys as well.

Data from the PSID on 4,766 male household heads aged between 25 and 65 was used by Geweke and Keane (2000) to address life-cycle earnings mobility. A dynamic reduced form model of earnings and marital status was developed and applied to male data covering the period 1968-89. The dynamic model of individual earnings (y) is written as:

$$(3.18) \quad \begin{aligned} y_{it} &= \gamma\, y_{i,t-1} + (1-\gamma)\beta' x_{it} + (1-\gamma)\tau_i + \varepsilon_{it} \\ \varepsilon_{it} &= \rho\varepsilon_{i,t-1} + \eta_{it} \end{aligned}$$

and the dynamic probit specification of marital status (m) is:

$$(3.19) \quad \begin{aligned} m_{it}^* &= \theta' s_{it} + \xi_{it} \\ \xi_{it} &= \lambda\xi_{i,t-1} + \psi_{it} \\ d_{it} &= \begin{cases} 1 & \text{if } m_{it}^* \geq 0 \\ 0 & \text{if } m_{it}^* < 0 \end{cases} \end{aligned}$$

where the vectors x and s are indicator variables explaining earnings and marital status, τ_i is random individual-specific effects constant over time, and $d_{it} = 1$ if individual i is married in period t. The model decomposes earnings into permanent and transitory components. Posterior distributions of these components show that in a given year, 60-70 per cent of the variation in the logarithm of earnings not explained by covariates is accounted for by the transitory components. Over a lifetime, the transitory component averages out. Geweke and Keane find transition probabilities in and out of low-earning states exhibiting variations over race and education classifications. Low earnings at a specific age, like 30, is a strong predictor of low earnings later in the life indicating the importance of unobserved permanent individual characteristics. This is also confirmed by Zandvakili (2002), who finds that the initial stage of labour market activity for young adults in the US influences their labour market engagement and earnings profiles over their lifetime. Education, marital status and race are the main contributors to the observed earnings inequality. Differences in personal and household circumstances are associated with differences in transition probabilities. The degree of genuine aggregate state dependence accounting for heterogeneity is estimated to be

52 per cent (see Cappellari and Jenkins, 2002). Here state dependence is estimated as the average predicted differences between the conditional probability of being poor at time t among those individuals who were poor at time t-1 and the conditional probability of being poor at t among those who were non-poor at t-1.

Ramos (2001) analyzed the dynamic structure of male fulltime employees' earnings in Great Britain for the period 1991-99 by decomposing the earnings covariance structure into its permanent and transitory components. The nested error component[5] model is:

$$
\begin{aligned}
y_{icat} &= \gamma_c \alpha_t [\mu_i + \eta_i AGE_{it} + u_{iat}] + \zeta_c v_{it} \\
u_{iat} &= u_{i(a-1)(t-1)} + \pi_{iat} \\
v_{it} &= \rho v_{i,t-1} + \lambda_t \varepsilon_{it}
\end{aligned}
$$
(3.20)

where the subscripts I, c, a, and t denote individual, cohort, age and period, μ_i and η_i are random time-invariant individual intercepts and slopes, γ_c and ζ_c are cohort shifters, u_{iat} is a random-walk innovation accommodating permanent ranking of individuals, and v_{it} is a transitory component. The model accounts for nested effects and reduces the number of unknown parameters to be estimated by allowing for non-linear interaction between α, μ and η. The results show that the persistence of earnings falls, and earnings dispersion causes earnings inequality to increase over time. Human capital and job related observable characteristics account for nearly all of the permanent earnings differences. Their degree of importance is however unknown. The transitory component is highly persistent. A number of job market related earnings instability factors are also identified.

The changes in Italian male earnings from 1970 to 1995 are analyzed by Cappellari (2000) using the minimum distance method. He analyses the earnings dynamics and the long-term inequality or short-term earnings volatility nature of aggregate earnings differentials. The earning autocovariance structure is decomposed into its persistent and transitory components. The complete model adopting an ARMA(1,1) process has the following structure:

$$
\begin{aligned}
y_{iat} &= \kappa_{(a-t)} \pi_t y_{iat}^P + \lambda_{(a-t)} \tau_t v_{it} \\
v_{it} &= \rho v_{i,t-1} + \varepsilon_{it} + \theta \varepsilon_{i,t-1}
\end{aligned}
$$
(3.21)

where y_{iat} is log-earnings of individual i, at age a, in year t, the superscript p denotes permanent, v captures the effects of random deviation from the permanent earnings, π_t and τ_t are the shifters on the permanent and transitory component, and $\kappa_{(a-t)}$ and $\lambda_{(a-t)}$ are sets of the birth cohort shifters. Cross-sectional earnings differentials are

---

[5] In nested error component models the data has more dimensions than the traditional two-way error component models, with individual-specific and time-specific effects. These effects are interrelated and vary in one or two dimensions. In industrial organization the extra dimensions to the firm and time are industrial sector, ownership, regions and countries. In the context of income data the extra dimensions can be distinguished for instance by the individuals' age group, family, gender, country of origin, or region(s) of residency.

growing over time. Such growth is determined by the permanent earnings component resulting from the divergence of the earnings profile over the working career and an increase in overall persistence during the first half of the 1990s. When allowing for occupation-specific components, the growing permanent earnings differentials arise from the earnings distribution of non-manual workers and the latter enjoy higher flexibility in pay settings. The introduction of technical innovations increased the relative demand and wages of skilled labourers (see also Borjas, 1994, 1999; and Atkinson, 1999). Another life cycle model of earnings dynamics with an ARMA(1,1) suggested by Moffitt and Gottschalk (2002) is written as:

$$(3.22) \quad y_{iat} = \alpha_t \mu_{iat} + v_{iat} = \alpha_t (\mu_{i,a-1,t-1} + \omega_{iat}) + (\rho_t v_{i,a-1,t-1} + \xi_{iat} + \theta_t \xi_{i,a-1,t-1})$$

where the parameters of the model shift over time. The objective is to investigate the driving force behind the trends in the US widening earnings distribution. They fit stochastic earnings processes to the empirical covariance structure and decompose it into its permanent and transitory parts. Results based on earnings of a sample of 2,988 male heads aged 20-59 from PSID during 1968-96 show that the variance of permanent earnings increased in the 1970s and 1980s, while the variance of transitory earnings rose in the 1980s and 1990s. The two components equally contributed to the growth of earnings inequality. Similar results were found by Baker and Solon (1998) using data on Canadian men. To compare the covariance structure of earnings by 16 cohorts and split the sample by occupation at age 22 into four skill groups, Dickens (2000) estimated the following model:

$$(3.23) \quad \begin{aligned} y_{iat} &= \alpha_t \mu_{iat} + v_{iat} \\ &= (1 + \alpha_1 t + \alpha_2 t^2)(\mu_{i,a-1} + \omega_{ia}) + (1 + \delta_1 t + \delta_2 t^2)(\rho_t v_{i,a-1,t-1} + \xi_{it} + \theta_t \xi_{i,a-1,t-1}) \end{aligned}$$

where the permanent and transitory components vary non-linearly over time according to a quadratic equation in $\alpha_1, \alpha_2, \delta_1$ and δ_2. The model is very complicated, yet the number of unknown parameters is reduced by using an interaction of vectors of parameters. Results using UK individual earnings data over the period 1975-95 suggest that an individual's earnings contain a highly permanent element, modelled by a random walk specification in age. The rise in earnings inequality was mainly driven by the permanent earnings differential in the first half of the 1980s, while later appear to be the outcome of earnings volatility. The increase in the variance of earnings is greater in the non-manual groups and is driven by the changes in the transitory variance.

In sum a further classification of inequality decomposition can be made by the transitory and permanent nature of inequality. Here the focus is on the dynamics or changes in individual earnings from one period to another. The earnings covariance structure is decomposed into persistent and transitory components. Their contributions to the growth of earnings inequality by sub-groups are quantified. This is important in the design of policy measures and expectations about their impact on earnings inequality. Estimated permanent earning dynamics allow analyses of individual specific earnings profiles, and a few examples are found in Baker (1997), Baker and Solon (1998) and Cappellari (2000). Cappellari finds that the earnings profiles diverge with characteristics, like age, implying a widening of permanent differentials over the working career, with skills implying differences in permanent earnings growth among skilled and manual workers due to an increase in permanent differentials over time. A distinction between permanent and transitory components of earnings differentials has important implications for the understanding of changing inequality, the segmented distribution of household's income and welfare. Rising earnings inequality may exacerbate a household's poverty, and calls for interventions and design of policies aimed at alleviating such welfare-worsening effects (Gottschalk, 1997 and Gottschalk and Smeeding, 1997).

The path from wage shocks to resulting changes in the observed consumption allocation decisions shows associations with factors deriving from the income processes. Attanasio *et al.* (2002) argue that the simultaneous analysis of earnings and consumption data can add to our insights of the evolution of inequality. It can be helpful in decomposing shocks to earnings and wages not only into transitory and permanent components, but also to distinguish shocks that households are able to smooth out from those they are not, differentiating the responses to shocks with primary and secondary earners' components of household earnings. Such information is important in the design of policy measures, in identification and quantification of their effects, and the distribution and the cost of their inequality alleviation. The presence of permanent and chronic inequality reduces the impact of inequality reducing policy measures.

STATISTICAL INFERENCE FOR INEQUALITY MEASUREMENT

Statistical inferences for inequality measurement, if any, are based on the asymptotic distribution of the index, the delta-method. One difficulty that arises in this context is the dependency in the data as inequality indices are often estimated based on a cross-section of a panel survey. To test for changes in the index over time, it is necessary to take into account the intertemporal covariance structure of incomes requiring calculation of covariances.

An alternative to the delta-method is the bootstrapping method. Previous studies suggest that bootstraping is an attractive alternative to the existing approximate asymptotic inference methods. It provides an estimate of the sampling distribution of inequality by resampling from the original survey, thus simulating the original sampling procedure. The method has advantages in small samples and accounts for stochastic dependencies without explicitly dealing with its covariance structure. Mills and Zandvakili (1997) used the bootstrap method to calculate confidence intervals for some inequality indices as well as for the components of a decomposition of the Theil coefficient by subgroups, and compare them with those obtained based on the delta-method. The results based on PSID and National Longitudinal Surveys (NLS) pre- and post-tax income data suggest that statistical inference is essential even when large samples are available, and that the bootstrap procedure appears to perform well in this setting.

The validity of the bootstrap method is also shown in the context of inequality, mobility and poverty measurement in Biewen (2002a), where additional scenarios consider correlated data, panel attrition or non-response, decomposition by sub-groups or income sources and the decomposition of inequality changes. The class of additively decomposable inequality (I) measure is employed. The contribution of the between-group component, the share of the within-group component of subgroup j and the within-group inequality to the overall inequality are computed. Experiments based on German wage data show that a higher coverage accuracy can be obtained by using bootstrap procedures. The decomposition of the changes in inequality following Mookherjee and Shorrocks (1982) is:

(3.24)
$$I^2 - I^1 = \Delta \approx \sum_{j=1}^{J} \overline{P}_j \Delta I^j + \sum_{j=1}^{J} \overline{I}^j \Delta P_j + \sum_{j=1}^{J} (\overline{r}_j - \log \overline{r}_j) \Delta P_j$$
$$+ \sum_{j=1}^{J} (\overline{P}_j \overline{r}_j - \overline{P}_j) \Delta \log(\mu_{1,1}^j (\mu_{1,0}^j)^{-1}) = \Delta_W + \Delta_{SW} + \Delta_{SM} + \Delta_M$$

where P and r denote population share and relation income, bars indicate average values over two periods, Δ is the difference operator, $\Delta_W, \Delta_{SW}, \Delta_{SM}$ and Δ_M stands for the contribution of changing levels of within-age group inequality, changes in population shares of the age groups on the within group and between group components, and changes in mean incomes to the changes in overall inequality. Monte Carlo results suggest that the confidence intervals based on the simplest possible bootstrap procedure achieve the same coverage accuracy as intervals obtained based on the conventional normal approximation and should be preferred in practice.

Maasoumi and Heshmati (2000) conduct bootstrap tests for the existence of first and second order stochastic dominance amongst Swedish income distributions over time and for several subgroups of immigrants and Swedes. Results are based on a sample of 43,724 individuals observed for the period 1982-90. Two income definitions are used; pre-transfer and taxes gross income, and post-transfer and taxes disposable income. A comparison of the distribution of these two variables affords a partial view of Sweden's welfare system. The focus is on the development of incomes of Swede's and immigrant groups of single individuals identified by: country of origin, period of residence, age, education, gender, marital status and household size. The results suggest that although the sample of singles studied is a relatively homogenous segment of the population of individuals, first order dominance is rare, but second order dominance holds in several cases especially amongst disposable income distribution. Income and welfare policies favour the elderly, females, and larger families, while taxes and public transfers are shown to be effective measures in reducing the variance of disposable income. The higher the educational credentials, the higher are the burdens of this welfare equalization policy. The development of income for immigrants has been different than those of Swedes and strongly affected by their length of residence and country of origin. Maasoumi and Heshmati (2003) using a panel of household data obtained from PSID, and a bootstrapping method, conditioning on household attributes, find a number of strong dominance rankings, both between groups and over time, and in both gross and disposable incomes.

Foster and Sen (1997) in their review of economic inequality after a quarter century suggest a new approach to inequality rankings based on normalized stochastic dominance. They find the new inequality criterion useful in ranking inequality of distributions with different means. Formby, Smith and Zheng (1999) show that coefficient of variation (CV) is closely related to this new criterion. Specially, a monotonic transformation of coefficient of variation, $\frac{1}{2}(CV)^2$ is equal to the area between the second-degree normalized stochastic curve and the line of perfectly equal distribution.

Van de gaer, Funnell and McCarthy (1999) indicate two ways of statistical inference with measures of inequality. One can use the bootstrap method to calculate bootstrapped standard errors of inequality or the functions of inequality measures as illustrated earlier. Alternatively, one can try to establish the large sample distribution of the inequality measure. These distribution-free statistical inferences are then extended to the cases where incomes are correlated. Accounting for correlated nature of samples is important in the comparison of inequality before and after taxes and transfers or looking at the evolution of the distribution of income over time using panel data. The framework is illustrated with data from the Irish household budget survey of 1994. The results suggest that the positive correlation between incomes before and after tax reduces the standard errors of the difference in inequality before and after taxation substantially.

INFERENCES ABOUT THE GINI INDEX

It is not common for empirical researchers to report Gini standard errors, though ideally they should be reported to enable researchers to make inferences about the index. Giles (2002) extends the OLS regression framework as an alternative to the jackknife, statistical resampling technique to get a large-sample approximation for the standard error of the Gini to seemingly unrelated regressions. The variance of Gini obtained from a three-step procedure is:

$$(3.25) \quad Var(G) = 4Var(\hat{\theta})/n^2$$

where Gini can be written as:

$$(3.26) \quad G = (2\hat{\theta}/n) - 1 - (1/n)$$

and

$$(3.27) \quad \hat{\theta} = \left[\left(\sum_{i=1}^{n} iy_i \right) \middle/ \left(\sum_{i=1}^{n} y_i \right) \right]$$

is the weighted least squares estimator of $i = \theta + v_i$, and v_i is a heteroscedastic disturbance term. Penn World Table Data for 133 countries in the years 1950, 1975, 1980 and 1985 is used, and Giles provides a basis for various ways to test the robustness of the Gini coefficient to the changes in the sample data. Karagiannis and Kovacevic (2000) suggest a method to calculate the jackknife variance estimator for the Gini coefficient by two passes through the data as:

$$(3.28) \quad Var_i = \frac{N-1}{N}(G_i - G)^2 + Var_{i-1}$$

where N is the sample size, G_i is the value of the Gini coefficient when the ith observation is taken out of the sample and G is the Gini coefficient based on all observations. The jackknife standard error is then obtained by taking the square root of the variance. The advantage with this procedure is that it is simple to use but not in the case of Gini if there are many observations and each time an observation is dropped and a new pseudo estimate of Gini must be calculated. Ogwang (2000) suggests an alternative regression interpretation of the Gini index which is then exploited to derive a simple algorithm in a seven-step procedure to compute its jackknife standard errors index using OLS regression. The method provides that incomes are sorted in ascending order and assuming heteroscedastic disturbances (weighted least squares).

The statistical approach to income inequality measurement is also discussed by Giorgi (1999) who focuses on the sampling properties of some inequality indices using distribution-free and parametric approaches. He considers two independent samples of size n_1 and n_2, then $\left[(I_1 - I_2)/((\hat{\sigma}_1/\sqrt{n_1}) + (\hat{\sigma}_2/\sqrt{n_2})) \right]$ is asymptotically distributed $N(0,1)$, where I denotes income inequality. The distribution-free approach involves (jackknife and bootstrap) methods of testing a hypothesis or setting up a confidence interval which does not require assumptions on the form of the parent distribution. The parametric approach hypothesis that the form of the underlying distribution is known means the inequality measure is expressed as a function of the considered distribution.[6] The iterated bootstrap method is applied in analysing the changes in income inequality over time based on sample data by Xu (2000). The results, based on a proposed method with bias correction on the US income in 1969, 1979 and 1988, verify the statistical significance of the changes in income inequality during the 1970s and 1980s.

Schechtman and Yitzhakai (1999) shows that the Gini correlation measures the dependence between two random variables, based on the covariance between one variable and the cumulative distribution of the other. Its properties are a mixture of Pearson's and Spearman's correlation measures, and they propose its application to decompose the Gini coefficient of household income into its components such as household heads, spouse and capital incomes. Another possible area of application is to analyze the variability of assets and their impacts on the stability of a finance portfolio.

The delta and bootstrapping methods are the two alternatives in making inference for inequality measurement. The latter has advantages in that it avoids complicated covariance calculations, and is used to calculate confidence intervals for different subgroups, inequality within and between subgroups, inequality decomposed by income sources and for the components of a decomposed inequality index. For instance one looks at the evolution of the distribution of income over time using panel data and compares inequality over time before and after taxes and transfers for different subgroups. Other approaches used include the jackknife and regression methods to report the Gini standard errors.

---

[6] The distributional assumptions involve: rectangular, exponential, Pareto, log-normal, Burr, Dagum and two-parameter gamma distributions.

SUMMARY

This review focused on recent developments of inequality decomposition and decomposition of the changes in poverty. The origin of the modern inequality decomposition literature is to be found in Shorrocks' work. Inequality is decomposed by subgroups, income sources, causal factors and by other unit characteristics. Regression-based methods of decomposition of inequality by income sources have been proposed where standard income-generating equations written in terms of covariances are estimated. Compared with the unconditional approach, the regression-based methods, depending on the way it is modelled, provide possibilities to quantify the conditional roles of various characteristics in a multivariate context and allowing for heterogeneity in responses. Furthermore, the confidence intervals for disaggregated contributions to the inequality index can be constructed.

Different methods of decomposing the changes in poverty into growth, redistribution, poverty standard and residual components were described, where the aim is to study the effects of growth on poverty accounting for changes in the distribution of income and the standard of poverty. The first two components differ by the base year and the Lorenz curve reference level chosen as a benchmark. Depending on data availability different measures of income and poverty can be used, and such an exercise is important in the evaluation of the inequality impact of growth and its impacts on poverty among regions, subgroups and sectors.

It is important to distinguish between the transitory and permanent components of earnings. In the long-term some effects of transitory shocks average out, while other persists. Economic policy aiming to change earnings inequality should distinguish shocks that households are able to smooth out and target those that they can not smooth out by accounting for subgroup heterogeneity and earnings instability. Several recently introduced dynamic earnings models with various degrees of complexity and a summary of their findings based on household surveys are given. These parametric approaches are conditional of various covariates. The main benefits of parametric approaches are that the changes are conditional on various attributes not all captured by the growth and the redistribution of components. Furthermore, confidence intervals for the effects are estimated. The main disadvantage is the assumption of functional forms of the relationship and its specification.

Statistical inferences for inequality measurement including delta and bootstrapping methods to provide estimates of the sampling distribution of inequality are discussed. The bootstrap method is used to calculate confidence intervals for different subgroups, within and between subgroups inequality, inequality decomposed by income sources, to compare inequality over time before and after taxes and transfers and for different subgroups. Jackknife and regression methods are employed to report Gini standard errors. The measurement, decomposition and modelling issues discussed here are crucial to the design of policy measures and expectations about their impacts on earnings inequality and poverty reduction.

Chapter 4

THE WORLD DISTRIBUTION OF INCOME AND INCOME INEQUALITY: A REVIEW OF THE ECONOMICS LITERATURE[*]

ABSTRACT

This review covers a range of measures and methods frequently employed in empirical analysis of global income inequality and global income distribution. Different determinant factors along with quantification of their impacts and empirical results from different case studies are presented. These results are further contrasted to those obtained based on the World Income Inequality Database. A number of issues crucial to the studies of global income inequality are also addressed. These are the concepts, measurement and decomposition of inequality, the world distribution of income and inequality measured at different levels of aggregation: global, international and intra-national. We analyse income at each of the three levels, discuss the benefits and limitations of each approach and present empirical results found in the literature and compare it with those based on the World Income Inequality Database. Research on the world income inequality supports increased awareness of the problem, its measurement and quantification, identification of causal factors and policy measures to affect global income inequality.

Keywords: Global income inequality, income distribution, inequality indices

INTRODUCTION

Inequality can have many dimensions. Economists are concerned specifically with the monetarily measurable dimension related to individual or household incomes. However, this is just one perspective and inequality is also linked to inequality in skills, education,

---

[*] This chapter is forthcoming as: Heshmati A. (2006), The world distribution of income and income inequality: A review of the economics literature, Journal of World System Research.

opportunities, happiness, health, life expectancy, welfare, assets and social mobility.[1] Here income inequality refers to the inequality of the distribution of individuals, household or some per capita measure of income. Lorenz Curve is the standard approach used for analysing the size distribution of income and measures of inequality and poverty. It plots the cumulative share of total income against the cumulative proportion of income receiving units. The divergence of a Lorenz curve for a given income distribution to Lorenz curve for perfect equality is measured by some index of inequality. The most widely used index of inequality is the Gini coefficient. Among the other measures of inequality are: the range, the variance, the squared coefficient of variation, the variance of log incomes, the absolute and relative mean deviations, and Theil's two inequality indices. There are three basic properties that one would expect the above indices to satisfy: mean or scale independence, population size independence and the Pigou-Dalton condition. The Gini coefficient, the squared coefficient of variation and the two Theil's measures satisfy each of the three properties (see Anand 1997). For the reviews of inequality see Subramanian (1997a), Cowell (2000) and Chapter 2 of this monograph.

The literature on economic inequality is growing as a result of increasing interest in measuring and understanding the level, causes and development of income inequality and poverty. In 1990s there was a shift in research which previously focused on economic growth, identification of the determinants of economic growth and convergence in per capita incomes across countries to analyze the distribution of income, its development over time and the identification of factors determining the distribution of income and poverty reductions.[2] This shift is among others a reflection of the changes in technology and increased awareness of the growing disparity and the importance of redistribution and poverty reductions. The growing disparity calls for the analysis of various aspects of income inequality and poverty including their measurement, decomposition, causal factors, inequality reduction, poverty elimination and redistribution policies. For a recent review decomposition of income inequality and poverty see Heshmati (2004b).

The extensive literature emerging in recent years has focused on the study of how the distribution of incomes across countries and globally has developed over time. Two empirical regularities identified in the distribution of income are the tendency for income per capita to converge, and an increase in inequality in the distribution of personal income in many countries. The increased interest in the studies of income inequality may be both cause and effect the availability of income distribution data. Availability of household surveys has been improved and several standardized databases have been created. These allow analysis of income distribution at the most disaggregate individual or per capita household levels. Income distribution is otherwise often analyzed at three levels of aggregation, namely global,

---

[1]   In chapter 2 we reviewed the recent advances in the measurement of inequality and gives attention to the interrelationship between income and non-income dimensions of inequality.

[2]   For a selection of studies of growth and convergence in per capita incomes see: Barro (1991), Barro and Sala-i-Martin (1995), Islam (1995), Mankiew, Romer and Weil (1992), and Quah (1996c). Quah (2002), Ravallion (2003b), Sala-i-Martin (2002a) analysed convergence in income inequality, while Acemoglu and Ventura (2002), Atkinson (1997), Bourguignon and Morrisson (2002), Gottschalk and Smeeding (1997) and Milanovic (2002a) focus on the distribution of income. Acemoglu (2002), Caminada and Goudswaard (2001), Cornia and Kiiski (2001), Gotthschalk and Smeeding (2000), Milanovic (2002a), O'Rourke (2001), Park (2001), Sala-i-Martin (2002b) and Schultz (1998) studied trends in income inequality. The relationship between inequality, poverty and growth is reviewed in Heshmati (2004a).

international and intra-national.[3] It can also be measured at the continental and sub-continental levels where one can examine inequality both between and within economic or geographic regions. There is evidence that poverty and inequality has developed differently between and within regions. The continental and regional inequalities are discussed in Chapter 5 and Chapter 6 respectively.

There are two empirical regularities in the distribution of income: the tendency for income per capita to converge (decrease in inequality), and the increase in inequality in the distribution of personal income in many countries (Schultz 1998). Inequality increased in Western countries in the 1980s and in transition countries in the 1990s. The reasons for increased interest in income inequality are the theoretical development and the availability of data on income distribution (Milanovic 2002a). The theoretical reasons are the better incorporation of inequality in economic theory, the growth–inequality relationship and the link between inequality and political economy. Availability of household surveys has improved in the former Soviet Union, Eastern Europe and Africa. Several standardized databases have been created, often based on the experiences gained from the Luxembourg Income Study (LIS), and now include the Household Expenditure and Income Data for Transition Economies (HEIDE), Africa Poverty Monitoring (APM), and the World Bank's Living Standards Measurement Study Household Surveys (LSMS). In several studies, based on these databases, inequality and poverty are related to a number of determinant factors. Due to the availability of data, the empirical results are mainly based on the second half of the twentieth century. We aim to cover a range of measures and methods frequently employed in empirical analysis of global income inequality and income distribution. Different determinant factors along with quantification of their impacts together with empirical results from different case studies are presented. These results are further contrasted to those obtained based on the World Income Inequality Database (WIID) covering almost the same period and the same group of countries.

This review addresses a number of issues crucial to the studies of global income inequality. These are the concepts, measurement and decomposition of inequality, the world distribution of income and inequality measured at different levels of aggregation: global, international and intra-national. In this chapter we analyse income at each of the three levels, and discuss the benefit and limitations of each approach and present empirical results found in the literature and those based on the World Income Inequality Database (WIID). Research on the world income inequality contributes to the increased awareness of the problem, its measurement and quantification, identification of causal factors and of policy measures to affect global inequality. Since several studies cover more than one dimension or aggregation level of inequality, there is some degree of overlapping in the three subsections of this study on global, international and intra-national.

It should be noted that this chapter is limited to review only the economic literature on income inequality. As such it does not cover the other large inequality literature in for

---

[3] Global or world income inequality refers to inequality differences between all individuals in the world (Milanovic 2002a; Schultz 1998; Quah 1999; Bourguignon and Morrisson 2002; Sala-i-Martin 2002a), while international income inequality refers to the economic disparity between countries (Acemoglu 2002; Cornia and Kiiski 2001; Gothscalk and Smeeding 1997; and Milanovic 2001). At the intra-national level inequality refers to the distribution of income among people within individual countries (Cameron 2000; Cowell, Ferreira and Lichtfield 1998; Gustafsson and Shi 2002; Liebbrandt, Woolard and Woolard 2000). Several of these studies cover two or all three dimensions.

instance sociology and political science. These literatures to a great extent overlap. A number of sociological literature reviews have been published on the issue of world income inequality and its development. Firebaugh and Goesling (2004), Firebaugh (1999 and 2000a) and Babones and Turner (2003) are among the major sociological review articles that have been published in recent years. Similar reviews for readers who are interested in the political science literature on the inequality are available in the series of edited volumes by Seligson and Passe-Smith (2003). The sociologists researches on empirics of world income inequality have resulted in the now-famous Korseniewicz-Firebaugh debate (Korzeniewicz and Moran, 2000; and Firebaugh, 2000b). The debate is related to the weighting procedures for assessing trends in world income inequalities. The debate centres round the reliance on the use of exchange rate per capita incomes or purchasing power parity based incomes in measuring world income inequality and its decomposition into between and within country components. Such debate on the premise and pitfalls in the use of secondary datasets and weighting procedures exists among the economists as well (Atkinson and Brandolini, 2001). There are also two special issues on the global income inequality published in the Journal of World-System Research (Babones 2002; Bata and Bergesen 2002a, 200b; Bergesen and Bata 2002; and Bornschier 2002).

Rest of the chapter is organised as follows. In the second section we review alternative approaches examining the distribution of income among representative world individuals and present some critiques on the approaches used. The third section is on the international level where the focus is on between country inequality and factors affecting the level and its development over time. The findings of trend are compared with those based on WIID database. In the fourth section the intra-national inequality is reviewed. The fifth section explores the factors affecting the shape of the world distribution of income. The factors include trade, education, growth, redistribution policies and globalisation. The final and sixth section is on the redistribution of the world income and a post-script and conclusion to the review.

DISTRIBUTION OF INCOME AMONG THE WORLD INDIVIDUALS

An analysis of the dynamics of distribution of income across people worldwide would ideally be based on data on individual incomes accruing over time. One could then estimate the entire income distribution across individuals and characterize its dynamics through time. Such data representative of populations, consistent over time and across countries is not available and is very unlikely to be produced globally anytime soon. A similar data but at smaller scale for the OECD and transition countries, the LIS and the HEIDE is available. There are, however, major differences in defining various pre- and post-taxes income components and transfers by countries and over time.

Despite the above problems, the LIS could serve as an example in the creation of a World Income Study (WIS) database. Ideally this database would allow testing alternative distributional hypotheses, a variety of concepts and measurements and to uncover different characteristics of income inequality.

In the absence of a WIS database or other appropriate databases, several researchers have attempted to develop alternative empirical frameworks based on aggregative statistics of the underlying data to serve in different ways as a substitute in the analysis of global income distribution and income inequality. A brief description of these data sets together with the outcomes is given in Chapter 7 of this volume.

Alternative Approaches to the Analysis of the World Distribution of Income

There are number of ways to estimate income distribution and global income inequality and to construct world indices of income distribution. One procedure is to use national household income (or expenditure) survey collected mainly since the mid 1980s providing direct income information by quintiles and deciles for individual countries to construct world income distribution over time (Milanovic 2002a). A short, unequal and unbalanced time periods is among the limitations of this approach.

A second approach is to use the mean income or GDP per capita for individual countries complemented by Gini coefficient or standard deviation as the measurement of income dispersion within the country and make an assumption of log-normality to construct income distribution for individual countries (Schultz 1998 and Quah 1999).

A third approximation is to use known actual income distribution of representative countries and apply it to other countries with geographical and economic similarities but with missing data (Bourguignon and Morrisson 2002). Among the limitations of this approach are variations in intertemporal patterns of income distribution and changing counterfactual countries over time.

The fourth way is to use aggregate GDP data and within-country income share to assign a level of income to each person in the world to estimate income distribution and global income inequality using different indices (Berry, Bourguignon and Morrrisson 1983 and Sala-I-Martin 2002b). The second and fourth alternatives are similar in the use of per capita GDP but they differ by additional information on within-country income shares used.

The fifth, and quite a simple approach, is to divide the global population into percentiles in terms of per capita income. In this approach, introduced by Park (2001), global income inequality refers to inequality among the global population. This method is similar to the second approach. Recently Dikhanov and Ward (2002) combined micro and macro approaches to reconstruct the world's income distribution.

It is to be noted that despite the limited number of time points the first alternative with direct income information at the individual (or household level) is the preferred approach. It allows analysis and comparison of inequality and distribution by subgroups, sectors, locations and household attributes across countries. Below we describe briefly each alternative to estimate the world income distribution.

Studies of the World Distribution of Income

Milanovic's Approach

The distribution of world income or expenditure classified based on the first approach at the individual level was derived by Milanovic (2002a).[4] This study is based on household surveys from 91 countries for 1988 and 1993.[5] Income and expenditure are adjusted for purchasing power parity (PPP) between countries. Inequality measured by the Gini coefficient increased from 0.63 in 1988 to 0.66 in 1993. The change is robust to the changes in the sample countries, PPP adjustment and inequality measurement (Gini coefficient and Theil). Inequality for each of the five regions (African; Asian; Latin American; Eastern Europe and FSU; and Western Europe, North America and Oceania) is decomposed. Using the Pyatt (1976) type decomposition, the overall inequality is decomposed into within-country (W), between-country (B) and overlapping (L) components. The decomposition formula for the Gini coefficient is:

$$(4.1) \quad Gini = W_i + B_i + L_i = \sum_{i=1}^{n} Gini_i \, p_i \pi_i + \frac{1}{\mu} \sum_{i=1}^{n} \sum_{j>i}^{n} (y_j - y_i) p_i p_j + L_i$$

where y_i is the mean income of country i, $Gini_i$ is the Gini coefficient for country i, π_i is the income share of the total income in the region, p_i is the population share of country i and μ the mean income of the region. Results show that the increase was driven by between-country rather than within-country differences in mean income. The main reason for low within-country inequality is the low and crowded per capita mean income. Results based on only two years of observation might be sensitive to different developments of business cycles in major countries or non-random (outlier) year differences. Furthermore, the uneven survey quality and differences in survey definition of income and expenditure are two potential problems. The assumption of equality of individuals within each decile, the problem of mixing income and expenditure, and the use of a single and PPP exchange rate may bias the overall inequality and its decomposition. Milanovic aims to establish the benchmark for world inequality in 1988 and 1993.

Schultz and Quah's Approach

In analysing inequality in the distribution of personal income in the world Schultz (1998) uses four different types of data; population estimates, PPP prices adjusted GDP per capita incomes, national estimates of the size distribution of household incomes, and intra-household gender differences in education inequality. Three indicators of income inequality are computed. The variance of logarithm of income, Gini concentration ratio, and the Theil mean log deviation are estimated based on the cumulative shares of income received by the

---

[4]   This paper is methodologically similar to those by Ravallion, Datt and van der Walle (1991) and Chen, Datt and Ravallion (1994). These are also based on household surveys, but limited to developing countries and focus on changes in world poverty, not on inequality.

[5]   In addition to the common sample (91), a number of countries are observed only in 1988 (10) and only in 1993 (28), or not included in either year (61). The common sample is extended in Milanovic (2001) to 126 countries.

quintile shares of income units. The variance in the logarithms of per capita GDP in PPP prices increased in the world from 1960 to 1968 and it has decreased since the mid 1970s. In the latter period the convergence in inter-country incomes offsets any increase in within-country income inequality. The variance measure is decomposed into between-country, within-country and within-household log income variance components. About two-thirds of overall inequality is due to the inter-country and one-third is from the intra-country components. The inter-household inequality and gender differences in education are the main contributors to the within-country inequality. The results are sensitive to the changes in sample size and the quality of the data underlying the inter-household component. For instance if China is excluded from the sample the decline in world inequality after 1975 is not anymore evident.

In another study using a similar approach as Schultz (1998), Quah (1999) combines distribution dynamics for per capita incomes across countries, with personal income distributions within countries over time. The result is expected to produce a picture of the worldwide income distribution dynamics across people. Given that information on actual distributions for economies in a number of periods are available, then the worldwide income distribution is obtained using the country and the world population sizes. The results based on country data from 1980-92 show that macroeconomic factors determine cross-country patterns of growth and convergence in growth determine world inequalities. However, the relation between a country's growth and its within-country inequality plays a small role in global inequality dynamics. The positive effect of economic growth on individual incomes and reductions in poverty overwhelms any potential negative impacts like increases in inequality. The increase in inequality between 1980 and 1992 is entirely due to the between-country inequality and derived from macroeconomic growth, not from microeconomic changes in within-country inequalities. Some numbers on inequality and poverty changes in India and China during the period 1980-92 are presented without much detail of the method used and underlying data. The advantage here is a sequence of annual observations for individual countries. However, the manuscript is incomplete and results are far from the final.

Bourguignon and Morrisson's Approach

Bourguignon and Morrisson (2002) attempts in estimating the world inequality of personal income and its evolution over time since 1820. Since data covering such a long period is sparsely available, the countries are divided into 33 groups of single and multiple countries. The groups of countries are in turn aggregated into 6 blocks defined on a geographical, economic or historical basis. From the early nineteenth century to the eve of the First World War, the Gini coefficient increased from 0.50 to 0.61. After a deceleration period between the two world wars, it increased to 0.64 in 1950. It had, however, stabilized during the latter half of the twentieth century. The increase in the Gini coefficient was 30 per cent between 1820 and 1992, while the Theil index increased by 60 per cent in the same period. The process of strong convergence in economic growth among industrialized countries and divergence between groups of countries together with the take off of China in the beginning of the 1980s have been significant factors in determining the evolution of the world inequality.

In estimating the distribution of income among individuals rather than countries, Bourguignon and Morrisson rely on real GDP per capita, population and the distribution of income summarized by 9 deciles income shares and the top two ventile shares. They use the income shares multiplied by PPP adjusted per capita GDP to derive the world income distribution. They acknowledge the importance of taking into account demographic weights in shaping the evolution of the world distribution of income. Hence, the contribution of this paper lies in quantifying the importance of aggregate economic growth, population growth, and the structure of domestic income inequalities in explaining the evolution of the world distribution of income. Inequality is measured by the Gini coefficient, the Theil index, the mean logarithmic deviation and the standard deviation of logarithm. The limitation of such two-century studies lies however in the fact that the entire first century and the first half of the second century are based on very few observations on a few industrialized countries and is a poor representation of the world's population or incomes. Also a country observed within a region can be a poor proxy for other countries with missing observation that are located in the same region. The third issue is the low comparability and quality of the data over time.

In addition to the income dimension, Bourguignon and Morrisson consider non-income dimensions such as life expectancy in analysing the inequality in (economic) well-being. The average life expectancy has increased from 26.5 years in 1820 to 61.1 in 1992. Differences in the economic growth, the demographic growth and the changes in domestic income distribution are the factors contributing to the world income inequality. The disequalising factors are: the high economic performance of the European countries and its divergence to Anglo-Saxon, poor growth performances of the rural China and India combined with their size effects, and the slow growth of Africa in post 1950s. The main equalizing factors are: income equalisation within the European countries, catching up of the European countries over the US after the Second World War and the high growth performances of the Asian Tigers and the urban China since the 1980s. The result of the analysis of inequality among world citizens is summarised as follows. First, the world income inequality exploded since the early 19th century. Second, the increase is because of inequality among countries or regions rather than within countries. Third, inequality is not increasing but poverty concentration is increasing in some regions. Fourth, the international disparity in life expectancy is increasing.

Sala-I-Martin's Approach

According to the fourth approach Sala-I-Martin (2002a) uses aggregate GDP data and within-country income shares (although in some cases estimated income shares) for the period 1970-1998 to assign a level of income to each person in the world. He then estimates the kernel density function for the worldwide distribution of income, computes poverty rates for individual countries, and finally estimates global income inequality using seven different inequality indices.[6] The overall inequality is decomposed into within and between-country inequality components. The results show a reduction in the global inequality between 1980 and 1998. Using the same data he estimates the poverty rates and headcounts for 125 countries (Sala-I-Martin 2002b). Assuming $1/day and $2/day poverty lines he finds that the overall poverty rates declined during the last 20 years. While it declined in Asia and in Latin America in 1980, it increased in Africa. A total of nine indices[7] of income inequality were

---

[6] The indices include: the Gini coefficient, the variance of log-income, two Atkinson's indexes, the mean logarithmic deviation, the Theil index and the squared coefficient of variation.

[7] In addition to the seven indices of income inequality listed in the previous footnote, the ratio of the average income of top 20 per cent of the distribution to the bottom 20 per cent, and the ratio of income of the persons

estimated. The results indicate substantial reductions in global income inequality during the 1980s and 1990s.

In a smaller regional scale Londono and Szekely (2000) expand the Deininger and Squire (1996) data to assess the changes in aggregate poverty and inequality in Latin America. Their empirical results are based on the data from 13 Latin America countries observed during 1970 to 1995. Despite the differences in the levels across countries, inequality and poverty in most of the countries follow similar trends. Aggregate inequality increased during the 1970s, it deteriorated further during the 1980s and remained around the level registered in 1990 level during the 1990s. The excess inequality (defined as the ratio of observed to expected inequality) is 25% and increasing over time. Lack of improvement in the inequality is related to the non-pro-poor distribution of growth.

Park's Approach

Park (2001) examines the trends in global distribution of income defined as the real GDP per capita in 133 countries over the period 1960-1992 using data from the Penn World Tables. The global population is divided into percentiles in terms of per capita income and he estimates the share of global income accruing to each percentile. The income shares are then used to estimate a global Gini coefficient for the 20 and 10 percentiles of the global population. The global income inequality here refers to the inequality among the nations of the world rather than the individuals of the world. It accounts for the population size of countries but neglect PPP. The key restrictive assumption is that all individuals of a country earn the same level of income and that all countries constitute a single world economy. Results show that while the global distribution of income has not been more equal during the period of study as a whole, inequality has been declining during 1976-1992.

Recently Dikhanov and Ward (2002) in an attempt to reconstruct the complex nature of the global income distribution during the later part of the twentieth century employed an intermediate aggregation approach labelled as quasi-exact interpolation technique. A combined micro (survey) and macro (national accounts) approach along with PPP is used to reconstruct the World's income distribution. The technique allows for analysis of the global income distribution taking into consideration both within and between-country inequalities and thus measuring inequality between average representative individuals. In analysing the structure of global distribution and its regional composition and distributional changes over time a small sample of 45 countries for the selected periods 1970, 1980, 1990 and 1999 is used. The results show that the partial global distribution has twin peaks: one concentrating around China, India and Africa, and another around the OECD indicating the absence of middle class among the citizens of the world.

Some Critiques on the above Approaches

Results based on a few yearly observations are likely to be sensitive to the changing economic situation of countries. The uneven survey quality, the differences in the survey's definitions of income and expenditure, the assumption of equality of individuals within each

---

located at the bottom of the top quintile divided by the income of the persons located at the top of the bottom quintile are estimated.

decile, the problem of mixing of income and expenditure, and the use of a single PPP exchange rate affect the quality of analysis. However, these studies might serve to establish the benchmark for analysis of world inequality.

Bourguignon and Morrisson (2002) find the treatment of world inequality in international studies, like many of those mentioned above, in general oversimplified because all citizens in a country (or population shares) are considered as perfectly identical. As a consequence, the extent of inequality is underestimated by ignoring income disparity and the evolution of the distribution of income within countries (and income shares). The inference here is on international rather than world inequality biasing the view about the temporal patterns of world inequality. In their own approach the deciles represent individuals, i.e. instead of one representative individual ten representative individuals represent the country. Again here the within deciles variations are not accounted for.

The results in Dikhanov and Ward (2002) showed that the partial global distribution has twin-peaks, indicating the absence of a middle class among the citizens of the world. Regardless of the partition level Milanovic and Yotzhaki (2001) using the national income/expenditure distribution data from 119 countries find that the world lacks a middle class. A similar twin-peaks was also observed earlier by Quah (1996a). Sala-I-Martin (2002b) used income shares from 97 countries from 1970 to 1998 to show that by 1998 the twin-peaks vanished giving rise to a large middle class when one instead of the aggregate country data uses the individual income data. Over the 39 years period the acute absolute poverty declined while under the broader definition of poverty the number of poor as well as global inequality increased.

A limitation of the study by Dikhanov and Ward (2002) compared with Milanovic (2002a) is the small sample size. Very little information about the micro-level data, its coverage, consistency and the interpolation technique used is given. Capeau and Decoster (2003) explain the driving forces behind the differences in the two extreme positions on whether inequality fell (Sala-I-Martin 2002a and 2002b) or rose (Milanovic 2002a and 2002b). They relate the diverging tendencies among others to the three key factors including: GDP per capita versus budget survey income measures used, the population weighted inequality measures and the inequality among citizens irrespective of location.

Summary of the World Individuals' Income Inequality

There are a limited number of ways to construct world indices of income distribution and to measure global income inequality reflecting both inequalities between and within countries. For the summary of several studies of global inequality see Appendix 4.A where the combined micro and macro approach is often used. These studies differ largely by the extent and variations in the quality of the micro data part. Mean income per capita complemented with Gini coefficient, the standard deviation as measure of income dispersion, or the direct information from household surveys by quintiles and deciles for individual countries and the demographic information is the standard data requirement to construct world income distribution. Empirical results show that the world inequality measured by Gini coefficient increased from 0.50 in 1920 to 0.66 in 1992. Poverty, measured by headcount (per cent) during the same period decreased from 94.4 to 51.3. The inequality based on shorter period but with a better quality of data increased from 0.625 in 1988 to 0.659 in 1993.

Economic growth, population growth, life expectancy, and the changes in the structure of income inequality are the important factors in determining the evolution of the world income distribution. Empirical results show also the evidences of disparity in the development of life expectancy and economic growth. The inequality within individual countries is not increasing but the inequality between countries and regions is increasing as well the poverty concentration is increasing in some regions. The limitation of these studies is the short time period and the lack of income surveys with a satisfactory country population and a continuous time period coverage. Results are often based on a few observations and sensitive to various data and the estimation method. Despite their limitations these studies can serve to establish a benchmark for world income inequality and poverty.

INTER-NATIONAL DISTRIBUTION OF INCOME

The inter-national inequality refers to the distribution of income between countries. The common approach is to use the mean income or GDP per capita for individual countries complemented by the Gini coefficient or the standard deviation as measure of income dispersion within the country and within-country income shares to construct income distribution for individual countries. In the following a brief review of the literature is presented and results are compared with those obtained from the WIID data.

Between-Country Disparities

As previously shown there is a comprehensive literature on the measurement of inter-national inequality focusing on disparity between nations and very often on its relation with economic growth. As mentioned previously, in several studies there is a certain degree of overlapping between inequalities at different levels of aggregation. Sala-I-Martin (2002a) uses aggregate GDP data and within-country income shares to estimate the worldwide distribution of income, compute poverty rates and estimate the global income inequality for the period 1970-1998. The poverty rates of $1/day and $2/day have fallen during the period of the study from 20 to 5 per cent and from 44 to 18 per cent respectively. The poverty reduction corresponds to 300 to 500 million people in 1998. Inequality is decomposed into within and between-country inequality components. In contrast to several studies reviewed previously, the results show also the reduction in the global inequality between 1980 and 1998. Most global disparities are of cross-country rather than within country characteristics. The main source of between-country reductions is due to the growth in the Chinese economy. The within-country inequality has slightly increased. The lack of growth in the African economies might cause further divergence and the increase in global inequality.

Unlike in Sala-I-Martin the results by Maddison (2001) showed evidences of rising disparities in the world economy due to the divergence in economic performance across regions and countries over time. Bourguignon and Morrisson (1999) study showed that the increase in total inequality during the entire period of 1820-1990 is driven by a rise in inequality between countries. The inequality between countries is the dominating factor in the evolution of the world income inequality. Milanovic (2002a) in a comparison of income in

1988 and 1993 shows that between 75-88 per cent of inequality is attributed to the differences in mean income between countries and only 12-25 per cent is explained by the inequality within countries. As mentioned previously, Capeau and Decoster (2003) explain the driving forces behind the differences in the two extreme positions on whether inequality fell or rose. They relate the diverging tendencies to income measures, the use of weights and the assumption of inequality among citizens irrespective of the location.

Factors Affecting Inter-National Income Inequality

Several factors have been identified and attempts have been made to quantify their impacts on the inter-national income inequality. In the following, we review a number of recent studies investigating the inequality effects of population weights on the Gini coefficient, the regional cost of living, openness, technology spillovers, specialization in production, economic growth, initial condition, skill-biased technology and wages, supply and demand of human capital and redistributive policies. The case in favour of population share weighted Gini is when countries or regions are aggregated. I do not see any case against population share weighted Gini coefficient when applied in aggregated cases.

Inter-national distribution of income based on the Gini coefficients of national per capita GDP for the period 1950 to 1998 and 120 countries computed by Milanovic (2001). The temporal patterns of inequality differ by whether the Gini coefficient is weighted by population or not. The unweighted Gini coefficient shows a declining inequality between 1965 and 1978 and an increasing trend in inter-national inequality after 1978. The increased inequality in Latin America, the jump in the inequality in Eastern Europe and the former USSR and the low performance of the African countries has contributed to the increased unweighted global inequality. The picture differs if the Gini coefficients are computed by weighting the GDP per capita by regional population shares. The weighted results show a declining world inequality due to the faster growth in the Indian and Chinese economies than the world economy. However, the rapid economic growth has increased the within country inequality in both countries. The increases in inequality are also found to be sensitive when market-based valuation methods are used and allowances are made for the differences in regional cost-of-living (Ravallion and Chen (1999), and Ravallion and Datt (2000)).

Acemoglu and Robinson (2000) used the log of income per worker relative to the world average in 1990 against its 1960 value to analyse the development and the dispersion of the world income distribution. Despite the large differences in income across countries, the dispersion of the world income distribution has been relatively stable. They show that even in the absence of diminishing returns in production and technological spillovers, degree of openness to the international trade and the extent of specialisation lead to a stable world income distribution. However, Milanovic (2002b) using data on $PPP incomes from 90 countries around 1988 and 1993 shows that the effect of openness on a country's income distribution depends on the country's initial income level. Openness makes the income distribution worse before making it better.

Acemoglu (2002) reviews the faster increase in supply of skills in Europe and their labour market institutions which prevented wage inequality from increasing as the two most popular explanations for different inequality trends in the US and UK over the past decades. He identifies an additional factor to be the difference in the relative demand for skills. In

Europe investment in technologies is encouraged by the states increasing productivity of less-skilled workers, reducing skill-biased technical change in Europe than in the US. Eicher and Garcia-Penalosa (2001) argue that stock of educated workers in an economy determines both the degree of income inequality and the rate of growth. They identify parameters that are central to the supply and demand of human capital[8] that are crucial for inequality changes. Democratisation and political reforms through redistributive programs prevented widespread social unrest and revolution in Western societies in the nineteenth century with implications on the dynamics of growth and the fall in inequality (Acemoglu and Robinson 2000). However, the traditional public finance concern about the excess burden of the within-country redistribution cannot explain why there is so little world redistribution (Kopczuk, Slemrod and Yitzhaki 2002).

In the early 1980s a number of factors have contributed to the increased interest to changes in the distributional issues in the US in general and cross-national comparisons in particular. Gottschalk and Smeeding (1997) names three major factors: (i) studies showing the rising inequality of labour market income and their transformation into a greater inequality in the distribution of total family income, (ii) cross-national micro data became available for a variety of rich OECD countries, and (iii) the debate in the public policy arena over the fairness issue and the distributive effects of changes in government policies. In their review of the literature, they lay out a number of stylized facts and present summaries for both level and trend in earnings and income inequality. There are wide differences in inequality across countries, over time and gender. Countries with centralized wage bargaining are more equal. Wage inequality is increasing over time and the trends differ across countries. It is affected by demand for skills, returns to education and experience and institutional constraints on wages. Post-tax and transfers disposable income is more equally distributed, but inequality has increased over time in most countries. The increased receipt of capital income and demographic and social changes played roles in accounting for the rise in inequality in the OECD countries. Gottschalk and Smeeding search for a better structural model of income distribution and redistribution that can be applied across nations. It is concluded that an ideal model is a simultaneous model of generation of all sources of income and the formation of income sharing units.

The WIID Data

The data used here are obtained from the UNU-WIDER World Income Inequality Database (WIID) which is an expanded version of the Deininger and Squire (1996) database. The WIID contains information on income inequality, income shares, and a number of variables indicating the source and the quality of data for 146 countries. The countries are observed on an irregular basis mainly during the period 1950 to 1998. To avoid distortions for graphing the trend in global income inequality over time the lower part of the data at 1950 is truncated. The number of excluded observations covering 1867-1949 is only 25 or 1.5 per

---

[8] Here changes in inequality depend on externalities in education, evolution of direct cost of education, the elasticity of substitution in production between skilled and unskilled, and the relative productivity and costs of learning by doing versus R&D.

cent of the sample. A statistical summary of the WIID data is presented in Table 4.1. For a description of WIID and other databases see the description in Chapter 7.

Table 4.1 Statistical summary of the World Income Inequality Database (WIID)

Variable	obs	mean	std dev	minimum	maximum
Gini without income shares	1376	38.110	10.910	15.900	79.500
Gini with income shares	1358	36.433	9.273	17.830	66.000
Gini with/out income shares	1631	38.065	10.517	15.900	79.500
Income share Q1	844	0.069	0.036	0.016	0.157
Income share Q2	844	0.112	0.026	0.020	0.204
Income share Q3	844	0.157	0.025	0.070	0.255
Income share Q4	844	0.220	0.022	0.124	0.313
Income share Q5	844	0.441	0.082	0.249	0.710
Q5/Q1 ratio	844	8.175	5.758	2.035	40.812

Note: Gini coefficient with/without income shares refer to a combination of two observations for a country in a given year where one is with and the other without information on distribution of income.

The Gini coefficient is measured in percentage points. It is the mean of multiple observations for a country in a given year. The multiplicity of observations is due to the differences in income definitions, data sources, reference units, and the population coverage. In constructing global inequality we have adjusted the Gini coefficient for the population as:

$$(4.2) \quad Gini_t = \sum_{i=1}^{N}(pop_{it}\,/\,pop_t)\,Gini_{it} = \sum_{i=1}^{N} ps_{it}\,Gini_{it}$$

where pop_{it} is the population of country I in period t, ps_{it} is the corresponding population share. Aggregate population in a given year (pop_t) is the reference population for the global population. However, since our sample does not cover all countries in the world in every year, it should be noted that the population adjusted Gini measure based on the partial sample of countries is very sensitive to the exit and entry of countries with a large population like China and India. Furthermore, given that Gini is not decomposable, it provides an aggregate measure of global inequality, which make it didfficult, to interpret. Although these are about within country inequality the differences in inequality among the countries can be used to quantify the extent of the between country income inequality. A limitation is however that with the exception of population no other adjustments made for data collection methodology or changing sample membership over time.

To provide a better picture of the distribution of the world inequality and its development over time we report the unweighted mean, median, standard deviation and populations weighted mean Gini coefficient in Table 4.2 and also in Figure 4.1. The deciles observations are transformed to quintile income shares to make the income distribution comparable across countries and over time. This procedure results in maximum number of comparable observations that can be obtained from the data but at the cost of losing information. In Figure 4.2 the mean quintile income shares over time are presented. As an alternative measure of inequality the ratio of the highest to the lowest quintiles is computed (see Table 4.3). The annual percentage changes in the unweighted mean Gini coefficient are also calculated and shown in Table 4.2. The development of the latter two measures is also shown in Figure 4.3.

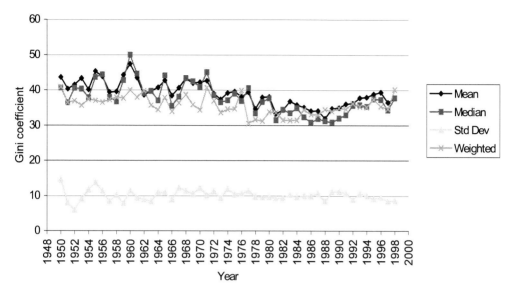

Figure 4.1. Global trends in income inequality.

**Table 4.2 Unweighted, population weighted and percentage changes
in global Gini coefficient over time**

Year	obs	minimum	mean	median	maximum	std dev	range	weighted	change
1950	7	23.36	43.63	40.60	70.00	14.46	46.64	40.90	-0.45
1951	6	35.60	40.33	36.42	55.70	7.92	20.10	36.41	-0.53
1952	8	35.60	41.47	40.57	53.00	5.85	17.40	36.93	1.94
1953	11	34.00	43.32	40.33	57.14	9.10	23.14	35.70	-7.76
1954	8	29.58	40.10	37.86	66.60	11.66	37.02	37.39	2.86
1955	11	23.27	45.30	43.68	67.20	13.74	43.93	36.99	0.87
1956	10	27.03	43.80	44.36	59.92	11.33	32.89	36.50	-1.14
1957	15	24.59	39.36	38.00	54.40	8.38	29.81	37.26	3.33
1958	18	20.47	39.50	36.73	55.19	10.14	34.72	37.97	-0.34
1959	17	35.25	44.24	42.79	60.60	7.84	25.35	37.72	4.23
1960	25	24.59	47.41	50.00	68.00	11.49	43.41	39.98	3.42
1961	21	25.30	43.45	44.59	62.48	9.44	37.18	38.01	-2.48
1962	25	21.18	38.64	39.15	53.50	8.90	32.32	39.84	-3.35
1963	25	22.50	39.69	39.71	58.20	8.38	35.70	35.69	-4.68
1964	21	20.89	40.70	37.00	63.00	10.99	42.11	34.40	6.62
1965	25	22.23	42.71	44.10	67.83	10.88	45.60	37.84	1.26
1966	17	25.56	38.38	35.50	53.89	8.88	28.33	33.94	-4.41
1967	28	19.87	40.61	38.09	66.00	12.26	46.13	36.35	-1.63

**Table 4.2 Unweighted, population weighted and percentage changes
in global Gini coefficient over time (Continued)**

Year	obs	minimum	mean	median	maximum	std dev	range	weighted	change
1968	34	15.90	43.33	43.36	66.27	11.38	50.37	38.67	2.19
1969	36	20.91	41.95	42.42	62.30	10.44	41.39	35.85	0.02
1970	42	20.15	42.16	40.84	79.50	12.20	59.35	34.38	0.17
1971	34	20.23	42.62	45.03	70.00	10.12	49.77	40.67	-0.78
1972	28	20.14	39.00	38.56	63.50	11.21	43.36	36.91	0.04
1973	31	19.22	37.34	36.53	65.10	9.40	45.88	33.64	1.11
1974	24	19.04	39.16	37.10	69.00	11.88	49.96	34.54	-2.51
1975	37	17.66	39.57	39.00	59.00	10.34	41.34	34.67	-0.50
1976	38	18.12	38.04	36.94	60.00	10.65	41.88	39.94	0.31
1977	33	18.60	39.40	40.56	59.00	11.34	40.40	30.51	0.55
1978	31	20.07	34.67	33.40	53.09	9.66	33.02	31.65	-0.73
1979	35	23.66	37.95	36.62	55.00	9.52	31.34	31.21	3.52
1980	41	20.70	38.05	37.65	65.50	9.49	44.80	33.83	-0.55
1981	56	19.72	33.33	31.44	57.30	9.37	37.58	33.60	-2.17
1982	31	20.88	34.34	34.47	56.00	9.34	35.12	31.49	1.58
1983	30	24.44	36.84	33.45	56.70	10.25	32.26	31.39	1.02
1984	34	21.30	35.77	34.92	58.01	9.49	36.71	31.47	0.28
1985	35	20.00	35.09	32.32	59.90	9.99	39.90	34.44	-1.80
1986	56	22.10	34.04	30.80	57.28	9.82	35.18	33.07	0.43
1987	40	19.40	34.13	31.84	59.01	10.59	39.61	32.99	0.04
1988	53	19.13	31.93	31.20	56.81	8.43	37.68	34.52	2.68
1989	66	20.57	34.76	30.87	62.90	11.04	42.33	33.98	-0.12
1990	63	19.55	34.94	31.99	63.00	11.11	43.45	34.90	2.86
1991	58	20.65	36.04	32.93	63.66	10.65	43.01	34.61	1.20
1992	60	22.62	36.21	35.64	56.07	8.88	33.45	36.22	4.98
1993	59	20.60	37.75	35.80	62.30	10.51	41.70	35.31	2.77
1994	56	20.00	37.95	35.35	60.90	9.90	40.90	35.15	2.86
1995	60	23.90	38.82	37.48	59.00	9.13	35.10	37.37	1.11
1996	53	23.70	39.32	37.27	58.85	9.45	35.14	35.36	2.26
1997	38	23.71	36.46	34.32	57.60	8.37	33.89	34.67	0.68
1998	15	25.30	37.72	37.75	59.11	8.70	33.82	40.12	3.66
Mean	49	23.05	39.02	37.74	60.48	10.09	37.43	35.65	0.50

Notes: Mean, median, standard deviation, minimum and maximum Gini values are based on the
unweighted country observations (obs) of the Gini coefficient in a given year, while weighted is
the mean value of the population weighted Gini coefficient. The population share is defined as the
share of total population of countries observed in a given year. The percentage change (change) is
based on the unweighted Gini.

The Global Trend in Inequality Based on the WIID Data

Simple descriptive statistics based on the WIID database are presented in Table 4.1. The summary statistics of the Gini coefficient for observations with and without income share distributions are given both separately and as well as jointly. The mean Gini coefficient for observations with income shares (36.43) is lower than for those without (38.11) income shares. There is a large variation in the distribution of income among the countries and over time. The income share of the poorest 20 per cent varies in the interval 0.016 and 0.157, with mean and standard deviation 0.069 and 0.036 respectively. The income share of the richest 20 per cent is 0.441 with relatively small standard deviation of 0.082. The disparity in income shares results in a Q5/Q1 ratio with a mean of 8.175 and a standard deviation of 5.758. The range varies within the interval 2.035 and 40.812.

There is a large disparity in inequality over time (see Table 4.2). It is to be noted that the numbers here reflect average of multiple observations for countries in a given year. The choice of measurement and the units of observation are not accounted for here. Therefore, the data lack uniform quality criteria and contains inconsistencies in distributions, definitions, sources, levels and coverage across countries and over time. If one chooses to use consistently segment of the data with the same definitions of income, of recipients and even the same welfare concept, the resulted sample will be very small and hardly sufficient to serve as a base for a discussion of global trends in income inequality.

The median value of Gini coefficient (37.74 per cent) is on the average 1.5 per cent lower than the mean value (39.02 per cent). The mean, median, standard deviation, minimum, maximum and range of unweighted and mean weighted Gini coefficient for the period 1950 to 1998 are presented in Table 4.2. There is a higher concentration of observations in the 1990s. Figure 4.1 shows that the mean and the median inequality follow the same pattern and are declining over time. The dispersion in inequality also declines after 1958.

The highest mean inequality values exceeding 55 per cent is found among the African countries (Central African Republic, Gabon, Kenya, Lesotho, Sierra Leone, Swaziland and Zimbabwe) and some Latin American countries exceeding 50 per cent (Bolivia, Brazil, Chile, Colombia and Honduras). The high levels of Gini, its concentration in conjunction with low average incomes are disastrous for aggregate welfare. The average range between maximum and minimum values observed for a country over time is 37.43 per cent and the standard deviation 10.09 per cent. A number of countries show quite large range of percentage variations, among others China, Brazil, Cuba, Guatemala, Jamaica, Morocco, Zimbabwe, Georgia, Finland, Netherlands, Spain, and the UK.

In the measurement of global or regional inequality it is a common standard to weight inequality by population. The population-weighted mean Gini coefficient is much lower (35.65 per cent) than the non-weighted (39.02 per cent). The drop is caused by the inclusion of countries with large populations and relatively low inequalities. Though India and China are frequently observed, the weighting procedure is not reliable, as the flow of population is very irregular over time. The average change in the Gini coefficient is 0.50 per cent indicating a small positive trend in non-weighted inequality over time. The change in Gini coefficient varies in the interval –7.76 (1952/1953) to +6.62 (1963/1964) per cent (see Figure 4.3 and Table 4.2). The shifts in the temporal patterns of Gini coefficient over the recent 50 years show that a simple time trend is not an appropriate way of modelling global trends in income inequality.

The distribution of income measured by quintile shares shows a large variation across countries and over time. The mean income quintile shares are 0.069, 0.112, 0.157, 0.220 and 0.441 (see Table 4.3). The lowest quintile share shows constant pattern prior to 1990 but increasing patterns post the 1990 period. The highest 3 quintiles show, on the other hand, variations before 1970 but a decreasing pattern in the post 1970s (see Figure 4.2). This resulted into a continuously increasing inequality change over time combined with a declining Q5/Q1 ratio (see Figure 4.2). The highest ratios are associated with countries involved in (domestic) conflicts like Iraq, Lebanon, Paraguay, Central African Republic, Guinea, Sierra Leone, South Africa and Georgia, while the lowest are associated with Egypt, Lao, Belarus and Luxembourg.

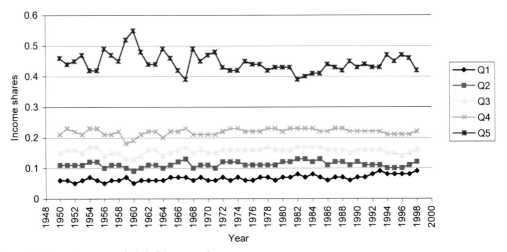

Figure 4.2. Development of global income shares

Table 4.3 Development of global Gini coefficient and distribution of income share over time

Year	obs	unweighted	weighted	Q1	Q2	Q3	Q4	Q5	Q5/Q1
1950	7	43.63	40.90	0.06	0.11	0.15	0.21	0.46	7.12
1951	6	40.33	36.41	0.06	0.11	0.16	0.23	0.44	7.65
1952	8	41.47	36.93	0.05	0.11	0.16	0.22	0.45	8.72
1953	11	43.32	35.70	0.06	0.11	0.15	0.21	0.47	7.62
1954	8	40.10	37.39	0.07	0.12	0.17	0.23	0.42	6.33
1955	11	45.30	36.99	0.06	0.12	0.17	0.23	0.42	6.89
1956	10	43.80	36.50	0.05	0.10	0.14	0.21	0.49	10.20
1957	15	39.36	37.26	0.06	0.11	0.15	0.21	0.47	7.61
1958	18	39.50	37.97	0.06	0.11	0.15	0.22	0.45	7.39
1959	17	44.24	37.72	0.07	0.10	0.13	0.18	0.52	7.43
1960	25	47.41	39.98	0.05	0.09	0.13	0.19	0.55	12.15
1961	21	43.45	38.01	0.06	0.10	0.14	0.21	0.48	7.79
1962	25	38.64	39.84	0.06	0.11	0.16	0.22	0.44	7.24
1963	25	39.69	35.69	0.06	0.11	0.16	0.22	0.44	7.03
1964	21	40.70	34.40	0.06	0.10	0.14	0.20	0.49	8.26

**Table 4.3 Development of global Gini coefficient and distribution
of income share over time (Continued)**

Year	obs	unweighted	weighted	Q1	Q2	Q3	Q4	Q5	Q5/Q1
1965	25	42.71	37.84	0.07	0.11	0.15	0.22	0.46	7.03
1966	17	38.38	33.94	0.07	0.12	0.16	0.22	0.42	5.82
1967	28	40.61	36.35	0.07	0.13	0.17	0.23	0.39	5.26
1968	34	43.33	38.67	0.06	0.10	0.15	0.21	0.49	8.62
1969	36	41.95	35.85	0.07	0.11	0.16	0.21	0.45	6.86
1970	42	42.16	34.38	0.06	0.11	0.15	0.21	0.47	7.72
1971	34	42.62	40.67	0.06	0.10	0.15	0.21	0.48	8.22
1972	28	39.00	36.91	0.07	0.12	0.16	0.22	0.43	5.91
1973	31	37.34	33.64	0.06	0.12	0.16	0.23	0.42	6.68
1974	24	39.16	34.54	0.07	0.12	0.16	0.23	0.42	6.35
1975	37	39.57	34.67	0.06	0.11	0.16	0.22	0.45	7.23
1976	38	38.04	39.94	0.06	0.11	0.16	0.22	0.44	6.97
1977	33	39.40	30.51	0.07	0.11	0.16	0.22	0.44	6.63
1978	31	34.67	31.65	0.07	0.11	0.17	0.23	0.42	6.09
1979	35	37.95	31.21	0.06	0.11	0.16	0.23	0.43	7.02
1980	41	38.05	33.83	0.07	0.12	0.16	0.22	0.43	6.39
1981	56	33.33	33.60	0.07	0.12	0.16	0.23	0.43	6.57
1982	31	34.34	31.49	0.08	0.13	0.17	0.23	0.39	5.11
1983	30	36.84	31.39	0.07	0.13	0.17	0.23	0.40	5.51
1984	34	35.77	31.47	0.08	0.12	0.17	0.23	0.41	5.40
1985	35	35.09	34.44	0.07	0.13	0.17	0.22	0.41	5.56
1986	56	34.04	33.07	0.06	0.11	0.16	0.22	0.44	6.91
1987	40	34.13	32.99	0.07	0.12	0.16	0.23	0.43	6.45
1988	53	31.93	34.52	0.07	0.12	0.16	0.23	0.42	6.19
1989	66	34.76	33.98	0.06	0.11	0.15	0.22	0.45	7.14
1990	63	34.94	34.90	0.07	0.12	0.16	0.22	0.43	5.95
1991	58	36.04	34.61	0.07	0.11	0.16	0.22	0.44	6.52
1992	60	36.21	36.22	0.08	0.11	0.16	0.22	0.43	5.36
1993	59	37.75	35.31	0.09	0.11	0.16	0.22	0.43	5.06
1994	56	37.95	35.15	0.08	0.10	0.15	0.21	0.47	6.08
1995	60	38.82	37.37	0.08	0.10	0.15	0.21	0.45	5.74
1996	53	39.32	35.36	0.08	0.10	0.14	0.21	0.47	6.20
1997	38	36.46	34.67	0.08	0.11	0.15	0.21	0.46	5.93
1998	15	37.72	40.12	0.09	0.12	0.16	0.22	0.42	4.86
Mean	49	39.02	35.65	0.07	0.11	0.16	0.22	0.45	6.80

Notes: The weighted Gini coefficient refers to the population weighted mean value calculated based on
the country observations in a given year. The Q1- Q5 are quintile income shares. The ration Q5/Q1
is a measure of the extent of income share inequalities in the world.

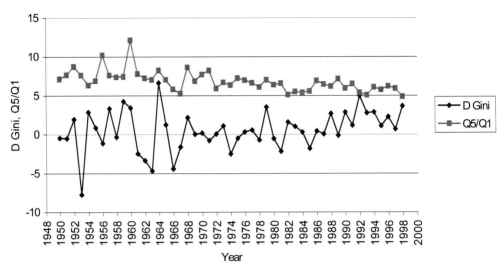

Figure 4.3. Development of changes in global Gini coefficient and Q5/Q1 ratio

Considering the global trends, due to the strong influence of the highest quintile income share, the inequality is volatile prior to 1970 and more stable and increasing during the period post 1986. There is evidence of the convergence in the mean, median and population weighted means over time (see Figure 4.1). In sum based on the WIID data, applied measurement methods and data irregularities, there is no convincing sign of a significant increasing or decreasing global trend in income inequality over the last 50 years. It should be noted that the inequality here is based on only within-country inequality but it is pooled and weighted such that the level differences reflect international inequality. The trend accounting for between-country inequality may be different.

Summary of Inter-National Income Inequality

Inter-national income inequality refers to economic disparity between countries of the world. Appendix B shows a summary of several studies of inter-national income inequality. Inter-national distribution of income is often based on Gini coefficient of national per capita GDP. The temporal patterns of inequality differ by whether Gini is weighted by the population of the countries or not. The results from a weighted Gini coefficient show that world inequality has declined due to the faster growth in India and China than the world economy but at the cost of an increased within-country inequality. The long run world income distribution involves substantial improvements in the income of many countries. Divergence in economic performance across regions and economies over time raises disparity in the world economy. Lack of growth in the African economies causes divergence and increases in the global inequality. In sum the total inequality is driven by a rise in inequality between countries affecting the evolution of world income inequality. Important factors affecting the convergence or divergence in the inter-national income gap are mass migration, barriers to migration, trade and capital flows. Political economy arguments affect the intertemporal (within country) variations in inequality, while the capital market imperfections affect the inter-national (between country) variations in inequality.

Considering the global trends in the income inequality results based on the WIID database show that, the inequality is volatile prior to 1970 and more stable with tendencies to increase post 1986. The overall pattern is very much similar with the patterns of the highest quintile income share. However, there is no convincing sign of a significant global trend in income inequality over the last 50 years. The inequality measure here is based on only the within-country inequality. The trend in the between-country inequality may be different. The cross-section of time-series data on inequality and income distribution using the Pyatt-type decomposition approach (Equation 4.1) described above could be used here to decompose the overall inequality into within-country, between-country and overlapping components as was done by Milanovic (2002a).

INTRA-NATIONAL DISTRIBUTION OF INCOME

Inequality Within Countries

The measurement of income distribution at the national level discussed here is based on aggregate data. Part of the information is taken from review of a number of inter-national studies. Within-country or intra-national inequality based on micro household data is not discussed in this section for the reason of limited space. The results of within-country inequality in selected large countries are found in Chapter 6 of this monograph.

As shown in the previous two sub-sections most of the research analysing changes in income distribution during the post World War II period concluded that income inequality within countries tends to be more stable over time, while the between-country inequality is more variable and deriving the level and temporal patterns of the world income inequality. This is interpreted as the lack of a strong association between growth and within-country inequality making poverty reduction through growth oriented policies more possible than redistributive policies. This view is challenged by Cornia (1999) and associates in a number of studies by referring to the declined inequality in several nations between the 1950s and 1970s and increased inequality in two-third of their sample of countries (77) during the last twenty years. Cornia suggests that the factors explaining the rise in income inequality are related to: shifts towards skill-intensive technologies, liberalization of domestic and international markets, decline in labour share during structural adjustment, trade liberalization, rise in financial rents, privatization of state assets, distribution of industrial assets, changes in labour institutions, and changes in the tax and transfer systems.

In a related study Cornia and Court (2001) in a policy brief using the WIID inequality database report changes in within-country income inequality over time and discuss the link between poverty, inequality and growth. In addition to the traditional common factors causing inequality such as land concentration, urban bias and inequality in education, a number of new causes of inequality[9] are discussed and policy measures to counteract inequality are provided. De Gregorio and Lee (2002) present empirical evidence on how education is related to a country's income distribution. The findings suggest that higher educational attainment

---

[9] In discussing major new causes of inequality they account for trade liberalisation, technological change, stabilisation and adjustment programmes in developing countries, financial liberalisation, privatisation and the distribution of industrial assets, changes in the labour market institutions, tax and transfer system.

and a more equal distribution of education makes income distribution more equal. Commander, Tolstopiateniko and Yemtsov (1999) point to wealth transfers through privatization programme, change in government expenditure, growth in earnings dispersion, shift in the structure of income as the deriving forces behind the increase in inequality in Russia. Fan, Overland and Spagat (1999) propose an early implementation of restructuring the education system in Russia and simultaneously reducing inequality.

Several studies show that between-country inequality explains a bigger share of inequality. Cornia and Kiiski (2001) advocate that from a policy perspective it is more important to focus on within-country inequality because the former is path-dependent and takes several generations to modify, while in the later case policy decisions to affect inequality are taken at the national level. Lindert and Williamson (2001) find that inequality has been driven by between countries rather than within countries income differences. However, heterogeneity in the magnitude of within-country effect is due to the factors of land and labour and the participant country's policies to exploit the benefits of globalization. During the interwar period the inequality between countries accelerated.

In sum the analysis of within-country income inequality is best studied based on representative micro household surveys. These are not discussed here. It is much easier to influence the within-country inequality by policy decisions than between-country international inequality under weak international institutions. The traditional common factors causing within-country inequality are identified in general to be land concentration, urban biased development, the ageing of population and inequality in education. The last two factors are more important in developed economies context. During a transition period wealth transfers during privatization programmes, changes in government expenditure and shift in the structure of income may also increase inequality. The major new causes of inequality associated with external relations are trade and financial liberalisation, technological change, stabilisation and adjustment programmes. However, the increase in inequality following the above changes may be transitory in nature. The degree of persistency in increased inequality will to the some extent depend on how active the counties studied are in their (tax and transfer) redistributive policies.

Stability and Convergence of Income Inequality

Li, Squire and Zou (1998) explored the issues of the relative stability of income inequality within countries over time and the significant variability among countries. The results suggest that inequality is largely determined by factors that change slowly within countries but are quite different across countries. The Gini coefficients are clearly different across countries and there is no evidence of a time trend in 65 per cent of the unbalanced panel of 49 countries used. The stability in the intertemporal variation in inequality is affected positively by political economy arguments (civil liberties and the initial level of secondary schooling), while the international variation in inequality is increasing in the capital market imperfections (financial depth and the initial distribution of land). The regression analysis of the variance of the Gini coefficient shows that after an adjustment for the differences in income definitions more than 92 per cent of the total variation is explained by country-specific effects.

Jones (1997), in characterising the evolution of the world income distribution, uses three different techniques. First, he uses a standard growth model and given 1980's conditions, to project the current dynamics of the income distribution forward. Results indicate small changes in the top of the income distribution. Second, following the insights from the cross-country growth literature, he interprets the variation in growth rates around the world as reflecting how far countries are from their steady state positions and predicts where countries are headed. Third, Jones considers how steady states are themselves changing over time. The increasing relative frequency of growth miracles indicates that the fraction of poor countries is falling and he projects that the long-run world income distribution involves substantial improvements in the incomes of many countries.

As a guideline for future research, in my view by using a similar approach as in the frontier literature the changes in the income distribution or distances to the steady state could easily be disaggregated into changes in the distribution of income over time and changes in the steady state to estimate the country-specific catch up rates.

There are several studies on the convergence in income inequality. It is applicable, for instance, to the studies of convergence in inequality among countries within an integrated economic region or the members of an economic union. The concept of convergence in income inequality (Benabou 1996) follows that of the conditional convergence of per capita income (e.g. Mankiw, Romer and Weil 1992). Iacoviello (1998) using LIS data investigated whether inequality converges to a steady state level of inequality during the process of income growth. Results showed that shocks to income yield short-run effects on the income distribution. A reversal link from inequality to income was not observed. Acemoglu and Robinson (2000) in their analysis of the development and dispersion of the world income distribution show that the increased openness to international trade and specialisation leads to a stable world income distribution.

FACTORS AFFECTING THE WORLD DISTRIBUTION OF INCOME

The literature on the distribution of income and income inequality identifies a number of factors important for the evolutions of the world income distribution. A summary of factors affecting the shape of the world distribution of income found in the literature is given in Appendix C. In this section we briefly introduce the arguments and empirical results on factors such as inheritance, wage inequality, supply of skills, labour market institutions, mobility, redistributive policies, growth, globalization, democracy, geography and institutions.[10]

The initial inequality related to parents and family environment affects education, opportunities, welfare and success rate of individuals in their life. The study by Bowles and Gintis (2002) is one recent example where they show evidence from the contribution of environmental, genetic and wealth effects to intergenerational transmission of economic

---

[10] The discussion here is related to factors that affect both within-country and between-country inequalities. It would be useful to broadly differentiate between factors affecting each of these two components and also allowing for their overlapping factors. It is desirable that emphasis should then be given to systematic discussion of colonialism, institutions and governance, international trade, international debt, defence spending, structural adjustment, and international aid. This will allow for heterogeneous perspectives on the problem. However, such systematic discussion is beyond the scope of this paper.

position. For instance, the parental income and wealth of an American are the strong predictors of the likely economic status of the next generation. However, in the following we focus on the factors affecting inequality at more aggregate level than individuals, household or sub-groups of population.

Trade Liberalization

Wage inequality has increased less in Europe than in the US and the UK for the same period (Lindert and Williamson 2001). The non-uniform increase in wage inequality among industrialised countries suggests that labour market policy matter. The 'transatlantic consensus' (Atkinson 1999) sees rising inequality as the product of exogenous inevitable events. Wage inequality in OECD countries or unemployment is increasing on account of technical change biased against unskilled workers or on account of the liberalization of international trade and the increased competition from the newly industrializing countries. Technology and reforms may change the size of the wage gap.

The Atkinson's alternative approach sees inequality in part socially generated related to wage/productivity relationship and changes in the labour markets, rather than trade or technology factors. Atkinson view about rising inequality is in contrast to the widely held belief that it is an unavoidable consequence of the present revolution in information technology or the globalisation of trade and finance. Redistributive policy measures of the governments can counteract the rise in the market income inequality.

The two most popular explanations for these differential trends are that: the relative supply of skills increased faster in Europe, and that the European labour market institutions in different ways prevented inequality from increasing. In relation with the effects of trade liberalization Fischer (2001) presents a general framework for the analysis of the evolution of the personal income distribution following trade liberalization. Here wages and interest rate determine the short-run and long-run evolutions of inequality respectively. Production factors and type of export determine the effects of liberalization on inequality.

Wood and Ridao-Cano (1999) using data from 90 countries during 1960-90 find that greater openness tends to cause divergence of secondary and tertiary enrolment rate between more-educated and less-educated countries, and also between land-abundant (such as sub-Saharan African) and land scarce countries.

Skills and Earnings

Acemoglu (2002) finds that the two traditional explanations (supply of skills and labour market institutions) to the different trends in inequality do not provide an entirely satisfactory explanation. A third explanation is that the relative demand for skilled labour increased differently across countries (see also Williamson 1996). Creation of wage compression and the encouragement of more investment in technologies increased the productivity of less-skilled workers, implying a less skilled biased technical change in Europe than in the US.

In relation with the analysis of inequality, economic growth and mobility Gottschalk (1997) presents some basic facts on how the distribution of earnings and employment has shifted. In a case with multi-period earnings, the inequality in each sub-period and the mobility across sub-periods would both impact the inequality of the permanent (or average) earnings of individuals. The relation incorporating price adjustments indicates that individual year variances (inequality) and cross year covariances (mobility) affect the variance of the average income. There is a controversy over the explanation of these patterns. In the US there has been an increase in demand for skilled labour and the relative price of skilled labour. Declines in the less skilled labours wages have resulted in unchanged average wages but the earnings inequality has increased. The earnings inequality has however increased less due to labour market institutions and the redistributive policies in the Nordic and the northern European countries than in other developed countries.

Variations in the distribution of skills and earnings among the major English-speaking countries (US, UK and Canada) and the continental European Union countries raise the possibility that the differences in the distribution of skills determine income inequality. Empirical results by Devroye and Freeman (2001) based on data from eleven advanced countries show that skill inequality explains only 7% of the cross-country inequality differences. Most part of inequality is related to the within-skill groups generated from the pay mechanism, rather than the between-skill groups.

Growth and Redistributive Policies

Acemoglu and Ventura (2002) offers an alternative framework to the new classical growth model for analysing the world income distribution. They show that even in the absence of diminishing returns in production and technological spillovers, international trade based on specialisation leads to a stable world income distribution. Specialisation in trade reduces prices and marginal product of capital and introduces diminishing returns. Concerning the role of institutions there is evidence that countries colonised by European powers that were relatively rich in 1500 are now relatively poor. This reversal is inconsistent with the geographical view that links economic development to geographic factors, but consistent with the role of institutions in economic development. European intervention created an institutional reversion by encouraging investment in poor regions. The institutional reversal accounts for the reversal in relative incomes during the 19th century. Diverging societies with good institutions for their economic development took advantage of industrialisation opportunities (Acemoglu, Johnson and Robinson 2002).

Atkinson (2000) has examined the redistributive impacts of the government budget in six OECD countries[11] over the period from 1980 to the mid-1990s. All countries experienced a rise in inequality of market income but differed both across countries and over time with regards to the distribution of disposable income. In reviewing the actual government policy responses by taking unemployment benefits and personal income taxation as case studies, the changes to policy parameters differed in extent and even in direction. However, no clear pattern was found in the nature of the relationship between inequality and redistribution. In a global perspective inequality reflects both elements of the within and the between-country income inequality components. The within-country components can be affected through policy interventions, but policy interventions to affect the global income inequality have proved to be a difficult task to co-ordinate (Cornia and Court 2001).

---

[11] The countries include United Kingdom, Canada, West Germany, Finland, Sweden and the United States.

Integration and its links to economic growth, poverty reduction and increasing inequality are important issues which are often addressed. Quah (2001) addresses several questions in his study of economic growth and income inequality. The two main questions asked are: how quantitatively important is the causal relation and why should that relation matter? Improvements in living standard overwhelm any deterioration due to increases in inequality. Other forces through their impacts on aggregate growth will also affect the poor – independently of the effect of inequality on the economic growth. Furthermore, the uses of the Gini coefficient might not reflect the true nature of inequality. Quah (2002) shows that neither of these possibilities (growth causing inequality and poor might be disadvantaged) is empirically testable for China and India. The findings indicate that only under inconceivably high increases in inequality would economic growth not benefit the poor, and the way inequality causes growth is empirically irrelevant for determining outcomes for the individual income distributions. With reference to the Dollar and Kraay (2001b) evidence on the gains and losses of growth to the poor, Ravallion (2001) finds large differences between and within countries on the impacts of growth on the poor. Ravallion expresses the need for a deeper micro empirical work on growth and distributional change to identify specific policies to complement the growth-oriented policies.

A view that any inequality-promoting effect of growth is unlikely to be large enough in magnitude to swamp the beneficent effect of growth on poverty is not probably sufficient case to concentrate on growth as the engine of poverty reduction. Growth combined with redistributive measures or simply redistributive measures alone could also reduce poverty.

Globalization

Globalization through the integration of economies and societies has been considered as a powerful force for economic development and poverty reduction. Although integration presents opportunities to reduce poverty, it also contains significant risk of increasing negative effects like inequality, polarisation, shifting power, cultural dominance and uniformity (Dollar and Kraay 2001b, and Dollar and Collier 2001).

The period of 1870-2000 is classified into: the first wave of globalization 1870-1913, the de-globalization period of 1913-1950, the golden age of 1950-1973, and the second wave of globalization of 1973 onwards (see O'Rourke and Williamson 2000, O'Rurke 2001, and Maddison 2001). The empirical evidence shows that during the first wave of globalization the convergence in per capita income and real wages took place within the Atlantic Economies due to an increase in international trade and massive international migration. The de-globalization period is characterised as a widening disparity between the richest and the poorest regions and among the Atlantic Economies. The golden age period is characterized as a period of rapid growth, relative stability and declining inequality.

In recent years, the research on the link between globalization and the world inequality has been intense. Three main approaches are distinguished (Wade 2001b). First, the neoclassical growth theory says that national economies will converge in their average productivity levels and average incomes because of the increased mobility of capital. Second, the endogenous growth theory states that diminishing returns to capital is offset by increasing returns to technological innovation in the developed countries. It is to be noted that the neoclassical theory predicts convergence (equality) while the endogenous theory predicts less convergence or divergence (inequality). Third, the dependency approach where convergence is less likely and divergence is more likely because of the differential benefits from the economic integration and trade, the restricted free market relations, and the locked developing countries to produce certain commodities.

The channels through which globalization affects the world inequality are identified by Wade (2001b) to be: commodity price equalisation, factor price convergence due to international migration and capital mobility reducing wage inequality and differentials in marginal products and rates of returns of capital among countries, and the dynamic convergence in per capital income growth where the growth rate is positively related to the distance to the steady state.

During the golden age period there was a considerable convergence among Western European economies and the OECD and a decline in the GDP gap in per capita income between the poorest and the richest regions (see Solimano 2001). In his survey of trends in both international economic integration and inequality over the past 150 years, O'Rurke (2001) distinguishes between the different dimensions of globalization and the within- and the between-country inequality. The 19th century globalization had large effects on the within-county income distribution, but also heterogeneous effects on inequality across countries making rich countries more unequal. The 20th century evidence on such link is however mixed.

Mahler (2001) studies the issues of economic globalization, domestic politics and income inequality in the developed countries in a pooled regression analysis using an unbalanced panel of LIS data on 14 countries where countries are observed between 1 to 3 periods during 1981-1992. This approach is different than the dependency approach of Wade.[12] The results show little evidence of a systematic relationship between any of the three main modes of economic globalization (trade, foreign direct investment and financial openness) and either of the distribution of disposable income or the earnings of households. The overall conclusion is that the integration into the world economy does not systematically lead to an egalitarian distribution of income or earnings across the entire economies. The modes of globalizations are weakly and positively related to the fiscal redistribution in the countries studied. Politics continues to play a critical role in determining the distributive outcomes in the developed world. Economic globalization is compatible with a wide variety of political interactions leading to a wide range of distributive outcomes.

With reference to a number of studies like Milanovic (2002a), and Dikhanov and Ward (2002), Wade (2001a and 2001b) argues that the global distribution of income is becoming ever more unequal. The inequality is increasing faster than hitherto suspected, and that governments should respond and be more proactive. In sum the studies reviewed here indicate that globalization has been a force for the between-country divergence. The unequal distribution of industrialization has been a divergence factor. For further discussion of globalization and its inequality effects see Williamson (1996).

Democracy and institutional structure of international society are also expected to have a relationship with income inequality. In a survey of the empirical relationship between

---

[12] The dependent variable is defined in three different ways as: (i) the 90/10 ratio of size-adjusted disposable household income, (ii) the 90/10 ratio of earnings inequality, and (iii) fiscal distribution defined as social benefit expenditures as proportion of GDP. The independent variables include: trade openness, outbound investment, financial openness, left party balance, electoral turnout, union density, wage-setting institutions, and log absolute GDP.

democracy and inequality Gradstein and Milanovic (2002) based on results from the transition economies show that there are some indications regarding a positive relation between democracy and inequality. Hurrell (2001) considers the link between the international institutions and the global economic justice. The institutional structure of the international society has developed but continues to constitute a deformed order. Hurrell examines why the international distributive justice remains so marginal to the current practice.

Heshmati (2003 and 2004b) presents measurement of a multidimensional index of globalization. The index is composed of four main components: economic integration, personal contact, technology, and political engagements, each developing differently over time. This breakdown of the index into major components provides possibilities to identify the sources of globalization and associate it with economic policy measures to bring about desirable changes in national and international policies. In a regression analysis Heshmati investigates the relationship between income inequality, poverty and globalization. Results show that the globalization index explains only 7-11 per cent of the variations in income inequality, and 9 per cent of poverty among the countries. By decomposing the aggregate globalization index into four components, results show that personal contacts and technology transfers reduce income inequality, while economic integration increases income inequality. Political engagement is found to have no significant effects on income inequality. Economic globalization component increases poverty, while personal contact reduces poverty. When controlling for regional heterogeneity, Heshmati finds that the regional variable plays an important role in explaining the variation in income inequality and poverty turning the globalization coefficient insignificant.

Summary of Factors Affecting the World Income Distribution

The non-uniform increase in wage inequality, the technical change biased against unskilled workers and the government's redistributive policies have resulted in the heterogeneous development of inequality among the industrialized countries. In addition to the geographic factors, the institutional structure and democracy play a role in economic development and inequality of countries. The between-country inequality dominates the within-country component. The later can easier be affected through policy interventions. Growth is found to increase income inequality. However, several studies conclude that the benefit of growth exceeds the disadvantages to the poor. More evidence based on better data is needed to make inferences on growth and the within-country distributional changes. Further studies are also needed to investigate the channels through which globalization affect the world income inequality. Finally, the multidimensional links and direction of the causal relationships between the determinant factors (other than inequality growth and openness) has been neglected in the previous research.

REDISTRIBUTION OF THE WORLD INCOME

In this review a number of ways to construct world indices of income distribution and to measure global income inequality reflecting both between and within-country inequalities were presented. Few studies compare the individuals' income distribution of the world. A combined micro and macro approach is often used where mean income per capita complemented with some measures of income dispersion, or income shares from household surveys and demographic information is the standard data requirement to construct the world income distribution. Economic growth, population growth, life expectancy, and the changes in the structure of income inequality are the important factors determining the evolution of the world income distribution. Empirical results show that the world inequality measured as the Gini coefficient increased and poverty measured as headcount decreased. In sum the inequality within individual countries is not increasing but the inequality between countries and regions is increasing and so is poverty concentration in some regions. Given the skewed World income distribution and its development, the rest of this section reviews engaging and creative studies on how to bring about necessary changes to the world income distribution in a desirable way. This section serves also as a summary of the review.

The issue of why to measure inequality is analysed by Kaplow (2002). From the public finance perspective the problems of the global redistribution has the same structure as the problem that an individual country is facing, namely the trading of the efficiency costs of a progressive tax-transfer system against the more equal distribution of the welfare it achieves. The world redistribution (cross-border transfers) is small relative to the world inequality. Kopczuk, Slemrod and Yitzhaki (2002) investigate whether these minimal transfers are optimal, what the optimal transfers are, and consider the hypothetical case of an optimal linear world income tax that maximises a border-neutral social welfare function. Using data from 118 countries a drastic reduction in the world consumption inequality, a dropping of the Gini coefficient from 0.69 to 0.25 is obtained. However, decentralised within-country redistribution has little impact on the overall world inequality. The actual foreign aid transfers, from the US and the other industrialized countries to the poor countries is a reflection of either placing a much lower value on the welfare of citizens of the poorest countries or expect that a very significant fraction of cross-border transfers is wasted.

The relative stability of income inequality within countries over time and the significant variability among countries is determined by political factors (of liberties and schooling) and the capital market imperfection (financial depth and distribution of land), respectively (Li, Squire and Zou 1998). From the previous discussion of the inter-national and the intra-national inequality we can conclude that inequality is determined by factors that change slowly within countries but are quite different across countries. An optimal combination of cross-boarder transfers and the within-country redistributive policies may simultaneously reduce substantially both within and between-country inequalities.

Cornia and Court (2001) in a policy brief using the WIID database, covering the second wave of globalization, report changes in within-country income inequality and on the link between poverty, inequality and growth. The analysis highlights five main issues. First, inequality has risen since the early-mid 1980s. Second, the traditional common factors causing inequality such as land concentration, urban bias and the inequality in education are not responsible for worsening the situation. The new causes identified are the liberal economic policy regimes and the way in which economic reform policies have been carried out. Land reform, expanding education and active regional policy are recommended as measures to reduce inequality among areas, gender and regions. Third, the persistence of inequality at high levels makes poverty reduction difficult. There is a negative relationship between inequality and the poverty alleviation elasticity of growth (see also Cornia and Kiiski 2001). Fourth, high level of inequality can depress the rate of growth, it affects the stability of the global economy and have undesirable political and social impacts by putting the market and globalization model at risk of a political backlash (see also Birdsall, 1998). Fifth, the developments in Canada and Taiwan show that the low inequality can be maintained at fast growth.

Economic growth has often been given priority as an anti-poverty measure, but the negative link between growth and inequality has often been ignored by policymakers. Rising inequality threatens growth and poverty reduction targets calling for more distributionally favourable pro-growth policies. Policies offsetting the inequality impact of new causes is designed and incorporated in a revised development approach 'the Post-Washington Consensus' (Stiglitz 1998). These policies include measures to offset the impacts of new technologies and trade, macroeconomic stability, careful financial liberalisation and regulation, equitable labour market policies, and innovative tax and transfer policies. Stiglitz conclude that the international community should include distribution issues in their policy advice, avoid distributive distortions, support to reduce output volatility and increase external budgetary support.

Caminada and Goudswaard (2001) study the association between international trends in income inequality and social policy. They investigate whether changes in the overall distribution of income in OECD countries during the last two decades can be attributed to social policy measures. For most countries they find a possible relationship between changing welfare policies and changing income inequality, especially in the UK and the Netherlands. Fundamental social security reforms have made the income distribution less equal. Social transfers varied enormously across 15 EU countries in 1994. Heady, Mitrakos and Tsakloglou (2001) analyse the comparative effects of these transfers on inequality using the European Community Household Panel data (ECHP). The results show increasing distributional impacts of these transfers and the share of GDP spend on them (high in Denmark and Netherlands and low in Greece and Portugal). However, the extent of means testing (high in UK), the distribution of different funds and the degree of targeting for each transfer also affects their impacts.

Locations in combination with immobility of factors are important for the incidence of poverty and justify regional targeting to reduce poverty. As an example Park, Wang and Wu (2002) evaluate the effectiveness of regional targeting in China's large scale rural poverty alleviation investment program that begun in 1986 using a panel of all counties in China for the period 1981-1995. A number of newly measures of targeting gaps, targeting error describing weighted mistargeting are defined. The evidence suggests that political constraints are likely to undermine regional targeting programs at the country level or higher. Targeting township is the preferred level of targeting. There exist tradeoffs between targeting and other social objectives deviating optimal targets from the perfect ones.

In view of the above and from a public finance perspective the global redistribution has the same structure as that of an individual country. The world redistribution in the form of cross border transfers is very small and not optimal relative to the world inequality. The within country redistribution has little impact on the global inequality. Political and capital market factors determine the stability, changes and levels of inequality across countries. Land reform, expanding education and active regional policy are found to be effective economic reform policy measures to reduce inequality. At a smaller regional scale such as EU, the social security reforms show evidence of the positive impacts of taxes and targeting transfers on the distribution of income and inequality within and between the EU member countries. The political constraint and the level of targeting are important to the success of the regional targeting programs to reduce poverty.

In analyzing the factors causing inequality, it would be useful to broadly differentiate between factors affecting each of the within-and between-country components of inequality and also allowing for their overlapping factors. In the case of developing countries, the emphasis should be given to a systematic discussion of important factors such as colonialism, institutions and governance, international trade, international debt, defence spending, infrastructure for economic development, structural adjustment programs and international aid. This will allow for heterogeneous perspectives on the inequality problem, available resources and measures to reduce inequality.

APPENDIX 4. A

A Selection of Studies of Distribution of Income among the World Individuals

No.	Author(s), Year	Measure of distribution	Measure of income	Period of study	No. of countries	Main results	Other issues
1	Bourguignon and Morrisson (2002)	Gini, Theil coefficient, Mean log deviation, and Std dev. of log.	GDP per capita in PPP, population, 9 decile + 2 vintile	Early 1820 to 1992	33 single and multiple groups of countries	Inequality increased until WWII, then stabilized or increased	During 19th century inequality in longevity increased
2	Milanovic (2002a)	Gini index	Disposable income or expenditure per capita	Unbalanced around 1988 and 1993	Three groups and a total of 91 countries	Inequality increased driven by between-country mean income	Based on household surveys and adjusted for PPP
3	Sala-I-Martin (2002a)	7 indices: Gini, Var. log Income, Atkinsons, MLD, Theil, CV	GDP data combined with within-country income share	Unbalanced 1970-1998	Three groups and a total of 125 countries	Reduction in global income between-country driven inequality 1980-1998	Unless Africa starts growing, inequality increases again
4	Sala-I-Martin (2002b)	9 indices: Gini, Var. log Income, Atkinsons, MLD, Theil, CV, 2 ratios of decile distr.	GDP data combined with within country income share (29 countries projected)	Unbalanced 1970-1998	Three groups and a total of 125 countries	Reductions in income inequality during 1980s and 1990s	To treat all citizens within a quintile equal give correct answer to inequality
5	Park (2001)	Gini index	GDP per capita (?), deciles of the world income distribution	1960-1992	133	Inequality increased 1960-68, volatile declined 1976-92	Inequality among nations
6	Quah (1999)		Combine per capita income & personal income distribution	1980 to 1992	No information	Increased between-country inequality derived from macroeconomic growth	Incomplete
7	Schultz (1998)	Variance of log income, Theil entropy index and Gini concentration ratio	Real income (GDP) converted to US 1985$ by foreign exchange rates and by PPP	1960-1989 1989, 1994	120	World inequality increased from 1960 to 1968, and decreased from mid 1970s.	Two-thirds of inequality is inter-country and one-third intra-country,

APPENDIX 4.B

A Selection of Studies of International Distribution of Income

No.	Author(s), Year	Measure of distribution	Measure of income	Period of study	No. of countries	Main results	Other issues
1	Acemoglu (2002)	Growth model	Real income	Unbalanced (2-4) periods, 1979-1997	12 OECD countries	Heterogeneous increase in wage inequality in US and UK than others	Differences in the increases in relative demand for skills
2	Acemoglu and Ventura (2002)	Log GDP 1965 vs 1985 Growth model	Log GDP	1965 and 1985	79 countries	International trade lead to stable world income distribution	Estimate the extend of terms of trade effects on income
3	Milanovic (2001 /2002a)	Gini index	Disposable income or expenditure per capita	Unbalanced around 1988 and 1993	Three groups and a total of 91 countries	Inequality increased driven by between-country mean income	Urban-Rural differences in China, slow grow of rural in S. Asia
4	Milanovic (2002b)	Mean-normalized average incomes of each decile across countries	Disposable income	Around 1988 (between 1985 and 1991) and 1993 (between 1992 and 1997)	87 countries	At very low average income level, rich benefit from globalization (openness, FDI).	The effect of openness on income distribution depend on initial income
5	Kopczuk, Selmrod and Yitzhaki (2002)	Gini index	Based on net or gross income and consumption	One period 1991-1997	118 countries	An optimal linear world income tax drop Gini from 0.69 to 0.25	Actual foreign aid is much lower than optimal income tax
6	Sala-I-Martin (2002a)	7 indices: Gini, Variance of log Income, Atkinsons, MLD, Theil, CV	GDP data combined with within-country income share	Unbalanced 1970-1998	Three groups and a total of 125 countries	Reduction in global income inequality, between country drive inequality 1980-1998	Unless Africa starts growing, inequality increases again
7	Li, Squire and Zou (1998)	Gini index	Expenditure or income	1947-1994, 5 years averages	49 countries	In equality stable over time and vary across countries	Political and market imperfection factors affect inequality
8	Jones (1997)	GDP per worker relative to US 1960 vs 1988	GDP per worker relative to US	1960 and 1988	121 countries	Fast growth, rapid growth in China and India new phenomenon	Use: growth model, where headed, how steady state changes

APPENDIX 4.C

Factors Affecting the Shape of the World Distribution of Income

No.	Author(s), Year	Measure of distribution	Measure of income	Period of study	No. of countries	Main results	Other issues
1	Acemoglu (2002)	Growth model	Real income	Unbalanced (2-4) periods, 1979-1997	12 OECD countries	Heterogeneous increase in wage inequality in US and UK than others	Differences in the increases in relative demand for skills
2	Acemoglu, Johnson and Robinson (2002)	GDP per capita, urbanization	GDP per capita, urbanization	1500-2000	Different in different periods	Institutional reversal accounts for reversal in relative incomes	Role of institutions in economic development
3	Acemoglu and Ventura (2002)	Log GDP 1965 vs 1985 Growth model	Log GDP	1965 and 1985	79 countries	International trade lead to stable world income distribution	Estimate the extend terms of trade effects on income
4	Dikhanov and Ward (2002)	Gini and Theil indices	Personal consumption expenditures	1970, 1980, 1990 and 1999	45 countries	Inequality grew in 1970-1990. Complex development in 1990s	Neither growth nor aid provide panacea to reduce poverty
5	Gradstein and Milanovic (2002)	Change in Gini	Disposable income or expenditure per capita	Average 1989-1997	21 transition countries	Positive relationship between democracy and equality	Method. Problem, inequality and democracy, data comparability
6	Milanovic (2002a)	Gini coefficient	Disposable income or expenditure per capita	Unbalanced around 1988 and 1993	Three groups and a total of 91 countries	Inequality increased driven by between country mean income	Urban-Rural differences in China, slow grow of rural in S. Asia
7	Quah (2002)	Gini coefficient	Per capita income	1980 and 1992	India, China and USA	Improvements from growth is greater than deterioration for poor	Does inequality cause growth?
8	Cornia and Court (2001)	Gini coefficient	Income	Unbalanced 1960-1997	73 countries	Technological change and globalization drive rises in inequality	Policies of education and labour market

No.	Author(s), Year	Measure of distribution	Measure of income	Period of study	No. of countries	Main results	Other issues
9	Fischer (2001)	Gini coefficient	GDP per capita?	Unbalanced 5 years averages	66 countries	Effects of trade and production factors on income distribution is mixed	In long run interest rate, in short run wage-wealth ratio
10	Mahler (2001)	Gini, 90/10 ratio of disposable and earnings inequality, fiscal redistribution	Disposable personal income, earnings, fiscal redistribution	Unbalanced 1981-1992, 1-4 periods	14 OECD countries	Little evidence on systematic relationship between inequality and globalization.	Policies play role in determining the distributive outcomes
11	O'Rurke (2001)	Gini coefficient, Theil, and Q5/Q1 ratio	Not defined	1960s, 1970s, 1980s, 1990s	Regional numbers	Globalization have impacts on within country inequality	More evidence on global and between country inequality
12	Quah (2001)	Gini coefficient	Per capita PPP adjusted real GDP	1980 and 1992	India, China and USA	Poor benefit from growth	Does inequality cause growth?
13	Ravallion (2001)	Gini coefficient	Private consumption per capita	Unbalanced 1980s – 1990s	47 developing countries	Heterogeneous impacts of growth on the poor, initial condition matter	Deeper micro empirical work, policies &programs
14	Atkinson (2000)	Gini coefficient	Market and disposable household income	Unbalanced 1961-1997	5 OECD countries	Rising wage dispersion and persistent unemployment. Explain inequality	Role of government budget on evolution of disposable Income
15	Dollar and Kraay (2001b)	Gini coefficient	Real per capita GDP at PPP in 1985 international dollars	Unbalanced 1950-1999	137 countries	Several determinants of growth have little systematic effects on income of poor (Q1)	Several factors may have direct effects on incomes of poor through their effect on income distribution
16	Atkinson (1999)	Gini coefficient	Market income, disposable household income	Unbalanced 1978-1999	8 OECD countries	Deriving force is social in origin not trade or technology	Rising inequality is not inevitable, policy affect social norm
17	Williamson (1996)		Real wages per day	1870, 1890, 1913	14 OECD countries	Globalization, labour saving tech. Change and trends affect inequality	Inequality is a side effects to globalization

Chapter 5

CONTINENTAL AND SUB-CONTINENTAL INCOME INEQUALITY[*]

ABSTRACT

Income inequality can be measured at different levels of aggregation such as global, continental, international and national levels. Here we consider income inequality at regions defined as equivalent of continental and sub-continental levels. We investigate the economic disparity between regions of the world and among countries within each continent or sub-continent. The empirical results, for data availability reasons, are mainly based on the second half of the 20th century. The review covers a whole range of measures and methods frequently employed in empirical analysis of the global and regional income inequality and income distribution. Different determinant factors along with quantification of their impacts are presented and empirical results from different case studies are discussed. Finally, these results are contrasted to those obtained based on the WIID covering almost the same period and group of countries.

Keywords: Income inequality, inequality indices, income distribution, continents, regions.

INTRODUCTION

It is well known that inequality is a multidimensional concept. Economists are concerned specifically with the economic or monetarily measurable dimension related to incomes. Inequality can be linked to, for instance, skills, education, opportunities, happiness, health, life expectancy, welfare, assets and social mobility.[1] This paper focuses on income inequality referring to the inequality of the distribution of individuals, household or some per capita measure of income. Lorenz Curve is used for analysing the size distribution of income. It plots the cumulative share of total income against the cumulative proportion of income

---

[*] This chapter is published as Heshmati A. (2005), Continental and sub-continental income inequality, ICFAI Journal of Applied Economics 5(6), 7-52.

[1] In Chapter 2 of this monograph we reviewed the recent advances in the measurement of inequality and gave attention to the relationship between income and non-income dimensions of inequality.

receiving units. The divergence of a Lorenz curve for a given income distribution to Lorenz curve for perfect equality is measured by some index of inequality. The most widely used index of inequality is the Gini coefficient. Among the other measures of inequality are: the range, the variance, the squared coefficient of variation, the variance of log incomes, the absolute and relative mean deviations, and Theil's two inequality indices. For the reviews of inequality see Subramanian (1997a), Cowell (2000) and Chapter 2 of this monograph.

The empirical literature on economic inequality is growing as a result of increasing interest in measuring and understanding the level, causes and development of income inequality and poverty and availability of the data of income distribution. In 1990s there was a shift in research previously focused on economic growth, determinants of economic growth and convergence in per capita incomes across countries for the analysis of the distribution of income, its development over time and the identification of factors determining the distribution of income and poverty reductions.[2] Empirical results show a tendency for income per capita to converge, and an increase in inequality in the distribution of personal income in particular in many developing and transition countries.

Availability of household surveys has been improved and several standardized databases have been created. These allow analysis of income distribution at the most disaggregate individual or per capita household levels. Income distribution is otherwise often analyzed at three levels of aggregation, namely global, international and national.[3] Income inequality can also be measured at a within-country regional level.[4] The international and national income inequality was reviewed in Chapter 4.

Different parametric and non-parametric methods have been developed to decompose inequality and changes in poverty. Inequality is decomposed by sub-groups, income sources, causal factors and by other income unit characteristics. Inequality can also be decomposed at different levels of aggregation. For instance, at the national level it can be decomposed into within-subgroup and between-subgroups of a population. In similar way at the international level inequality can be decomposed into within-country and between-country components.[5] Income inequality, in addition to the levels mentioned above, can be measured at the continental and sub-continental levels where one examines both between and within economic or geographic regions.

[2] Quah (2002), Ravallion (2003b), Sala-i-Martin (2002a) analysed convergence in income inequality, while Acemoglu and Ventura (2002), Atkinson (1997), Bourguignon and Morrisson (2002), Gottschalk and Smeeding (1997) and Milanovic (2002a) focus on the distribution of income. Acemoglu (2002), Caminada and Goudswaard (2001), Cornia and Kiiski (2001), Gotthschalk and Smeeding (2000), Milanovic (2002a), O'Rourke (2001), Park (2001), Sala-i-Martin (2002b) and Schultz (1998) studied trends in income inequality.

[3] Global or world income inequality refers to inequality differences between all individuals in the world (Milanovic 2002a; Schultz 1998; Quah 1999; Bourguignon and Morrisson 2002; Sala-i-Martin 2002a), while international income inequality refers to the economic disparity between countries (Acemoglu 2002; Cornia and Kiiski 2001; Gottschalk and Smeeding 1997; and Milanovic 2001). At the intra-national level inequality refers to the distribution of income among people within individual countries (Cameron 2000a; Cowell, Ferreira and Lichtfield 1998; Gustafsson and Shi 2002; Liebbrandt, Woolard and Woolard 2000). Studies of continents or regions include: transition economies (Ivaschenko 2002, Wan 2002b), East Asian countries (Kakwani and Krogkaew 2000 and You 1998), the European Union (Belbo and Knaus 2001, Gottschalk and Smeeding 2000), Latin American countries (LondoNo and Szekely 2000, Wood 1997) and sub-Saharan African countries (Milanovic and Yitzhaki 2001, Svedborg 2002).

[4] Recent such studies focus on large countries like China (Xu and Zou, 2000; Gustafsson and Shi, 2002), Russia (Luttmer 2001; Fedorov 2002), India (Jha 2000; Datt and Ravallion, 1992) and the USA (Patridge, Rickman and Levernier, 1996; Moffitt and Gottschalk, 2002). For a recent review see Chapter 6 of this monograph.

[5] For recent reviews of the measurement and decomposition of inequalities see Shorrocks and Wan (2003) and Chapters 2 and 3 of this monograph.

There is evidence that poverty and inequality has developed differently between and within regions. Here the focus is on inequality in income distribution within and between geographic and economic regions. Such analysis can reveal effects of openness, convergence due to factor mobility, and may also indicate regional polarization, or disintegration and widening inequality driven by structural differences between regions. Furthermore it is important to consider heterogeneity in income inequality in both level and development over time among the countries within a region.

Data availability of household surveys has improved in the regions such as former Soviet Union, Eastern Europe and Africa. Several standardized databases have been created. These data cover mainly the second half of the twentieth century. This review aims to cover empirical analysis of continental or regional income inequality and income distribution. We discuss the benefit and limitations of this approach compared to the global and international levels and present empirical results found in the literature and those obtained based on the World Income Inequality Database (WIID) covering almost the same period and the same group of countries. Research on the world income inequality increases awareness of the problem, its measurement and quantification, identification of causal factors and of policy measures to reduce the within and between continents income inequality.

Rest of the Chapter is organised as follows. In section 2 the WIID database is described. Section 3 and 4 are on inter-regional and intra-regional income inequalities. The regions based on available studies include Eastern Europe and former USSR, Scandinavian, Western Europe, OECD countries, small and medium sized developing countries, sub-Saharan Africa, Latin America, East Asia, South Asia, South-East Asia and Pacific. The final Section summarises the reviews and empirical results.

THE DATA

The data used here are obtained from the WIDER World Income Inequality Database (WIID) which is an expanded version of the Deininger and Squire (1996) database. WIID contains information on income inequality, income shares, and a number of variables indicating the source of data, and the quality classification for 146 existing industrialized, developing and transition countries.[6] The countries are observed on an irregular basis mainly covering the period post 1950 until 1998. To avoid distortions for graphing the trend in global and regional inequality over time we have truncated the data at 1950. The number of the excluded observations covering 1867-1949 is only 25 or 1.5% of the sample.

The Gini coefficient is measured in percentage points. It is the mean of multiple observations for a country in a given year. The multiplicity of observations is due to the differences in income definitions, data sources, reference units, and the population coverage. The population adjusted Gini coefficient is also reported. However, the population adjusted Gini measure is very sensitive to the exit and entry of countries with large populations like China and India.

To provide a better picture of the distribution of inequality we report the first, the last, the period range and the number of years a country is observed. In addition to the mean Gini

---

[6] The WIID data originally contains 151 countries. The number of countries in our analysis differs due to the disintegration of the Soviet Union, Czechoslovakia and Yugoslavia, and reunification of Germany.

coefficient, the median, the minimum, the maximum, the standard deviation, the range and the annual changes in Gini coefficient are provided for individual countries grouped by the regional location in Table 5.3. In Table 5.4 we report the Gini coefficient and the population weighted Gini coefficient together with the distribution of income. The decile observations are transformed to quintile income shares to make the income distribution comparable across countries and over time. As a second measure of inequality the ratio of the highest to the lowest quintiles are calculated and reported in Table 5.4.

INTER-REGIONAL INCOME INEQUALITY

The relative high degree of homogeneity in the economic development within regions combined with a high degree of heterogeneity between regions makes analysis of the inter-regional inequality an interesting dimension to be explored. Maddison (2001), using data on GDP across countries and over time reports a steady increase in the inter-regional inequalities since 1870. As a measure of the regional dispersion the ratio of income per head of the richest to the poorest region of the world is used. The ratio has increased from 5:1 in 1870 to 19:1 in 1998. There is, however, evidence of substantial convergence and divergence patterns across regions. In addition to income ratios Maddison uses income share as a second measure to compare regions of the world. The global GDP share of the Western off-shoots (US, Canada, Australia and New Zealand) increased from 10.2 per cent in 1870 to 30.6 per cent in 1950. It declined to 25.1 per cent in 1998. The Western Europe share of the global GDP decreased from 33.6 per cent to 20 per cent during the same period. A similar decrease was observed in the case of Latin America from 8.7 per cent to 2.5 per cent, while the Africa's share remained constant at around 3.0-3.5 per cent. The Asia's share declined prior to 1952 but it increased from 18.5 per cent in 1973 to 37.2 per cent in 1998. The Eastern Europe and the former USSR enjoyed a constant share of the world GDP in the range of 11-13 per cent until 1973. Thereafter this region experienced a decline from 12.9 per cent in 1973 to 5.3 per cent in 1998. It is to be noted that in the case of the GDP shares no correction for changes in the population size or the purchasing power parity is made. The decline in the shares is reflecting negative relative changes in the shares in total and not necessarily declines in the absolute Global GDP levels.

Maddison's two measures only account for the level differences between regions. They neglect the distributional inequality within regions. Milanovic (2002a) derives the world income or the expenditure distribution of individuals for 1988 and 1993 based on the household data from 91 countries and adjusted for PPP between countries. The data has a high coverage. It covers 84 per cent of the world population and 93 per cent of the world GDP. Inequality measured by Gini coefficient increased from 0.63 in 1988 to 0.66 in 1993.[7] The increase is attributed by 75-88 per cent to inter-country rather than intra-country differences in the mean income. The main contributors were from the rising urban-rural differences in China, the slow growth in the rural South Asia and the declining income in the transition countries. The estimated Gini coefficients in 1988 and 1993 by regions are: Africa 0.43 and 0.47, Asia 0.56 and 0.62, Latin America and Caribbean 0.57 and 0.56, Eastern Europe and USSR 0.26 and 0.46 and Western Europe, North America and Oceania 0.37 and

0.37 respectively. Despite the benefits concerning the high coverage and the disaggregation level of data, the period is short covering only late 80s and early 90s. Thus, the direction of changes might not be representative for the true long-run changes in the regional income inequality, but extreme observations, measurement errors, or differences in definitions and sources of income.

The data described above is extended in Milanovic (2001) to 126 countries over the last 50 years. Three different concepts of the world or international inequality are defined: the unweighted countries' GDP per capita, the population weighted GDPs per capita, and a combination of the international and internal country income distributions. Using the above concepts and based on income or expenditures calculated from household surveys, the world income distribution is derived. The unweighted measure shows an increasing global inequality over time driven by the development in Latin America, Eastern Europe and Africa. The population-weighted measure indicates a declining inequality driven mostly by China's fast growth during the last two decades. The increasing inequality by the third combined concept is attributed to the fast growth and the rising urban/rural differences in China, the slower growth in the rural Asia and the declining income in transition economies. The longer time period and better country coverage together with the adjustment for population by Milanovic improves the quality of analysis significantly.

Dikhanov and Ward (2002) using data from a sample of 46 countries for the period 1970 to 1999 find that the absolute number of the poor, broadly defined, increased and the global income distribution became less equal. The regional structure has undergone major changes during the period of the study reflecting the unprecedented economic performance of China and the economic progress in India. Eventhough the sample contains large countries like India and China and cover a period of significant development in those two countries, it is too small to serve as a basis for making an inference about the development of income distribution at the global level. The picture provided is partial rather than global.

Deininger and Squire (1998) used country data for 108 countries during 1960-1992 on distributions of income and land. Similar to Milanovic (2002a) it is recommended that inequality analysis should preferably be based on the household data with a comprehensive coverage of sources of income and being representative of population. Deininger and Squire showed that: there is a strong negative relationship between the initial inequality in land and the long-term growth. Inequality reduces income growth for the poor, and there is little support for the Kuznets hypothesis. Growth and inequality are affected by the redistribution of assets and the increased aggregate investment. A comparison of decadal medians of the Gini coefficient for the income distributions by regions during the period 1960-1990 demonstrates a large variation in inequality between regions. It is the highest in Latin America (0.50-0.53) and the sub-Saharan Africa (0.40-0.50) and lowest in Eastern Europe (0.22-0.29), but increasing over time during the transition period in the latter case.

Parker and Gardner (2002) used seven different approaches[8] including three transition matrices and measures, three changes in raw incomes and one inequality reduction principle to measure the international income mobility. Income mobility analysis is concerned with

---

[7]   The two periods of 1988 and 1993 are not exact. They cover surveys collected around those two periods.
[8]   The transition matrices and measures include Bartholomew (1982), Shorrocks (1978a) and Parker and Rougier (2001). The measures are based on changes in raw incomes include King (1983), Fields and Ok (1996 and 1999). Finally, the measure based on the inequality reduction principle is based on Shorrocks (1978b). Alternative, for mobility measures see also Zandvakili (1999).

measuring changes in the economic status of individuals and movements of their incomes over time. The measure based on the income inequality principle proposed by Shorrocks (1978a) uses the arithmetic mean incomes corresponding to two different periods. The results using GDP per capita from 106 countries divided into five regions[9] for the years 1972, 1982 and 1992 indicate that 1982-1992 period to be more mobile than the 1972-1982 period. An increase in mobility counteracts the rise in international income inequality. Mobility is characterised as small transitory movements and takes place in the middle deciles of the distribution. Tropical Africa is the next mobile region, but unlike the North region most of the observed income changes were negative.

Table 5.1 Summary of distribution of Gini coefficient by country group, based on WIID.

Region	Min	Max	Nyear	Range	Min	Mean	Median	Maxi-mum	StdDev	Range	Wgini
MENA	1944	1997	57	53	23.36	39.97	37.08	59.92	8.23	36.56	41.31
East Asia	1953	1998	93	45	18.60	33.67	31.20	55.80	7.65	37.20	28.81
SEAAsia & Pacific 1956	1998	87	42	30.40	43.17	43.90	57.16	5.87	26.76	39.80	
South Asia	1950	1997	106	47	28.86	36.94	35.75	53.00	5.37	24.14	34.49
Latin America	1948	1998	320	50	27.00	47.39	47.25	67.83	7.47	40.83	51.79
sub-Saharan Afr.	1914	1999	157	85	28.90	49.26	50.00	79.50	10.05	50.60	46.53
East Europe	1955	1998	191	43	15.90	25.14	25.04	44.81	5.06	28.91	31.57
Former Soviet Rep	1972	1998	125	26	22.90	31.56	29.60	57.60	7.06	34.70	33.99
Industrialized	1867	1998	495	131	19.87	34.79	33.83	67.20	7.90	47.33	36.08
All regions	1867	1999	1631	132	15.90	41.12	40.24	79.50	9.61	27.91	35.65

Min   First year of observation
Max   Last year of observation
Nyear   Number of years observed
Range   The difference between the last and first years of observation
Minimum   Minimum Gini value
Mean   Mean Gini value
Median   Median Gini value
Maximum   Maximum Gini value
StdDev   Standard deviation of the Gini
Range   The difference between maximum and minimum Gini values
Wgini   Population weighted mean Gini

The interregional income inequality derived from the WIID where the sample countries (146) are divided into 9 regions is reported in Table 5.1 and the distribution of income by quintiles in Table 5.2. The results show a significant interregional heterogeneity. Here we define heterogeneity as the standard deviation of the Gini coefficient. The highest rate is found to be associated with the sub-Saharan Africa (10.05 per cent) and Middle East and

---

[9] The five regions are North (23), South (9), Tropical America (23), Tropical Asia (18) and Tropical Africa (33). The numbers in parenthesis are number of countries in each region.

North Africa (8.23 per cent), while a low dispersion is observed in South East Asia (5.87 per cent), South Asia (5.375), and Eastern Europe (5.06 per cent). The variation despite the comprehensive redistribution systems is unexpectedly high in the industrialised countries (7.90 per cent). The dispersion and ranges between minimum and maximum Gini values are highly correlated. Sub-Saharan Africa and Latin America again display the lowest levels of income (0.06 and 0.04) allocated to the first quintile of the population and the highest share to the highest quintile (0.52 and 0.54), respectively. With the exception of Eastern Europe and the former Soviet Republics, the variation in inequality within regions is stable or declining over time. South East Asia and South Asia show the least dispersion within region (see Figure 5.1). However, the development of inequality in Latin America, Eastern Europe and the former Soviet Republics show increasing trends in the post 1970s.

Table 5.2 Summary of Gini coefficient and quintile shares by country group, based on WIID

Region	Min	Max	Nyear	Range	Gini	Wgini	Q1	Q2	Q3	Q4	Q5	Q5/Q1
MENA	1944	1997	57	53	39.01	41.31	0.07	0.10	0.15	0.21	0.47	7.09
East Asia	1953	1998	93	45	33.67	28.81	0.07	0.12	0.16	0.23	0.41	5.55
SEAsia & Pacific	1956	1998	87	42	43.17	39.80	0.07	0.10	0.14	0.21	0.49	7.39
South Asia	1950	1997	106	47	36.94	34.49	0.08	0.12	0.16	0.21	0.42	5.13
Latin America	1948	1998	320	50	47.39	51.79	0.04	0.08	0.13	0.21	0.54	12.50
sub-Saharan Afr.	1914	1999	157	85	49.26	46.53	0.06	0.09	0.13	0.20	0.52	8.21
East Europe	1955	1998	191	43	26.14	31.57	0.10	0.14	0.18	0.22	0.35	3.54
Former Soviet Rep	1972	1998	125	26	31.56	33.99	0.09	0.12	0.16	0.22	0.42	4.78
Industrialized	1867	1998	495	131	34.79	36.08	0.07	0.12	0.17	0.24	0.40	5.72
All regions	1867	1999	1392	132	38.06	38.26	0.07	0.11	0.16	0.22	0.44	6.88

Min   First year of observation
Max   Last year of observation
Nyear   Number of years observed
Range   The difference between the last and first years of observation
Gini   Mean Gini value
Wgini   Population weighted mean Gini value
Q1-Q5   Income shares of the first-fifth quintiles of population
Q5/Q1   the ration of the fifth quintile share to the first quintile income share

To sum up there are a number of measures traditionally used in the studies of inter-regional income inequality. The ratio of income per head of the richest to the poorest region of the world is one such measure. The ratio has increased over time and results show evidence of both convergence and divergence among the regions. A second measure is the regions' GDP share of the global income. Different regions' share has developed differently over time. A third, measure is based on the Gini coefficient of income inequality. The focus is on its variations across regions and its regional development over time. Several studies indicate that the Gini coefficient has increased. A fourth measure is based on the development of the absolute number of poor. The number of poor has declined but its regional concentration has increased. Land distribution and redistribution of assets are a fifth measure of inequality. A sixth measure is based on income mobility that counteracts increasing income inequality. A seventh measure is computed based on the ratio of the regions highest to lowest quintile share of income.

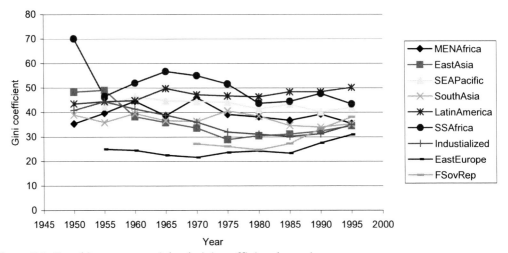

Figure 5.1. Trend in mean unweighted gini coefficient by region.

Regardless of the chosen measure when applicable the transformation of income to PPP and its adjustment for the population size, the coverage in terms of the number of countries and their populations share are important factors affecting the development of the inter-regional inequality in the world (for a detailed discussion of these issues see Chapter 7 of this manuscript). Several studies prefer the use of the household data with comprehensive coverage of income sources and representative population. Results based on WIID database show a large interregional heterogeneity in both the level and the development of income distribution and income inequality over time. The inequality in Latin America, Eastern Europe and the former Soviet Republics show increasing trends post 1970s.

INTRA-REGIONAL INCOME INEQUALITY

Intra-regional inequality refers to the disparity in income distribution within a geographical region consisting of a number of countries which may or may not be members of an economic union. Here we review a few recent studies on each geographical region. The regional classification differs from that used to group countries based on the WIID database or the classifications found in international data sources. Thus, the review here is based on a less standardized classification employed by individual researchers in the inequality literature to group countries into different regions. In many cases regions overlap or countries across two or more regions are compared to each other. We use the concepts of region, continent and sub-continents interchangeably. The regional income inequality within a selection of large countries is reviewed in Chapter 6 of this monograph.

Eastern Europe and the Former USSR

The transformation process of Eastern Europe from planned economies to market economies has been the focus of attention of many researchers. Milanovic (1998) is concerned with the social dimensions of the transition to market economies in the Central and the Eastern Europe and the former Soviet Union. The main emphasis is on the incidence of poverty in the transition economies. Here GDP per capita and the income inequality across the region are used as a backdrop to the poverty analysis. The state of inequality and poverty during the period before transition 1987-1993 is compared with the transition period during 1993-1996. Using data including 18 of the region's 27 countries it is shown that poverty has increased greatly across the region as a result of the combined decline in real incomes and the increased income inequality. Nine countries were excluded because of the effects of shocks due to the internal and external military conflicts. Empirical results show that while the real incomes have declined across the region, inequality has not increased homogeneously everywhere. The wage distribution and the failure in the welfare transfer system might have caused the increase in the income inequality. Milanovic and Yitzhaki (2001) using data from 22 transition economies for 1988 and 1999 found that 61 per cent of the overall inequality is associated with the within country inequality. The high and increasing within country inequality contrary to many studies, which expect a positive relationship between democracy and equality contradicts the existence of such relationship (Gradstein and Milanovic, 2002). The WIID data show significant variations in the mean inequality over the region. The Russian Federation, Georgia and Kyrgyze Republics, Estonia and the republics that engaged in conflicts experienced high inequality (see Table 5.3, Section 7).

Table 5.3 Distribution of Gini coefficient by country, based on WIID

Obs Country	Idnr	Region	PERIOD				GINI COEFFICIENT							
			Min	Max	Nyear	Range	Minimum	Mean	Median	Maximum	Std Dev	Range	Wgini	Dgini
1. Middle East and North Africa:														
1 Algeria	1	1	1988	1995	2	7	35.30	37.01	37.01	38.73	2.43	3.43	36.87	-1.27
2 Cyprus	32	1	1966	1966	1	0	25.56	25.56	25.56	25.56	.	0.00	.	.
3 Djibouti	37	1	1996	1996	1	0	38.10	38.10	38.10	38.10	.	0.00	38.10	.
4 Egypt	40	1	1959	1995	6	36	28.90	33.72	35.03	35.84	2.73	6.94	33.08	-0.62
5 Iraq	65	1	1956	1956	1	0	59.92	59.92	59.92	59.92	.	0.00	.	.
6 Israel	67	1	1944	1995	17	51	23.36	32.70	32.48	38.20	3.76	14.84	33.74	0.27
7 Jordan	71	1	1980	1997	7	17	30.95	35.51	35.35	42.03	3.87	11.08	35.92	-1.52
8 Lebanon	78	1	1960	1960	1	0	55.00	55.00	55.00	55.00	.	0.00	.	.
9 Sudan	124	1	1963	1969	3	6	37.95	40.73	39.65	44.60	3.46	6.65	.	0.75
10 Tunisia	135	1	1961	1990	8	29	40.25	44.92	44.16	53.00	4.84	12.75	44.24	0.34
11 Turkey	136	1	1952	1994	9	42	40.00	49.21	50.42	56.45	5.10	16.45	48.39	-2.16
12 YemenRep	147	1	1992	1992	1	0	39.50	39.50	39.50	39.50	.	0.00	39.50	.
Mean region 1	1	1944	1997	57	53	23.36	39.97	37.08	59.92	8.23	36.56	41.31	.	

Table 5.3 Distribution of Gini coefficient by country, based on WIID (Continued)

Obs Country	Idnr	Region	PERIOD				GINI COEFFICIENT							
			Min	Max	Nyear	Range	Minimum	Mean	Median	Maximum	Std Dev	Range	Wgini	Dgini
2. East Asia:														
13 China	25	2	1953	1998	26	45	18.60	29.35	29.34	55.80	7.18	37.20	28.59	3.37
14 HongKong	60	2	1957	1996	12	39	37.65	44.65	45.09	52.00	4.11	14.35	44.50	1.70
15 KoreaRep	74	2	1953	1993	17	40	29.82	34.18	34.00	40.22	2.95	10.40	34.28	0.80
16 Mongolia	92	2	1995	1997	2	2	28.57	30.88	30.88	33.20	3.28	4.63	.	-6.98
17 Taiwan	129	2	1953	1996	36	43	28.14	33.04	30.33	55.80	7.16	27.66	31.92	-0.41
Mean region 2	2		1953	1998	93	45	18.60	33.67	31.20	55.80	7.65	37.20	28.81	.
3. South East Asia and Pacific:														
18 Cambodia	19	3	1997	1997	1	0	40.40	40.40	40.40	40.40	.	0.00	.	.
19 Fiji	44	3	1968	1977	3	9	42.25	43.05	42.50	44.41	1.18	2.16	43.00	-0.55
20 Indonesi	63	3	1964	1996	17	32	31.38	36.36	34.20	51.00	5.74	19.62	36.09	5.06
21 Lao	76	3	1992	1992	1	0	30.40	30.40	30.40	30.40	.	0.00	.	.
22 Malaysia	86	3	1957	1995	18	38	37.26	47.71	48.16	57.16	4.03	19.90	47.83	0.97
23 Myanmar	94	3	1958	1958	1	0	34.97	34.97	34.97	34.97	.	0.00	.	.
24 Philippi	106	3	1956	1997	12	41	43.06	46.94	47.35	50.26	2.42	7.21	46.43	-0.06
25 PopuaNG	108	3	1996	1996	1	0	50.90	50.90	50.90	50.90	.	0.00	50.90	.
26 Singapor	118	3	1966	1993	15	27	37.00	42.49	42.83	48.83	3.20	11.83	42.27	1.05
27 Thailand	132	3	1962	1998	16	36	41.08	45.03	43.91	51.43	3.16	10.34	45.33	0.64
28 Vietnam	146	3	1992	1998	2	6	35.70	35.90	35.90	36.10	0.28	0.40	35.70	0.19
Mean region 3	3		1956	1998	87	42	30.40	43.17	43.90	57.16	5.87	26.76	39.80	.
4. South Asia:														
29 Banglade	8	4	1959	1996	22	37	31.76	37.68	37.57	45.00	3.81	13.24	37.36	-0.49
30 India	62	4	1950	1997	41	47	28.86	34.55	34.94	46.25	3.63	17.39	34.12	0.24
31 Iran	64	4	1960	1984	8	24	41.88	45.59	44.53	50.18	3.71	8.30	45.29	0.17
32 Nepal	95	4	1976	1996	4	20	30.06	42.50	43.46	53.00	10.93	22.94	41.19	0.40
33 Pakistan	102	4	1963	1996	19	33	29.69	34.26	33.60	40.23	3.11	10.55	34.33	-0.28
34 SriLanka	123	4	1953	1995	12	42	30.10	40.40	42.38	47.70	5.40	17.60	39.98	-1.20
Mean region 4	4		1950	1997	106	47	28.86	36.94	35.75	53.00	5.37	24.14	34.49	.
5. Latin America:														
35 Argentin	2	5	1953	1998	20	45	34.35	41.88	43.34	46.68	4.09	12.33	42.28	0.11
36 Bahamas	7	5	1970	1993	11	23	40.64	46.35	45.29	53.19	4.28	12.56	.	1.31
37 Barbados	9	5	1951	1981	20	30	31.10	36.04	34.35	48.86	4.51	17.76	35.98	-1.22
38 Bolivia	12	5	1968	1993	5	25	47.26	50.53	51.57	52.23	2.10	4.97	50.61	-1.38
39 Brazil	15	5	1958	1996	26	38	34.70	54.99	55.97	63.66	5.82	28.96	55.50	1.59
40 Chile	24	5	1964	1996	28	32	44.00	50.93	51.51	55.67	3.74	11.67	51.26	0.72
41 Colombia	26	5	1960	1996	24	36	43.40	51.79	51.21	59.22	4.41	15.82	51.74	-0.04
42 CostaRic	28	5	1961	1996	22	35	39.71	45.31	45.10	51.00	2.88	11.29	.	0.51
43 Cuba	31	5	1953	1978	4	25	27.00	35.06	28.06	57.14	14.72	30.14	.	-2.13
44 DominRep	38	5	1969	1996	7	27	43.15	47.73	48.70	50.56	2.76	7.42	47.97	0.04
45 Ecuador	39	5	1965	1995	7	30	41.88	52.12	47.73	67.83	10.25	25.95	50.53	1.74
46 ElSalvad	41	5	1961	1996	10	35	42.40	48.73	49.31	53.89	4.08	11.49	48.69	0.83
47 Guatemal	55	5	1948	1990	8	42	29.96	48.86	50.09	59.50	10.27	29.54	51.53	2.21
48 Guyana	58	5	1956	1993	2	37	46.11	51.13	51.13	56.16	7.11	10.05	49.90	-0.48
49 Honduras	59	5	1967	1998	10	31	50.00	55.57	54.98	63.00	3.53	13.00	55.19	-0.86
50 Jamaica	69	5	1958	1996	13	38	36.40	47.23	41.79	65.50	10.84	29.10	46.29	-0.09
51 Mexico	90	5	1950	1996	18	46	40.26	51.08	51.93	59.00	4.88	18.74	50.95	0.48

Table 5.3 Distribution of Gini coefficient by country, based on WIID (Continued)

Obs Country	Idnr	Region	PERIOD				GINI COEFFICIENT							
			Min	Max	Nyear	Range	Minimum	Mean	Median	Maximum	Std Dev	Range	Wgini	Dgini
52 Nicaragu	98	5	1993	1993	1	0	50.30	50.30	50.30	50.30	.	0.00	50.30	.
53 Panama	103	5	1960	1997	13	37	36.09	49.22	50.39	56.50	6.66	20.41	50.45	0.68
54 Paraguay	104	5	1983	1995	4	12	39.80	47.96	47.05	57.92	7.64	18.12	48.48	7.44
55 Peru	105	5	1961	1997	13	36	37.19	49.46	49.01	62.48	7.55	25.29	48.07	1.51
56 PuertoRi	110	5	1953	1989	6	36	38.70	45.69	46.15	51.96	5.53	13.26	.	2.73
57 Suriname	125	5	1962	1962	1	0	30.00	30.00	30.00	30.00	.	0.00	.	.
58 Trinidad	134	5	1957	1992	7	35	40.30	45.71	46.02	52.45	4.16	12.15	45.44	0.35
59 Uruguay	143	5	1961	1997	16	36	36.61	41.39	41.94	44.18	2.17	7.57	41.45	0.11
60 Venezuel	145	5	1962	1997	24	35	38.28	42.90	42.94	49.42	3.22	11.14	42.84	0.13
Mean region	5	5	1948	1998	320	50	27.00	47.39	47.25	67.83	7.47	40.83	51.79	.
6. Sub-saharan Africa:														
61 Botswana	14	6	1971	1986	3	15	52.00	53.90	52.30	57.40	3.03	5.40	53.54	-1.15
62 BurkinaF	17	6	1994	1995	2	1	39.00	43.60	43.60	48.20	6.51	9.20	43.55	-19.09
63 Burundi	18	6	1992	1992	1	0	33.30	33.30	33.30	33.30	.	0.00	33.30	.
64 Cameroon	20	6	1983	1983	1	0	49.00	49.00	49.00	49.00	.	0.00	49.00	.
65 CenAfRep	22	6	1992	1993	2	1	55.00	58.15	58.15	61.30	4.45	6.30	58.19	11.45
66 Chad	23	6	1958	1958	1	0	34.36	34.36	34.36	34.36	.	0.00	.	.
67 Congo	27	6	1958	1958	1	0	43.30	43.30	43.30	43.30	.	0.00	.	.
68 CotedIvo	29	6	1959	1995	8	36	36.90	43.50	42.15	52.56	6.06	15.66	42.33	-3.21
69 Dahomey	35	6	1959	1959	1	0	41.96	41.96	41.96	41.96	.	0.00	.	.
70 Ethiopia	43	6	1981	1996	3	15	32.42	38.87	40.00	44.20	5.97	11.78	39.68	6.09
71 Gabon	47	6	1960	1977	4	17	48.86	57.29	58.70	62.90	6.38	14.04	56.80	1.33
72 Gambia	48	6	1992	1992	1	0	43.40	43.40	43.40	43.40	.	0.00	43.40	.
73 Ghana	53	6	1988	1997	5	9	32.70	34.27	33.97	35.90	1.19	3.20	34.18	-1.27
74 Guinea	56	6	1991	1995	3	4	40.40	43.58	43.55	46.80	3.20	6.40	43.47	-4.77
75 GuineaBi	57	6	1991	1991	1	0	56.16	56.16	56.16	56.16	.	0.00	56.16	.
76 Kenya	73	6	1914	1994	19	80	48.80	60.69	60.00	70.00	6.49	21.20	59.92	-1.21
77 Lesotho	79	6	1987	1987	1	0	59.01	59.01	59.01	59.01	.	0.00	59.01	.
78 Liberia	80	6	1974	1974	1	0	43.00	43.00	43.00	43.00	.	0.00	.	.
79 Madagasc	84	6	1960	1993	4	33	39.10	46.08	46.59	52.05	5.64	12.95	45.93	-3.92
80 Malawi	85	6	1969	1993	5	24	46.08	55.30	56.70	62.00	6.43	15.92	56.64	1.60
81 Mali	87	6	1994	1994	1	0	52.25	52.25	52.25	52.25	.	0.00	52.25	.
82 Mauritan	88	6	1988	1995	2	7	38.35	40.41	40.41	42.47	2.91	4.11	40.21	-1.38
83 Mauritiu	89	6	1980	1991	3	11	36.69	40.67	39.63	45.70	4.59	9.01	40.52	-1.85
84 Morocco	93	6	1955	1999	12	44	32.16	45.81	48.80	59.00	8.59	26.84	.	-1.52
85 Niger	99	6	1960	1995	3	35	31.60	39.40	36.10	50.50	9.87	18.90	41.88	6.87
86 Nigeria	100	6	1959	1997	13	38	35.18	43.20	41.24	59.97	7.45	24.78	42.73	-2.01
87 Reunion	111	6	1977	1977	1	0	51.00	51.00	51.00	51.00	.	0.00	.	.
88 Rwanda	114	6	1983	1984	2	1	28.90	28.90	28.90	28.90	0.00	0.00	28.90	0.00
89 Senegal	115	6	1959	1995	6	36	41.30	49.96	52.07	57.37	6.38	16.07	48.47	-2.59
90 Seychell	116	6	1978	1984	2	6	46.00	46.50	46.50	47.00	0.71	1.00	46.52	0.36
91 SierraLe	117	6	1967	1989	5	22	49.00	57.73	59.00	62.90	5.42	13.90	.	0.84
92 SouthAfr	121	6	1959	1995	12	36	48.00	54.89	54.00	63.00	5.21	15.00	55.53	0.62
93 Swazilan	126	6	1974	1994	2	20	60.90	62.30	62.30	63.70	1.98	2.80	.	-0.22
94 Tanzania	131	6	1964	1993	8	29	38.20	49.12	49.67	58.00	6.30	19.80	48.96	-4.12

Table 5.3 Distribution of Gini coefficient by country, based on WIID (Continued)

Obs Country	Idnr	Region	PERIOD				GINI COEFFICIENT							
			Min	Max	Nyear	Range	Minimum	Mean	Median	Maximum	Std Dev	Range	Wgini	Dgini
95 Togo	133	6	1957	1957	1	0	33.80	33.80	33.80	33.80	.	0.00	.	.
96 Uganda	141	6	1970	1993	4	23	34.66	37.19	37.06	39.97	2.78	5.30	37.59	0.98
97 Zambia	150	6	1959	1996	9	37	43.51	54.57	51.00	79.50	10.36	35.99	53.02	-3.06
98 Zimbabwe	151	6	1945	1990	4	45	46.00	57.85	59.56	66.27	8.80	20.27	60.59	-1.50
Mean region	6	6	1914	1999	157	85	28.90	49.26	50.00	79.50	10.05	50.60	46.53	.
7. East Europe:														
99 BosniaHe	13	7	1991	1991	1	0	32.88	32.88	32.88	32.88	.	0.00	.	.
100 Bulgaria	16	7	1957	1997	36	40	15.90	23.88	23.28	35.70	4.54	19.80	31.08	1.78
101 Croatia	30	7	1987	1998	6	11	21.10	25.68	25.80	30.07	2.95	8.97	25.84	6.53
102 CzechRep	33	7	1958	1997	12	39	19.27	23.22	23.26	28.14	3.07	8.87	24.36	1.96
103 Hungary	61	7	1955	1998	28	43	20.47	24.61	23.49	31.89	3.46	11.42	25.00	0.61
104 Macedoni	83	7	1990	1997	8	7	23.34	26.34	27.09	27.90	1.68	4.55	26.66	2.45
105 Poland	107	7	1956	1998	29	42	20.88	26.60	25.94	33.20	2.84	12.32	26.66	0.94
106 Romania	112	7	1988	1997	10	9	20.57	26.38	25.03	36.38	4.99	15.81	26.34	5.79
107 RussianF	113	7	1981	1998	13	17	25.10	34.14	36.55	44.81	7.64	19.71	39.35	4.39
108 SlovakRe	119	7	1958	1997	11	39	19.13	21.99	20.65	30.60	3.35	11.47	21.14	1.26
109 Slovenia	120	7	1987	1997	11	10	19.90	25.66	25.61	29.69	2.93	9.79	26.98	4.32
110 Ukraine	142	7	1968	1997	17	29	21.50	28.43	25.00	37.25	5.42	15.75	30.01	0.51
111 YugoslFR	148	7	1989	1997	9	8	25.96	31.30	31.30	35.35	3.19	9.38	.	2.64
Mean region 7	7	1955	1998	191	43	15.90	25.14	25.04	44.81	5.06	28.91	31.57	.	
8. Former Soviet Republics:														
112 Armenia	3	8	1986	1997	11	11	26.90	33.77	32.49	47.67	6.72	20.77	37.96	5.68
113 Azerbaij	6	8	1972	1996	8	24	25.20	30.82	28.72	45.02	6.57	19.82	45.02	3.37
114 Belarus	10	8	1981	1998	12	17	23.30	26.50	26.20	33.64	3.13	10.34	27.79	-0.27
115 Estonia	42	8	1981	1998	12	17	24.00	32.15	35.31	38.00	5.75	14.00	36.70	2.27
116 Georgia	49	8	1981	1997	11	16	24.80	39.93	36.41	57.60	12.87	32.80	53.70	6.90
117 Kazakhst	72	8	1981	1996	8	15	25.70	30.14	29.40	35.40	3.28	9.70	34.19	2.10
118 KyrgyzRe	75	8	1981	1997	11	16	24.30	34.39	36.68	42.60	7.09	18.30	41.61	3.80
119 Latvia	77	8	1981	1998	13	17	24.00	28.86	27.00	35.32	4.38	11.32	30.49	3.19
120 Lithuani	81	8	1981	1997	11	16	23.70	30.82	33.60	39.19	6.18	15.49	35.79	2.44
121 Moldova	91	8	1981	1995	9	14	22.90	30.86	26.70	40.16	7.10	17.26	38.08	3.90
122 Tajikist	130	8	1981	1990	5	9	25.20	29.29	28.83	33.40	3.34	8.20	.	4.14
123 Turkmeni	137	8	1981	1998	7	17	25.20	31.30	30.80	41.45	5.74	16.25	.	3.18
124 Uzbekist	144	8	1981	1994	7	13	24.80	29.48	29.30	33.30	3.28	8.50	33.00	2.64
Mean region 8	8	1972	1998	125	26	22.90	31.56	29.60	57.60	7.06	34.70	33.99	.	
9. Industrialized countries:														
125 Australi	4	9	1962	1998	18	36	31.60	37.68	38.65	44.60	4.84	13.00	38.08	4.60
126 Austria	5	9	1970	1991	21	21	24.50	25.91	25.50	29.30	1.21	4.80	25.90	-0.09
127 Belgium	11	9	1969	1994	11	25	24.02	33.50	30.78	43.75	7.31	19.73	33.46	-0.52
128 Canada	21	9	1951	1994	26	43	25.13	30.83	31.44	35.78	2.41	10.65	30.63	-0.17
129 Denmark	36	9	1939	1995	29	56	22.49	34.04	35.52	45.00	6.67	22.51	32.92	0.35
130 Finland	45	9	1952	1998	27	46	20.00	29.33	28.37	46.57	5.21	26.57	29.16	1.08
131 France	46	9	1956	1995	11	39	28.72	38.14	34.95	50.46	7.74	21.74	37.58	-0.03
132 Germany	50	9	1950	1997	28	47	19.87	31.67	30.93	43.68	6.26	23.81	.	3.65
133 Greece	54	9	1957	1993	19	36	32.70	41.56	43.18	46.26	3.95	13.56	41.39	0.57
134 Ireland	66	9	1973	1987	3	14	35.74	36.80	36.96	37.69	0.99	1.95	36.77	-0.13

Table 5.3 Distribution of Gini coefficient by country, based on WIID (Continued)

Obs Country	Idnr	Region	PERIOD Min	Max	Nyear	Range	GINI COEFFICIENT Minimum	Mean	Median	Maximum	Std Dev	Range	Wgini	Dgini
135 Italy	68	9	1948	1995	25	47	29.18	35.68	35.53	42.00	3.85	12.82	35.45	-0.66
136 Japan	70	9	1890	1993	33	103	24.90	35.53	34.80	46.70	4.55	21.80	33.98	-0.02
137 Luxembo	82	9	1985	1994	3	9	25.20	25.89	25.40	27.06	1.02	1.86	25.86	-0.64
138 Netherla	96	9	1950	1997	24	47	27.62	32.10	31.27	44.80	4.88	17.18	31.72	0.42
139 NewZeala	97	9	1954	1997	31	43	30.04	45.61	43.90	67.20	11.48	37.16	44.20	-0.80
140 Norway	101	9	1957	1996	23	39	23.40	30.74	29.39	39.87	5.07	16.47	30.56	1.79
141 Portugal	109	9	1973	1995	5	22	34.14	36.26	35.60	40.58	2.49	6.44	36.15	0.54
142 Spain	122	9	1965	1996	15	31	23.70	30.93	32.97	36.68	4.79	12.98	30.79	1.40
143 Sweden	127	9	1948	1996	45	48	20.07	38.14	37.56	55.70	12.36	35.63	37.47	1.03
144 Switzerl	128	9	1978	1992	4	14	31.22	33.20	33.47	34.66	1.47	3.44	33.21	0.11
145 UK	138	9	1867	1996	41	129	23.15	30.87	28.77	57.51	6.18	34.36	30.19	0.63
146 US	139	9	1944	1997	53	53	35.18	38.65	37.93	44.78	2.35	9.60	38.85	0.03
Mean region	9	9	1867	1998	495	131	19.87	34.79	33.83	67.20	7.90	47.33	36.08	.
Mean all regions			1867	1999	1631	132	15.90	41.12	40.24	79.50	9.61	27.91	35.65	0.34

Obs   Observation number
Country   Country
Idnr   Country ID number
Region   Regional location
Min   First year of observation
Max   Last year of observation
Nyear   Number of years observed
Range   The difference between the last and first years of observation
Minimum   Minimum Gini value
Mean   Mean Gini value
Median   Median Gini value
Maximum   Maximum Gini value
Std Dev   Standard deviation of the Gini
Range   The difference between maximum and minimum Gini values
Wgini   Population weighted mean Gini
Dgini   Average percentage change in Gini
Note: USSR, Yugoslavia and Czechoslovakia are excluded and East and West Germany are averaged.

A combination of a number of existing linear, log linear and reciprocal models to an exponential model proposed by Ram (1995) is used by Wan (2002b) to analyse the relationship between income inequality and the growth in transition economies:

$$(5.1) \qquad INEQ = (1 - \exp(-\beta_1 Y)) \exp(-\beta_2 Y) + \beta_3 Z + \beta_4 Z^2 + \varepsilon$$

where $INEQ$ is measured by an indicator like the Gini coefficient, Y is level of development like GDP per capita, Z is some transformation variable (linear, logarithmic, or reciprocal) of the development, and ε a random error term. Using data on 24 transition economies Wan finds a positive inequality growth relationship. However, the results indicate that rising inequality is neither a part of the inevitable Kuznets curve, nor a part of the empirical regularity found by Barro (2000). Barro finds little overall relation between income inequality and the rates of growth and investment. Higher inequality tends to retard the growth in poor countries and encourages the growth in richer countries. In parallel to the rising inequality and the variation in the observed inequality levels in the transition economies spending on education has declined. Aghion and Commander (1999) simulate the effects of such education policy choices on the path of inequality over the transition. The Kuznets curve representation does not apply. They show how trade liberalization and technological and organizational changes affect the relative demand for types of labour resulting in an increase in inequality. Persistent of inequality is expected to depend on the pace of skill acquisition and on the evolution of the educational system. Policies raising the quality of education dampen the increase in wage inequality. For explanations of the observed increase in the between-group and the within-group wage inequality in the developed countries over the past thirty years in association with the transition to the new technological paradigm and the application of growth enhancing policies (in education and training) see Aghion (2002).

Ivaschenko (2002) investigates the causes of the unprecedented changes in the income distribution and the dramatic increase in the income inequality facing the transitional economies of Eastern Europe and the former Soviet Union in the 1990s. Panel data from 24 transitional countries for the period 1989-1998 is used in a regression analysis:

$$(5.2) \qquad GINI_{it} = \beta_i + \sum_{j=1} X_{jit} + \varepsilon_{it}$$

The subscripts i, t, and j denote country, period and inequality determinant (X) variables. The aim is to identify and to estimate the impacts of a number of potential determinants of the rising inequality. These determinants are per capita GDP, economic liberalisation, privatisation and deindustrialization, hyperinflation, unemployment and the size of government consumption, civil conflict, political rights and civil liberties. Inequality is measured by the Gini coefficient obtained from the WIID. In the base model specification, variations in the Gini coefficient is explained by it determinants including per capita GDP, its square, inflation rate, unemployment rate, the general government consumption, industry value added as percentage of GDP, and the private sector share of GDP. The results support a U-shaped relationship between income inequality and per capita GDP. The relationship between income inequality and growth is positive for Eastern Europe and negative for the former Soviet Union republics. Hyperinflation, civil conflict and unemployment increase inequality. Economic liberalisation, privatisation and deindustrialization have also contributed to the rise in income inequality. Alexeev and Leitzel (2001) demonstrate that the state-sector queue rationing and price controls are preferable to the imperfectly targeted income subsidies in providing a social-safety net to counteract the rapid changes in the relative well being during transition.

In examining the problem of ensuring health-care coverage to rural and poor areas of the developing countries Luttmer (2001) decomposes the total income into transitory and persistent components. Luttmer measured income as a monthly consumption expenditure or an income adjusted for the household size using an equivalent scale. The aim is to distinguish the underlying income inequality and changes in poverty from the effects due to measurement error or transitory shocks:

$$(5.3) \qquad C_{it} = C_{it}^* + \varepsilon_{it} = (C_{i,t-1}^* + \alpha_t + \eta_{it}) + \varepsilon_{it}$$

where the log consumption expenditure (C) of individuals over time is function of the underlying level of consumption (C^*), a transitory shock possibly including measurement error (ε), a time-specific trend (α), a term representing persistent shocks (η), and i is individual and t time period. The empirical analysis is based on the household level data from Poland 1993-1996 and Russia 1994-1998. The results show that accounting for noise in the data reduces the inequality measured as Gini coefficient by 10-15 per cent. About half of the median absolute annual changes in income or spending in Poland (20 per cent) and in Russia (50 per cent) reflect measurement error or transitory shocks. This suggests the underlying levels of income and spending which are more stable than the data suggests. The high levels of economic mobility were found to be largely driven by transitory events and noisy data. Around 80 per cent of the poor in these two countries remain in poverty for at least one year. One possible way of reducing the negative role of the transitory events and measurement error, which get averaged out over the year, is to examine the inequality in average incomes.[10]

Results based on the WIID database suggest that the dynamics of inequality in the transition economies is characterised by an increasing inequality and a large variation in inequality levels across transition countries. Prior to 1985 the range of inequality was quite small. Both the mean and the range between countries increased substantially (see Figures 5.2 and 5.3). The increase and dispersion is much higher for the former Soviet republics (7.06 and 34.70) than the Eastern Europe (5.06 and 28.91). The numbers in the parenthesis are the standard deviation and ranges of income inequality as measured by the Gini coefficient. The standard deviation and ranges of inequality over time are the highest for the Russian Federation (7.64 and 19.71) among the East European countries and the lowest for Macedonian (1.68 and 4.55). In the case of the former Soviet republics the highest dispersion is associated with Georgia (12.87 and 32.80) and the lowest to Tajikistan (3.34 and 8.20). For more details on individual countries see Table 5.3, Sections 7 and 8.

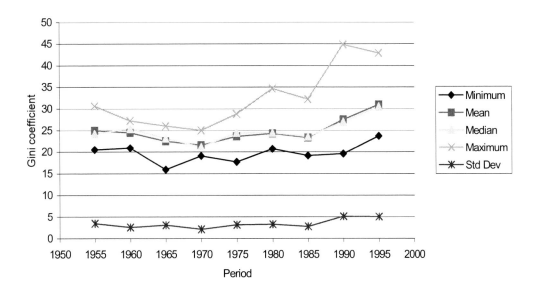

Figure 5.2. Development of gini coefficient, East Europe.

----

[10] Here average incomes are based on the current month, and the last 12, 24 and 36 months ago.

The discussion above can be summarized as the path of inequality over the transition and is explained by the differences in the initial conditions, the countries subsequent policy choices and key variables like ownership and restructuring programmes. Empirical result does not support the Kuznets curve for the transition economies, but confirms the association between inequality and growth. The analysis is extended to look at how trade liberalisation, technological and organisational change affects the relative demand for labour resulting in the rising inequality. Labour market policies, improved institutional capacities for taxation and redistribution and policies aimed at rising quality of education by rising adaptability are expected to dampen the increase in income inequality.

Scandinavia

The high quality, comparable and comprehensive household surveys and various public service registers in Scandinavia have been accessible to researchers. The excellent data situation together with the need for the evaluation of impacts of decades of tax and benefit reforms on labour supply, welfare and the inequality between and within different income groups have resulted in many single or cross-Scandinavian income distribution studies (e.g. Aronsson and Palme, 1998, Fellman, Jäntti and Lambert, 1999, and Maasoumi and Heshmati, 2000). A few of such recent studies will be reviewed below.

A two-way causal relationship between income mobility and income inequality can be expected. Shorrocks (1978b) introduced as an alternative to the transition matrix approach a family of mobility measures that incorporates the relationship between mobility and inequality. Mobility is measured as the relative reduction in the weighted average of a single-year inequality when the accounting period is extended. The opposite state of no mobility is defined to occur when the relative income or rankings of individuals are constant over time. Aaberge et al. (2002) compare the income inequality and the income mobility based on household data in the Scandinavian (Denmark, Norway and Sweden) countries and the US during 1980s. In a somewhat modified version of the approach proposed by Shorrocks income mobility (M) is defined by the function of Gini coefficient and the overall mean (μ) and the means of the distribution of income in different years (μ_t):

$$(5.4) \qquad M = 1 - \frac{GINI}{\sum_{t=1}^{T} (\mu_t / \mu) GINI_t}$$

Income is measured as earnings, market income and disposable income. The results demonstrate that inequality is greater in the US and that the ranking of the countries by degree of inequality remains stable when the comparison period is extended to up to 11 years, 1980-1990. The period average income inequality is for Denmark 0.22, Norway 0.26, Sweden 0.23 and the US 0.34. The US has the highest mobility for earnings and disposable income, while Sweden seems to be the most income mobile country for market income in the sample. However, the results suggest that there is no evidence of a positive relationship between inequality and mobility.

The studies of several countries focus on the distributional impacts of various policies on the welfare of sub-groups. Björklund and Palme (1997) decomposed the overall income inequality over 18 years into two parts: one showing the inequality of long-run (permanent) income, and a second showing the variability of individual income over time. A welfare state affects both components, but the equalising impact on income of the group with a low long-run income is higher. Fellman, Jäntti and Lambert (1999) by decomposition techniques use inequality impact of optimal policy as a yardstick to gauge the effectiveness of tax and benefit policies in reducing inequality in Finland 1971-1990. In comparison with the distribution of incomes of single immigrants and Swedes by various attributes Maasoumi and Heshmati (2000) find that welfare policies favour the elderly, females, larger families, and immigrants with longer periods of residency. The higher the educational credentials, the higher are the burden of these equalisation policies.

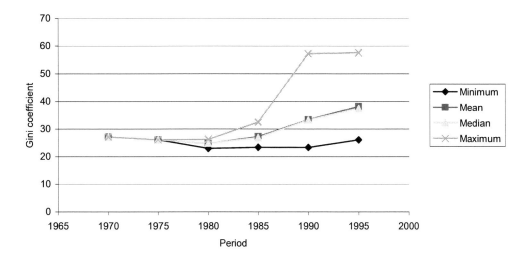

Figure 5.3. Development of Gini coefficient, Former Soviet Republics.

The evolution of the income distribution of a small number of developed countries during two centuries is analysed by Morrisson (2000). The use of long time series data rather than cross sections is preferred to test the Kuznets inverse U-curve hypothesis. Data from the Scandinavian countries (Denmark, Sweden, Finland and Norway), Netherlands, Germany and France is used for the purpose. The inverse U-curve hypothesis is verified in four (France, Sweden, Germany, and Finland) cases. Using the Theil inequality indicator:

$$(5.5) \qquad T = T_B + T_W = T_B + s_1 T_1 + s_2 T_2$$

is decomposed into between (T_B) and within (T_W) agricultural (1) and non-agricultural (2) sectors in each country. The variable s indicates the shares of two sectors in the total income. Political (the two World Wars and French revolution) and economic (taxes and transfers and government interventions) factors explaining the long-term evolution of distribution are discussed. The economic factors playing a key role in the evolution of the income distribution are found to be the market structures, the diffusion of education and saving, and dualism.

The concept of convergence in inequality (Benabou 1996) follows the conditional convergence of per capita incomes (Mankiw, Romer and Weil, 1992). Iacoviello (1998) using LIS data including Denmark, Finland, Norway and Sweden investigates whether inequality converge to a steady state level of inequality during the process of income growth. In addition Iacoviello studies the linkage between the income and inequality movements, the factor influencing this growth process, as well as the reverse causation from the Gini income inequality to growth. The post-tax Gini coefficient during the country specific periods covering 1965-1993 is used to measure income inequality. Results show that the shocks to income can yield short run effects on the income distribution. However, a reversal link from inequality to income was not observed.

The pre tax and transfer income inequality among the Scandinavian countries is increasing. Analysis of the WIID data shows that the mean inequality is highest in Sweden (38.14 per cent) and the lowest in Finland (29.33 per cent). The corresponding for Denmark and Norway are 34.04 per cent and 30.74 per cent respectively. The dispersion measured as standard deviation and range is the highest for Sweden (12.36 and 35.63) and the lowest for Norway (5.07 and 16.47). The distribution at the tails is however different and more equal in the case of Finland and Sweden (see Section 9 of Tables 5.3 and 5.4).

Western Europe

The West European region is the single region most intensely studied at different levels of aggregation when income distribution is concerned. Ritakallio (2001) studies the trends in the income inequality and poverty and the effectiveness of income transfer systems between 1980 and 1995 in nine countries in Western Europe, US and Canada. These countries represent three[11] different ideal types of social policy or welfare state models: mean testing (UK, Canada and USA), corporatist (Netherlands, France and Germany) and institutional models (Norway, Finland and Sweden). The empirical analysis is based on LIS database containing the national household annual income (earnings, transfers and income from capital and employment) survey data. The LIS data is found to be a reliable starting point for the comparison of welfare states and their social policy. Comparisons by Rotakallio are made at three levels: between the population sub-groups, between points of time, and between the countries or the welfare state models.

The analysis of inequality and poverty by Ritakallio produced similar picture of the differences across the countries and the models of social policy. Income inequality measured as the Gini coefficient for earnings is increasing over time. However, the income inequality for disposable income in the Nordic countries and Canada has not increased over time, while the USA and the UK represent the opposite developments of disposable income. The countries are found to be different in their effectiveness in reducing poverty and income inequality using income transfer measures. Here poverty is defined using the relative income method where poverty line is both country and time specific. Poverty line is defined as half of the per capita median annual income. Poverty rates (share of the poor in the whole population) and poverty profiles (share of the poor in each population category) for the total

---

[11] A fourth type of social policy or welfare state model is the basic security model.

population and disaggregated by household type, number of children, age and labour participation show a large heterogeneity among the population sub-groups and the countries.

Belbo and Knaus (2001) propose an aggregate measure of inequality for the founding[12] countries of the European Monetary Union. The comparison is based on the distribution of the total annual household income after taxes and transfer payments from the European Community Household Panel and LIS in 1994. The Theil inequality index (T1) is used here and inequality is decomposed into the between and the within components for different household types within Euroland:

$$(5.6) \qquad T = T_W + T_B = \sum_{k=1}^{K} s_k \left(\frac{1}{N} \sum_{i=1}^{N} (y_i / \mu) \ln(y_i / \mu) \right) + \sum_{k=1}^{K} s_k \ln(\mu_k / \mu)$$

where y_i is income of individual i, s_k is the share of total income of sub-group k, μ and μ_k are the mean income of the population (N) and sub-group k. The population sub-groups are defined based on age and the number of children in each household. Using sub-group shares of the total income determine each country's as well as each group's contribution to the overall income inequality. Results show that the between country differences make up 9 per cent of the overall inequality indicating large differences in mean income levels across Euro countries. Social transfer payments contribute positively to the between country inequality differences and the between-household differences make up 2 per cent of the total inequality indicating a homogenous distribution of income across demographic groups.

The overall changes in the result when integrating new countries into the existing entity is decomposed by Belbo and Knaus into four effects: the direct inequality effect, the between group or the mean income effect, and the re-weighting the within and between inequality effects. The decomposition in above allows the assessment of the contribution of each member states or demographic groups to the overall inequality. The results show that the Theil inequality ranges from a minimum of 0.15 (the Netherlands) to a maximum of 0.24 (Portugal) and the average for Euroland has a value of 0.18. The between country post (pre) social transfer payments make up a 9.0 (3.0) per cent of the overall inequality and responsible for the overall inequality than the differences between household types. They find great disparities within and between the economic situations of the different demographic groups across the countries. A common social policy should target to reduce the within specific household inequality. An expansion of the Union to other members (Greece, the UK and Denmark) increases inequality from 0.18 to 0.19.

Heady, Mitrakos and Tsakloglou (2001) in their analysis of the comparative effects of social policy on inequality using the European Community household data found increasing distributional impacts of transfers and their share of GDP. The extent of means testing, the distribution of different funds and the degree of targeting for each transfer also affect their effectiveness.

Economic globalization, domestic politics and income inequality in 14 developed countries using LIS data is studied by Mahler (2001). The results show little evidence of a systematic relationship between economic globalization and either of the distribution of

---

[12] The founding countries of the European Monetary Union are: Austria, Belgium, France, Germany, Ireland, Italy, Luxembourg, Netherlands, Portugal and Spain.

disposable income or the earnings of households. Integration into the world economy does not systematically lead to an inegalitarian distribution of income or earnings across the entire economies. Politics continues to play a critical role in determining distributive outcomes in these countries. Economic globalization is found to be compatible with a wide variety of political interactions leading to a wide range of distributive outcomes.

As mentioned previously Iacoviello (1998) using the LIS data from eight continental European countries investigates whether inequality converges to a steady state level of inequality during the process of economic growth, the linkage between income and inequality movements, factors influencing this growth process, reverse causation from Gini coefficient to growth and its consequences concerning the simultaneity bias. Results show that shocks to income can yield short run dynamics in the income distribution, while the reverse link is not well supported by the LIS data. Quah (1996b) argue that physical location and geographical spillovers matter more than national macro factors to the observed distribution dynamics across the European regions. However, both factors are important for explaining the inequality dynamics.

In sum several studies analysing the distribution of income among the West European countries are based on LIS database. In comparison with other data sources LIS is a reliable database for the comparison of welfare states and their social policy. It allows comparison at different levels like between and within population sub-groups, between and within countries and also over time. Differences in welfare models make the countries different in their effectiveness in reducing poverty and inequality using taxes and income transfer measures. Therefore despite a high degree of homogeneity there are still significant variations in the levels of the inequality within and between the different population sub-groups and across the West European countries.

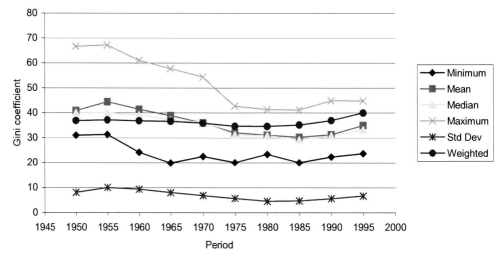

Figure 5.4. Development of Gini coefficient, industrialized countries.

Our results based on the WIID database show that the between country inequality in the industrialised countries region is relatively high but the patterns of inequality over time is relatively stable. However, there is a negative trend in the mean inequality between 1955 and 1985 followed by a positive trend post 1985 (see Figure 5.4). This is valid when both population-weighted and unweighted averages are considered. During post 1975 the level of inequality is converging in the West European region. The countries differ mainly in the distribution where the US tops the list among industrialised countries with a Q5/Q1 ratio of 9.17, compared to for instance Luxembourg with a low ratio of 2.98 (see Section 9 of Tables 5.3 and 5.4).

OECD Countries

Most of the OECD countries are already covered in previous 3 sections. The inclusion of a separate section for the OECD countries labeled as a region is simply due to the fact that several empirical studies investigates the income distribution among the OECD countries a group. Despite the risk of possible overlapping a short review of the findings in the literature follows.

Gottschalk and Smeeding (2000) study the income inequality in the OECD. Availability of the LIS-data and the improved cross-national comparability has made it possible to produce some consistent patterns and provide answers to concerns about the growing inequality in income, earnings and wealth amongst the OECD countries. The range of income inequality is very wide. Absolute and relative comparisons show a higher level of inequality in the US. Income inequality has been steadily increasing in the mid-1980s through mid-1990s. The increased inequality in several countries offset the equality gains made in the 1960s and 1970s.

Duro and Esteban (1998) present a decomposition of the Theil index of inequality into four components:

$$(5.7) \quad T = T^y + T^e + T^a + T^w = \sum_{i=1}^{N} s_i \ln\left(\frac{\mu^4}{x_i^y \times x_i^e \times x_i^a \times x_i^w}\right) = \sum_{i=1}^{N} s_i \ln(\mu / x_i)$$

where the components are productivity per employee worker (y), the employment rate (e), the active over working age population rate (a), and the active over total population rate (w). The s_i is the share of country i in the world population and x_i per capita income of sub-groups. It is applied to 23 OECD country's data. The results suggest that there is a rise in the international inequality between 1960 and 1975 and a decline thereafter until 1989. About one third of the inequality is attributed to factors other than productivity differentials. Inequalities in unemployment rates play an increasing role indicating a high degree of sensitivity of the local economies to sector-specific shocks. The results based on the Penn World Tables and OECD Labour Force Statistics give a somewhat different picture than those of Gottschalk and Smeeding. Data sources and decomposition of inequality may explain the differences. The factorial decomposition proposed by Duro and Esteban is extended by Georlich-Gisbert (2001) and is applied to a set of 23 OECD countries for the period 1962-1993. Here instead of population share income share is used. All factors are found to contribute significantly to the income inequality.

Real wages and living standards have converged among the OECD countries between 1850 and 1910. Part of this convergence in real wages and GDP per worker or GDP per capita has been due to the mass migration. The mass migration from countries with low real wages and low GDP per worker to countries with higher wages and GDP per capita were an important equalising effect on world incomes (Lindert and Williamson 2001). New barriers to trade and capital flow post 1929 have widened the international income gap. The differences in activity rates, unemployment, the working age population and the inequality in productivities affect the overall inequality. The overall cross-country inequality is lower within the 23 OECD countries compared with the worldwide level.

As mentioned in Duro and Esteban (1998) inequalities in unemployment rates play an increasing role indicating a high degree of sensitivity of the local economies to specialization in production and the effects of sector-specific shocks. For example, the negative relationship between wages and unemployment at the regional level within Germany is discussed in Pannenberg and Schwarze (2000). The aim is to link inequality with the difference in the level of unemployment in the East and West regions of Germany. Parikh (2002) examines the interregional labour mobility, inequality and wage convergence after the reunification between 16 regions of the East and West Germany for the period 1992-1995. The relationship between income inequality and the migration of skilled workers did not turn out to be strong.

In the unequal societies the median voter[13] will relatively be poorer because his/her factor gross and disposable incomes are lower in relation to the mean income. The more unequal the distribution of income is, if net transfer is positive, the more a median voter gains through tax and transfer policy, the more probable he/she votes for higher taxes and transfers, and the more unequal societies choose a greater redistribution. Given the expectations above Milanovic (2000) study the median voter hypothesis, income inequality and income distribution based on the LIS household budget survey data. The data covers 24 democracies observed 1 to 7 years in 1980s and 1990s. The results strongly support the conclusion that countries with a greater inequality of the factor income redistribute more to the poor, but it only weakly describes the collective choice mechanism. The bottom half receives 19.4 per cent of the factor income, while it receives 32.1 per cent of the post taxes and the transfers income. The gain of the bottom quintile and bottom half of the factor income distributions are 9.75 per cent and 12.44 per cent, respectively. The average Gini coefficient among the 24 countries reduces from 0.46 to 0.32. The reduction in Gini coefficient differs by income definition, country and over time. The largest inequality reduction is in Belgium (23-28 per cent) and Sweden (20-24 per cent) and the lowest in Taiwan (less than 1 per cent).

Riphahn (2001) in studying the social assistance take-up in Germany shows that more than half of all households eligible for transfers under the German social assistance program did not claim their benefits. It seems as in the case of the natural rate of unemployment there is a natural rate of poverty that can't be eliminated using transfers. Therefore the possible reductions in the Gini coefficient by accounting for non-claimed benefit transfers could be much larger.

Jäntti (1997) also uses the LIS data to examine levels and trends in the income inequality in five OECD countries[14] in the 1980s. A number of decomposition methods are discussed to decompose the level of income inequality and the changes in the income inequality into

---

[13] Median voter is defined as an individual with the median level of income. For further discussion of inequality, median voter hypothesis and redistribution see also Lee and Roemer (1999).

[14] The countries and periods include Canada 1981 and 1987, Netherlands 1983 and 1987, Sweden 1981 and 1987, UK 1979 and 1986 and USA 1979 and 1986. Income is measured as household disposable equivalent income.

between and within components by nine income sources[15] and a number of population groups.[16] Two methods, the squared coefficient of variation (CV^2) and the mean logarithmic deviation (*MLD*), are chosen to estimate each component's share in their contribution to the overall inequality and compare the changes across the years:

(5.8) $\qquad CV^2 = \sum_k \rho_k CV_k CV (\mu_k / \mu)$

(5.9) $\qquad MLD = \sum_j v_j MLD_j + v_j \log(1/\lambda_j)$

where CV is the coefficient of variation, ρ_k is the correlation coefficient between population and sub-group income, y and y_k, $v_j = N_j / N$ is the population share and $\lambda_j = \mu_j / \mu$ is the relative income for jth sub-group, j and k are sub-group and income components. The annualised changes in terms of the percentage changes in each component's contribution calculated. Results show that inequality increased in Sweden, the UK and US, but it did not increase in Canada and the Netherlands. Changes are mainly associated with the changes in the labour earnings. Increased inequality of the head of the household's earning and the increased share of spouse's earnings in the family income accounts for much of the observed income inequality. Demographic shifts are given a minor role in increasing inequality, while taxes and transfers are responsible for a decreasing effect on income inequality. The marginal impacts of various income sources on the overall income inequality applied to the US income distribution is also analysed by Lerman and Yitzhaki (1985):

(5.10) $\qquad G = \sum_{k=1}^{K} \rho_k G_k s_k$

where each source's (k) contribution is viewed as the product of the source's own within-group Gini coefficient (G_k), its share of the total income (s_k), and its correlation with the rank of the total income (ρ_k). The results indicate that the marginal effect of the spouse's earnings exceeded the marginal effects of the capital income.

Atkinson (2000) has examined the redistributive impacts of the government budget in six OECD countries (the UK, Canada, West Germany, Finland, Sweden and the US) over the period from 1980 to the mid-1990s. All countries experienced rise in inequality of market income but differed both across countries and over time with regards to the distribution of the disposable income. In reviewing the actual government policy responses by taking unemployment benefits and personal income taxation as case studies, the changes to policy parameters differed in extent and even in direction. However, no clear pattern was found in the nature of the relationship between inequality and redistribution. Atkinson and Brandolini

---

[15] The nine income sources are: earnings of head, earnings of spouse, self-employment, property income, other private, social insurance, means-tested, income taxes, and payroll taxes.

[16] The population groups are: partitions by family structure (single person, married couple with no children, single parent, and married couple with children), by age groups (less than 20, 20-24, 25-29, and so on), and by the number of income earners (0, 1, 2, and 3 earners).

(2001) compare four secondary data sets on income distribution covering the 40s until 70s. A number of OECD countries are used to illustrate the impacts of various factors on the outcome of inequality comparison. They suggest alternative ways to deal with the differences in the definition across countries or across time.

Results based on the LIS-data with improved cross-national comparability show growing income inequality amongst the OECD countries since mid-1980s. The range is wide indicating a significant inequality between countries. The redistributive policies in form of taxes and transfers have reduced the negative impacts of high unemployment, the wage inequality and the within country market income inequality resulting in a more equal distribution of the disposable income. With integration of economies and local specialization if sector-specific shocks result in persistent unemployment, they increase the inequality among countries and population sub-groups.

As previously mentioned results based on the WIID database show that the between country inequality in the OECD (labelled as industrialised) countries is relatively high but the patterns of inequality over time compared to other regions is less volatile. Many studies point to a positive relationship between democracy and equality, but the transition experience of the East European countries seems to go against this conclusion (Gradstein and Milanovic 2002). There is a negative trend in the mean inequality between 1955 and 1985 followed by a positive trend in the post 1985 (see Figure 5.4). During post 1975 the inequality is converged in the West European region. For detailed information on individual countries see Section 9 of Tables 5.3 and 5.4.

Small and Medium Sized Developing Countries

The relationship between inequality and growth or inequality and development is studied extensively to quantify the impacts of macroeconomic variables (see Alesina and Rodrik 1994; Person and Tabellini 1994). Bourguignon and Morrisson (1998) suggest an empirical approach to the relationship between inequality, as observed in microeconomic data and development-related macroeconomic variables. Major determinants of country differences in income distribution previously ignored in the literature concerning the dualistic nature of developing countries and the nature of the agricultural sector. Data from 38 developing countries around 1970s is used by Bourguignon and Morrisson for this purpose. Income distribution data comprises various combinations of income shares and the determinant variables are GDP per capita, GDP share of agriculture, schooling, exports, income source, cultivated land, and the relative labour productivity of agriculture/non-agriculture. The result is robust with respect to the composition of the sample, the observation period and the inclusion of country-specific fixed effects. The results suggest that the increasing level of productivity in agriculture can serve as an important measure to reduce inequality and poverty in the developing countries. However, the important role of the growing service sector at the cost of agriculture and manufacturing as a source of employment and infrastructure for development and equality should not be ignored.

There are few data observations covering the Middle East and North African countries. The existing data suggest that inequality is stable but the range and dispersion is declining over time (see Figure 5.5). Given several of these economies are oil based consumption societies with low level skill, production and in general development potential very unlikely inequality would have decreased.

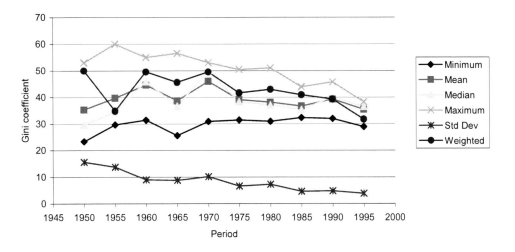

Figure 5.5. Development of Gini coefficient, Middle East and North Africa.

Sub-Saharan Africa

Several studies based on income or expenditures calculated from household surveys studying the world income distribution show increasing global inequality over time driven by the development in Latin America, Eastern Europe and Africa. Africa has been a single diverging region when growth, equality and poverty reduction is concerned. Svedborg (2002) in his survey of the measurement and results from the cross-country income distribution studies points to a number of limitations with Gini coefficient and similar measurements. He concludes that the relative differences in income between the richest and the poorest countries (located in Africa) have increased since the 1960s, but the distribution of income across countries has remained unchanged. The initially poorest (African) countries have continued to become more impoverished relative to other countries. Their future development will depend on economic growth and the relative population growth in the region. Despite its importance to the global distribution, it has not been possible to trace relevant studies based on household data comparing the income inequality among multiple African countries and over time.[17] In the absence of such multi-country studies in the following briefly we review a number of single country studies.

The average income per capita in Africa is the lowest among the continents. Milanovic and Yitzhaki (2001) find the overall inequality quite high, with the average Gini coefficient

---

[17] For a comprehensive study of poverty comparisons over time and across countries in Africa, see Sahn and Stifel (2000). For empirical analysis various household attributes using demographic and health surveys conducted during 1986-1998 covering 12 countries are used in factor analysis to compute a wealth index based on assets. The index is used to compare intertemporal and intraregional poverty. The results show declines in poverty in the previous decade in rural areas. The improvements are largely due to the increased economic openness and removal of distortions that discriminate against rural areas.

equal to 52.1 per cent in around 1988 and 1993. The between and within country inequality components of the world inequality are 20.3 (39 per cent) and 33.3 (61 per cent) respectively. The numbers in the parentheses are the components' shares of the overall inequality. Unlike the global level and despite the significant heterogeneity at the continent level among the 27 African countries studied by Milanovic and Yitzhaki, the between country component is relatively low.

Turning to the individual country level, the extremely high inequality of South Africa has often been explained by the racial legacy. Leibbrandt and Woolard (2001) present evidence that the between race contribution to inequality has declined from a contribution of 62 per cent in 1975 to 33 per cent in 1996, although the within each race group inequality widened from 38 per cent in 1975 to 67 per cent in 1996. As shown, the empirical results suggest trade off between the between race and the within race inequality components. In the decomposition of inequality by income source (Liebrandt, Woolard and Woolard 2000) using data from the rural former homelands of South Africa reveals that wage income is both the most important income component and also the most important source of inequality. Policy induced changes to wage income will have major impacts on inequality in the rural areas.

Another empirical picture of the changing racial dimensions of income inequality and the changing inequality patterns in South Africa linked to labour market is provided by Whiteford and Seventer (2000). They used the Theil index decomposition method to decompose the overall inequality into (urban and rural) sectors, different sub-groups, and income sources. The racially rigged labour market is the underlying key force changing the inequality patterns across and within racial groups. The link between the labour market access, the market wage variation and the household inequality is investigated. The results suggest the existence of complex patterns of inequality generation. It confirms the dominance of labour market in deriving the total inequality but finds the contribution of the wage income low and uneven.

Despite the important role of the labour market and wages, Whiteford and Seventer find evidence of a less income mobility between 1993 and 1998 at the top and the bottom of the distribution than in the middle for sample of African households in Kwazulu-Natal. They attempt to identify the key determinants of this mobility using a series of profiles and also a multivariate model of the real income changes. The proposed model explains changes in the log household income adjusted for adult equivalent household size by asset and the set of characteristics of the economic environment in which households are operating. Unemployment and demographic changes are other important variables explaining changes in income per adult equivalent. Leibbrandt, Woolard and Woolard (2000) find that wage income is an important source driving the inter-household inequality and the poverty in the rural former homelands of South Africa. For other similar studies decomposing the income inequality by income sources see Lerman and Yitzhaki (1985), Haddad and Kanbur (1997) and Jänttio (1997).

The distribution of earnings in the rural Ghana and Uganda examined by Caragarajah, Newman and Bhattamishra (2001) show major differences by gender and types of income. The non-farm earnings are mainly in the form of self-employment income which contributes to the inequality, but also affects positively the earnings of lower income groups. Wage income reduces inequality. The inequality impact of self-employment is higher among households headed by female. The non-farm sector is an alternative activity to agriculture and determinants of the non-farm income are related to location, education, age, and the regional characteristics like distance to market. The rural economy in both countries is lacking in many basic functional capacities, most notably infrastructure, which limits the degree and returns to the rural diversification.

In sum very few comprehensive multi-country studies of income inequality among the sub-Saharan African countries can be found in the inequality literature. The existing studies show different patterns in the within and between country inequality components compared to those of the global levels. Despite the heterogeneous income levels and development among African countries, the within country inequality is much higher than the between country component. Even though extreme observations, probably due to data problem caused a large dispersion in inequality among the countries and over time. Several country-level studies points to the importance of racial factor, labour market, gender, sectoral and infrastructure to the within country income inequality. In particular the heterogeneous contribution of the different income sources to the overall income inequality is emphasized.

Analysis of the WIID data shows an increasing income inequality among the sub-Saharan countries. The mean inequality is the highest in Kenya (60.69 per cent) and Swaziland (62.30 per cent) and the lowest in Rwanda (28.90 per cent) and Togo (33.80 per cent). However, these inequality numbers represent extreme cases which are based on only 1 or 2 observations. Most African countries are observed only few periods. The mean inequality based on more than 10 observations lie in the interval 43.20-60.69 per cent indicating a relatively high and persistent inequality. The overall mean is 49.26 per cent with the standard deviation of 10.05 per cent together with a range of inequality up to 35.99 per cent (Zambia) indicate a relatively high and persistent level of income inequality in the region. This is confirmed by the high *Q5/Q1* ratio as well. The sample mean *Q5/Q1* ratio is 8.21. It varies in the interval 4.53 (Niger) and 25.89 (Sierra Leone). For more details see Section 6 of Tables 5.3 and 5.4 and Figure 5.6.

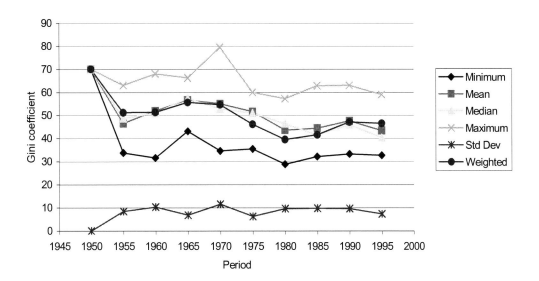

Figure 5.6. Development of Gini coefficient, Sub-Saharan Africa.

Latin America

In analysing poverty and inequality in Latin America and the Caribbean LondoNo and Szekely (2000) divide the period 1970-1995 into three stages. The 70s is characterized by macroeconomic stability and high growth rates, the 80s by volatility and stagnation, while the first half of 90s as a return to more stale environment and positive growth rates. Using data covering 13 countries LondoNo and Szekely shows that poverty and inequality have not declined in the spite of recovery in 1990s. There are differences in levels between countries, but inequality and poverty follow similar trends. The aggregate inequality and poverty reduced in 70s, deteriorated during the 80s but remained high in 90s. The lower tail of the distribution has not benefited from growth indicating lack of a distributive progress. The within country inequality has not been stable. The analysis of inequality at the individual level in the region indicates 25% excess inequality. Inequality is found to be the source of the lack of progress in poverty reduction in the region. Wood (1997) argues that unlike the experience in the East Asia, openness to trade has widened the wage inequality in Latin America. Wood suggests that the conflict of evidence is probably the result of differences between the 1960s and the 1980 (the entry of China into the world market) and the advent of new technology biased against unskilled workers, rather than differences between the two regions. Wood and Ridao-Caso (1999) analysis of data on 90 countries during 1960-1990 indicate that a greater openness tends to cause the divergence of level of education and enrolment rate between countries.

Milanovic and Yitzhaki (2001) find the overall global inequality high, with the average Gini coefficient equal to 0.555 in around 1988 and 1993. The between and the within country inequality components are 0.041 (7 per cent) and 0.514 (93 per cent), respectively. Due to the high level of homogeneity among the Latin American countries at the continental level, the 19 Latin American countries are distinguished by a very high within country inequality. Several countries are identified as potentially unstable countries (Gini coefficient exceeding 0.50).

Since there are not many empirical studies covering multiple of the Latin American countries, we rely to a larger extent on single country studies to review the literature on the income inequality across Latin America and over time. One such study is by Birchenall (2001) who used the Colombian data from 1983 to 1990 to show that the polarisation of income is the variable most strongly and dynamically correlated with income inequality and GDP growth. In another study, changes in the shape of the Brazilian income distribution during 1981 to 1990 using micro data is examined by Cowell, Ferreira and Litchfield (1998). It is shown that the income inequality and the average real incomes increased. They examine the difficulties in modelling the shape of the income distribution due to the highly skewed nature of the distribution of Brazilian income. The results show that inequality in general and amongst the very rich in particular increased during the 1980s. A logarithmic transformation of income gave satisfactory result. The inequality in Brazil is explained by the differences between households of different types, different levels of education, and other spatial differences. Changes in inequality over time can be explained by the high rate of inflation.

Table 5.4 Distribution of Gini coefficient and quintile shares by country, based on WIID

Obs Country	Idnr	Region	Min	Max	Nyear	Range	Gini	WGini	Q1	Q2	Q3	Q4	Q5	Q5/Q1
1. Middle East and North Africa:														
1 Algeria	1	1	1988	1995	2	7	37.01	36.87	0.08	0.11	0.15	0.21	0.44	5.39
2 Egypt	40	1	1959	1995	6	36	33.72	33.08	0.13	0.12	0.16	0.21	0.39	3.00
3 Iraq	65	1	1956	1956	1	0	59.92	.	0.02	0.06	0.08	0.16	0.68	34.00
4 Israel	67	1	1944	1995	17	51	32.70	33.74	0.06	0.12	0.17	0.23	0.42	6.69
5 Jordan	71	1	1980	1997	7	17	35.51	35.92	0.08	0.10	0.14	0.21	0.47	6.02
6 Lebanon	78	1	1960	1960	1	0	55.00	.	0.03	0.04	0.16	0.16	0.61	20.33
7 Sudan	124	1	1963	1969	3	6	40.73	.	0.07	0.09	0.18	0.20	0.47	6.80
8 Tunisia	135	1	1961	1990	8	29	44.92	44.24	0.06	0.09	0.13	0.19	0.53	8.51
9 Turkey	136	1	1952	1994	9	42	49.21	48.39	0.04	0.08	0.13	0.20	0.54	12.39
10 YemenRep	147	1	1992	1992	1	0	39.50	39.50	0.08	0.11	0.15	0.21	0.45	5.49
Mean region	1	1	1944	1997	57	53	39.01	41.31	0.07	0.10	0.15	0.21	0.47	7.09
2. East Asia:														
11 China	25	2	1953	1998	26	45	29.35	28.59	0.08	0.12	0.16	0.25	0.39	5.21
12 HongKong	60	2	1957	1996	12	39	44.65	44.50	0.05	0.10	0.14	0.20	0.51	9.99
13 KoreaRep	74	2	1953	1993	17	40	34.18	34.28	0.07	0.12	0.16	0.22	0.42	5.73
14 Mongolia	92	2	1995	1997	2	2	30.88	.	0.10	0.12	0.16	0.22	0.40	4.02
15 Taiwan	129	2	1953	1996	36	43	33.04	31.92	0.08	0.13	0.17	0.23	0.38	4.59
Mean region	2	2	1953	1998	93	45	33.67	28.81	0.07	0.12	0.16	0.23	0.41	5.55
3. South East Asia and Pacific:														
16 Cambodia	19	3	1997	1997	1	0	40.40	.	0.10	0.10	0.14	0.20	0.46	4.87
17 Fiji	44	3	1968	1977	3	9	43.05	43.00	0.04	0.08	0.13	0.22	0.52	13.08
18 Indonesi	63	3	1964	1996	17	32	36.36	36.09	0.09	0.12	0.16	0.21	0.42	4.79
19 Lao	76	3	1992	1992	1	0	30.40	.	0.13	0.12	0.16	0.20	0.39	2.93
20 Malaysia	86	3	1957	1995	18	38	47.71	47.83	0.05	0.09	0.13	0.21	0.53	11.16
21 Myanmar	94	3	1958	1958	1	0	34.97	.	0.10	0.13	0.13	0.15	0.49	4.85
22 Philippi	106	3	1956	1997	12	41	46.94	46.43	0.05	0.09	0.13	0.20	0.53	10.14
23 PopuaNG	108	3	1996	1996	1	0	50.90	50.90	0.06	0.08	0.12	0.19	0.56	9.12
24 Singapor	118	3	1966	1993	15	27	42.49	42.27	0.06	0.11	0.14	0.23	0.46	7.27
25 Thailand	132	3	1962	1998	16	36	45.03	45.33	0.05	0.09	0.13	0.21	0.52	9.72
26 Vietnam	146	3	1992	1998	2	6	35.90	35.70	0.11	0.11	0.15	0.20	0.43	3.88
Mean region	3	3	1956	1998	87	42	43.17	39.80	0.07	0.10	0.14	0.21	0.49	7.39
4. South Asia:														
27 Banglade	8	4	1959	1996	22	37	37.68	37.36	0.08	0.12	0.16	0.22	0.42	4.95
28 India	62	4	1950	1997	41	47	34.55	34.12	0.09	0.12	0.16	0.21	0.41	4.83
29 Nepal	95	4	1976	1996	4	20	42.50	41.19	0.08	0.11	0.14	0.20	0.47	5.88
30 Pakistan	102	4	1963	1996	19	33	34.26	34.33	0.09	0.14	0.16	0.21	0.40	4.60
31 SriLanka	123	4	1953	1995	12	42	40.40	39.98	0.07	0.11	0.15	0.20	0.47	6.96
Mean region	4	4	1950	1997	106	47	36.94	34.49	0.08	0.12	0.16	0.21	0.42	5.13
5. Latin America:														
32 Argentin	2	5	1953	1998	20	45	41.88	42.28	0.05	0.09	0.14	0.20	0.51	9.40
33 Bahamas	7	5	1970	1993	11	23	46.35	.	0.03	0.09	0.16	0.24	0.47	13.88
34 Barbados	9	5	1951	1981	20	30	36.04	35.98	0.03	0.08	0.14	0.22	0.52	15.39
35 Bolivia	12	5	1968	1993	5	25	50.53	50.61	0.05	0.09	0.13	0.19	0.54	10.69
36 Brazil	15	5	1958	1996	26	38	54.99	55.50	0.03	0.06	0.10	0.18	0.63	21.88
37 Chile	24	5	1964	1996	28	32	50.93	51.26	0.04	0.08	0.12	0.19	0.58	15.49
38 Colombia	26	5	1960	1996	24	36	51.79	51.74	0.04	0.08	0.12	0.18	0.58	14.28
39 CostaRic	28	5	1961	1996	22	35	45.31	.	0.05	0.09	0.13	0.21	0.53	11.52
40 DominRep	38	5	1969	1996	7	27	47.73	47.97	0.05	0.08	0.13	0.21	0.52	9.59
41 Ecuador	39	5	1965	1995	7	30	52.12	50.53	0.07	0.09	0.14	0.21	0.48	7.18
42 ElSalvad	41	5	1961	1996	10	35	48.73	48.69	0.05	0.07	0.12	0.20	0.56	11.27
43 Guatemal	55	5	1948	1990	8	42	48.86	51.53	0.04	0.07	0.12	0.19	0.58	14.35
44 Guyana	58	5	1956	1993	2	37	51.13	49.90	0.06	0.10	0.15	0.22	0.46	7.95
45 Honduras	59	5	1967	1998	10	31	55.57	55.19	0.03	0.07	0.11	0.19	0.60	17.92

Table 5.4 Distribution of Gini coefficient and quintile shares by country, based on WIID (Continued)

Obs Country	Idnr	Region	Min	Max	Nyear	Range	Gini	Wgini	Q1	Q2	Q3	Q4	Q5	Q5/Q1
46 Jamaica	69	5	1958	1996	13	38	47.23	46.29	0.06	0.10	0.15	0.22	0.48	8.03
47 Mexico	90	5	1950	1996	18	46	51.08	50.95	0.04	0.09	0.13	0.20	0.55	13.33
48 Nicaragu	98	5	1993	1993	1	0	50.30	50.30	0.06	0.08	0.12	0.20	0.54	9.52
49 Panama	103	5	1960	1997	13	37	49.22	50.45	0.03	0.07	0.12	0.20	0.57	16.94
50 Paraguay	104	5	1983	1995	4	12	47.96	48.48	0.03	0.06	0.11	0.19	0.62	20.80
51 Peru	105	5	1961	1997	13	36	49.46	48.07	0.06	0.08	0.12	0.20	0.55	9.98
52 PuertoRi	110	5	1953	1989	6	36	45.69	.	0.03	0.08	0.14	0.23	0.53	17.40
53 Suriname	125	5	1962	1962	1	0	30.00	.	0.11	0.12	0.15	0.21	0.42	3.96
54 Trinidad	134	5	1957	1992	7	35	45.71	45.44	0.04	0.09	0.16	0.24	0.48	12.99
55 Uruguay	143	5	1961	1997	16	36	41.39	41.45	0.07	0.10	0.14	0.21	0.47	6.45
56 Venezuel	145	5	1962	1997	24	35	42.90	42.84	0.05	0.09	0.15	0.22	0.50	10.93
Mean region	5	5	1948	1998	320	50	47.39	51.79	0.04	0.08	0.13	0.21	0.54	12.50
6. Sub-saharan Africa:														
57 Botswana	14	6	1971	1986	3	15	53.90	53.54	0.03	0.07	0.12	0.20	0.59	19.33
58 BurkinaF	17	6	1994	1995	2	1	43.60	43.55	0.08	0.09	0.12	0.18	0.54	7.15
59 Burundi	18	6	1992	1992	1	0	33.30	33.30	0.11	0.12	0.16	0.21	0.40	3.69
60 CenAfRep	22	6	1992	1993	2	1	58.15	58.19	0.03	0.05	0.10	0.18	0.65	24.08
61 Chad	23	6	1958	1958	1	0	34.36	.	0.08	0.12	0.15	0.22	0.43	5.38
62 CotedIvo	29	6	1959	1995	8	36	43.50	42.33	0.07	0.10	0.14	0.20	0.47	6.42
63 Dahomey	35	6	1959	1959	1	0	41.96	.	0.08	0.10	0.12	0.20	0.50	6.25
64 Ethiopia	43	6	1981	1996	3	15	38.87	39.68	0.10	0.11	0.14	0.19	0.46	4.73
65 Gabon	47	6	1960	1977	4	17	57.29	56.80	0.03	0.05	0.09	0.16	0.67	23.08
66 Gambia	48	6	1992	1992	1	0	43.40	43.40	0.06	0.09	0.13	0.20	0.52	8.95
67 Ghana	53	6	1988	1997	5	9	34.27	34.18	0.09	0.12	0.16	0.22	0.42	4.62
68 Guinea	56	6	1991	1995	3	4	43.58	43.47	0.06	0.09	0.14	0.22	0.48	7.58
69 GuineaBi	57	6	1991	1991	1	0	56.16	56.16	0.02	0.06	0.12	0.21	0.59	25.28
70 Kenya	73	6	1914	1994	19	80	60.69	59.92	0.05	0.08	0.12	0.19	0.55	10.42
71 Lesotho	79	6	1987	1987	1	0	59.01	59.01	0.03	0.06	0.11	0.19	0.60	18.29
72 Madagasc	84	6	1960	1993	4	33	46.08	45.93	0.05	0.09	0.12	0.19	0.54	10.11
73 Mali	87	6	1994	1994	1	0	52.25	52.25	0.06	0.08	0.12	0.19	0.55	8.79
74 Mauritan	88	6	1988	1995	2	7	40.41	40.21	0.06	0.11	0.16	0.22	0.45	7.45
75 Mauritiu	89	6	1980	1991	3	11	40.67	40.52	0.07	0.11	0.17	0.23	0.43	6.56
76 Morocco	93	6	1955	1999	12	44	45.81	.	0.08	0.10	0.14	0.19	0.48	6.02
77 Niger	99	6	1960	1995	3	35	39.40	41.88	0.09	0.11	0.15	0.21	0.43	4.53
78 Nigeria	100	6	1959	1997	13	38	43.20	42.73	0.06	0.09	0.13	0.20	0.51	8.43
79 Rwanda	114	6	1983	1984	2	1	28.90	28.90	0.12	0.13	0.16	0.21	0.38	3.33
80 Senegal	115	6	1959	1995	6	36	49.96	48.47	0.05	0.08	0.12	0.18	0.56	10.87
81 SierraLe	117	6	1967	1989	5	22	57.73	.	0.02	0.03	0.10	0.21	0.63	25.89
82 SouthAfr	121	6	1959	1995	12	36	54.89	55.53	0.03	0.05	0.10	0.21	0.62	23.65
83 Swazilan	126	6	1974	1994	2	20	62.30	.	0.04	0.06	0.10	0.17	0.64	17.41
84 Tanzania	131	6	1964	1993	8	29	49.12	48.96	0.05	0.08	0.12	0.19	0.57	11.50
85 Uganda	141	6	1970	1993	4	23	37.19	37.59	0.08	0.11	0.15	0.21	0.45	5.57
86 Zambia	150	6	1959	1996	9	37	54.57	53.02	0.05	0.09	0.13	0.20	0.53	10.04
87 Zimbabwe	151	6	1945	1990	4	45	57.85	60.59	0.05	0.06	0.10	0.17	0.62	12.77
Mean region	6	6	1914	1999	157	85	49.26	46.53	0.06	0.09	0.13	0.20	0.52	8.21
7. East Europe:														
88 Bulgaria	16	7	1957	1997	36	40	23.88	31.08	0.10	0.14	0.19	0.23	0.33	3.20
89 Croatia	30	7	1987	1998	6	11	25.68	25.84	0.10	0.13	0.17	0.22	0.39	4.04
90 CzechRep	33	7	1958	1997	12	39	23.22	24.36	0.12	0.14	0.17	0.21	0.37	3.17
91 Hungary	61	7	1955	1998	28	43	24.61	25.00	0.10	0.14	0.18	0.23	0.35	3.39
92 Poland	107	7	1956	1998	29	42	26.60	26.66	0.09	0.14	0.18	0.23	0.36	3.88
93 Romania	112	7	1988	1997	10	9	26.38	26.34	0.10	0.14	0.18	0.23	0.35	3.33

Table 5.4 Distribution of Gini coefficient and quintile shares by country, based on WIID (Continued)

Obs Country	Idnr	Region	Min	Max	Nyear	Range	Gini	WGini	Q1	Q2	Q3	Q4	Q5	Q5/Q1
94 RussianF	113	7	1981	1998	13	17	34.14	39.35	0.09	0.12	0.16	0.22	0.41	4.56
95 SlovakRe	119	7	1958	1997	11	39	21.99	21.14	0.11	0.15	0.18	0.22	0.33	2.94
96 Slovenia	120	7	1987	1997	11	10	25.66	26.98	0.11	0.14	0.17	0.22	0.36	3.32
97 Ukraine	142	7	1968	1997	17	29	28.43	30.01	0.09	0.13	0.16	0.22	0.39	4.17
Mean region	7	7	1955	1998	191	43	26.14	31.57	0.10	0.14	0.18	0.22	0.35	3.54
8. Former Soviet Republics:														
98 Armenia	3	8	1986	1997	11	11	33.77	37.96	0.03	0.09	0.15	0.23	0.50	19.24
99 Belarus	10	8	1981	1998	12	17	26.50	27.79	0.14	0.14	0.17	0.21	0.33	2.44
100 Estonia	42	8	1981	1998	12	17	32.15	36.70	0.07	0.11	0.16	0.22	0.45	6.34
101 Georgia	49	8	1981	1997	11	16	39.93	53.70	0.02	0.07	0.12	0.20	0.59	26.95
102 Kazakhst	72	8	1981	1996	8	15	30.14	34.19	0.10	0.12	0.16	0.22	0.40	4.14
103 KyrgyzRe	75	8	1981	1997	11	16	34.39	41.61	0.09	0.11	0.15	0.22	0.44	4.88
104 Latvia	77	8	1981	1998	13	17	28.86	30.49	0.10	0.13	0.17	0.22	0.38	3.78
105 Lithuani	81	8	1981	1997	11	16	30.82	35.79	0.10	0.12	0.16	0.21	0.41	4.28
106 Moldova	91	8	1981	1995	9	14	30.86	38.08	0.09	0.12	0.16	0.22	0.40	4.33
107 Turkmeni	137	8	1981	1998	7	17	31.30	.	0.08	0.11	0.15	0.22	0.45	5.62
108 Uzbekist	144	8	1981	1994	7	13	29.48	33.00	0.10	0.12	0.16	0.22	0.40	3.90
Mean region	8	8	1972	1998	125	26	31.56	33.99	0.09	0.12	0.16	0.22	0.42	4.78
9. Industrialized countries:														
109 Australi	4	9	1962	1998	18	36	37.68	38.08	0.05	0.11	0.17	0.24	0.43	8.07
110 Austria	5	9	1970	1991	21	21	25.91	25.90	0.07	0.14	0.18	0.23	0.37	5.02
111 Belgium	11	9	1969	1994	11	25	33.50	33.46	0.09	0.14	0.19	0.23	0.35	3.91
112 Canada	21	9	1951	1994	26	43	30.83	30.63	0.07	0.13	0.18	0.24	0.38	5.48
113 Denmark	36	9	1939	1995	29	56	34.04	32.92	0.06	0.12	0.18	0.25	0.40	6.72
114 Finland	45	9	1952	1998	27	46	29.33	29.16	0.09	0.13	0.18	0.23	0.37	4.30
115 France	46	9	1956	1995	11	39	38.14	37.58	0.07	0.12	0.16	0.23	0.43	6.25
116 Germany	50	9	1950	1997	28	47	31.67	.	0.09	0.13	0.17	0.22	0.39	4.44
117 Greece	54	9	1957	1993	19	36	41.56	41.39	0.08	0.12	0.15	0.23	0.42	5.54
118 Ireland	66	9	1973	1987	3	14	36.80	36.77	0.05	0.11	0.17	0.24	0.43	8.26
119 Italy	68	9	1948	1995	25	47	35.68	35.45	0.08	0.13	0.17	0.23	0.39	4.87
120 Japan	70	9	1890	1993	33	103	35.53	33.98	0.07	0.12	0.17	0.23	0.42	6.39
121 Luxembo	82	9	1985	1994	3	9	25.89	25.86	0.12	0.13	0.17	0.22	0.35	2.98
122 Netherla	96	9	1950	1997	24	47	32.10	31.72	0.08	0.13	0.18	0.23	0.38	4.77
123 NewZeala	97	9	1954	1997	31	43	45.61	44.20	0.06	0.12	0.17	0.25	0.40	7.03
124 Norway	101	9	1957	1996	23	39	30.74	30.56	0.06	0.12	0.18	0.24	0.40	6.80
125 Portugal	109	9	1973	1995	5	22	36.26	36.15	0.07	0.12	0.16	0.23	0.42	5.94
126 Spain	122	9	1965	1996	15	31	30.93	30.79	0.08	0.14	0.18	0.23	0.37	4.46
127 Sweden	127	9	1948	1996	45	48	38.14	37.47	0.07	0.14	0.18	0.24	0.37	5.12
128 Switzerl	128	9	1978	1992	4	14	33.20	33.21	0.08	0.12	0.17	0.22	0.41	4.96
129 UK	138	9	1867	1996	41	129	30.87	30.19	0.09	0.13	0.17	0.23	0.38	4.17
130 US	139	9	1944	1997	53	53	38.65	38.85	0.05	0.11	0.17	0.24	0.43	9.17
Mean region	9	9	1867	1998	495	131	34.79	36.08	0.07	0.12	0.17	0.24	0.40	5.72
Mean all regions			1867	1999	1392	132	38.06	38.26	0.07	0.11	0.16	0.22	0.44	6.88

Note: USSR, Yugoslavia and Czechoslovakia are excluded and East and West Germany are averaged.

Obs   Observation number
Country   Country
Idnr   Country ID number
Region   Regional location
Min   First year of observation
Max   Last year of observation
Nyear   Number of years observed
Range   The difference between the last and first years of observation
Gini   Mean Gini value
WGini   Population weighted mean Gini value
Q1-Q5   Income share of the first-fifth quintiles of population
Q5/Q1   the ration of the fifth quintile share to the first quintile income share

In similarity with the sub-Saharan African countries, the Latin American countries also are distinguished by a higher within country inequality than the between country inequality. The polarisation of income and the high rate of inflation explain the high level and the undesirable development of inequality over time in the region. Nine out the 26 Latin American countries included in the WIID database have an average inequality rate higher than 50 per cent (see Section 5 of Table 5.3). The mean income inequality in the region is 47.39 and a small standard deviation of 7.47. The range is quite high, 40.83. Honduras is the most unequal (55.57), while Cuba is the most equal (35.06) country in the region. The inequality has increased fastest in Paraguay and the $Q1/Q1$ ratio is after Brazil (21.88) the second highest (20.80) ratio. For more details see also Section 5 of Table 5.4. The dispersion in inequality is declining over time indicating a process of convergence in inequality. However the convergence is towards a higher level of inequality (see Figure 5.7).

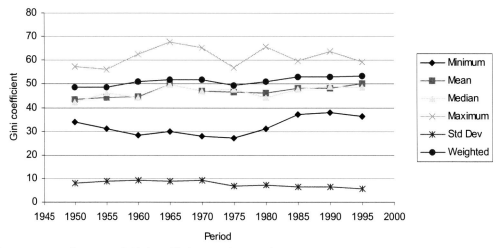

Figure 5.7. Development of Gini coefficient, Latin America.

East Asia, South Asia, South-East Asia and Pacific

As in the case of the African and the Latin American countries, it has not been possible to trace studies based on household data comparing income inequality among multiple of the East and the South-East Asian countries. In the following we briefly review available mainly single country studies.

Warr (2001) has studied the incidence of poverty and inequality in Thailand using household and population data for the period of 1988-1999. The poverty and inequality results in a regional perspective indicate that inequality is increased post 1997. There was a 21.4 per cent decline in the percentage of poor, from 32.6 per cent to 11.2 per cent, prior to the economic crisis of 1997, but the poverty rate again increased during the post crisis period to 15.9 per cent in 1999. Inequality is measured by the Gini coefficient and the ratio of the highest to the lowest quintile income shares using both household and individual as the unit of observation. In the later case Warr accounts for the gender and ages of household members to reflect their needs. In comparison with the need-based measure, the unweighted household measure underestimates the inequality, but the two measures move closely together over time.

Despite the major reduction in poverty rate, Thailand has failed to reduce the widening gaps between individuals, areas and regions predominately the Northern region. Droughts in the dry season, the floods in the wet season, lack of support from the central government, large sized household, employment patterns, low educational attainment, limited access to credit, and inadequate rural-urban linkage are among the underlying causes of poverty (Hossain 2001). Hossain focuses on the income poverty and inequality in the Northern region and suggests some employment, income and equality policy measures to mitigate regional as well as rural-urban disparities in Thailand. Cameron (2000b) also finds changes in the income distribution in Java being related to the ageing of population, educational attainment and agricultural/industrial structure. Unexpectedly, there is little evidence that economic crisis has had a large, systematic and negative impact on the well-being of children in Indonesia (Cameron 2000a).

Several East Asian economies tried to couple economic growth with reductions in poverty and income disparity. The economic crisis of 1997 has deteriorated these prospects. Analysis of the relationship between growth, inequality and poverty in nine countries in the East Asia and the Pacific region[18] is summarised by Kakwani and Krongkaew (2000). The individual study results are published in a special issue of the Journal of the Asia Pacific Economy 2000, Volume 5(1/2). In the Australian case the focus on the taxes and transfers and on the growth rates of the various income components rather then on the growth rate of the total income as of the other countries. The distribution of income has remained relatively equal in Japan despite the changes in the welfare post the World War II. The regional income distribution in Korea has been very egalitarian and affected by the domination of the political and the military leaders. The increasing development of the income disparity in Taiwan is related to the industrial transformation and changes in the factor intensity of production.

It is widely believed that the East Asian economies performed exceptionally well both in generating growth and in keeping income inequality low. You (1998) investigated the income distribution in East Asia and found that only Japan, Korea and Taiwan enjoy low inequality. However, in general the East Asian countries have been successful in translating high profit shares into high savings and investment rates. The high profits and the low inequality have resulted in an even distribution of wealth. Bourguignon, Fournier and Gurgand (2001) applied a decomposition method to isolate the impact of the changes in earnings structure, labour-force participation behaviour, and the socio-demographic structure of the population on stability of the income distribution in Taiwan during 1979-1994. Wage structure, changes in female labour force participation, educational structure and changes in composition of household have in different ways served both as deriving and off-setting forces to the inequality changes.

Based on the WIID database, the mean income inequality in the East Asian region is quite low, 33.67 (see Figure 5.8). It is the highest in Hongkong (44.65) but the lowest in China (29.35). Inequality has declined in Mongolia, but it increased in China over time. The mean income inequality in the South Asian region is higher than East Asia, 36.94. Inequality

---

[18] The countries include advanced industrialised countries (Australia and Japan), newly industrialised countries (Korea and Taiwan), low- to middle-income developing countries (China, Indonesia, Malaysia, The Philippines and Thailand).

is the highest in Iran (45.59) but the lowest in Pakistan (34.26). Changes in the inequality over time have been the highest in Nepal.

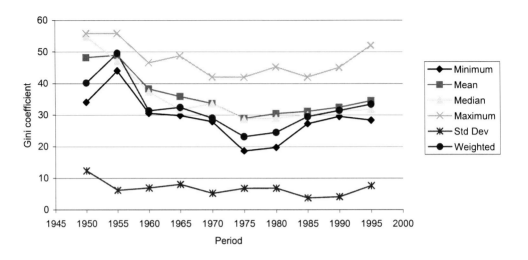

Figure 5.8. Development of Gini coefficient, East Asia.

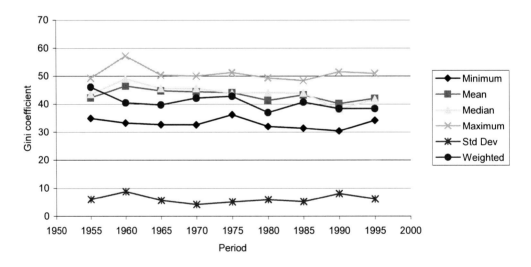

Figure 5.9. Development of Gini coefficient, South East Asia and Pacific.

The mean income inequality in South East Asia and Pacific (Figure 5.9) is much higher that the East and the South Asian regions, 43.17, but not when the dispersion in inequality is concerned (see Figure 5.10). Inequality is the highest in Malaysia (47.71) and Philippines (46.94). The ranking here is based on more than one survey observation and less influenced by outliers or measurement errors. The increase in inequality has been the highest in Indonesia. The ratio of the highest to the lowest quintiles with the exception of Hongkong (9.99) is below 7 in the East and the South Asian countries. However, it exceeds 10 in several of the South East Asian and the Pacific countries including Fiji, Malaysia and Philippines. For more details on the level and variations in inequality across the three regions see Sections

2 to 4 of Table 5.3 and 5.4. Inequality in East Asia declined prior to 1975 but it increased post 1980, while it declined over time in South Asia and South East Asia and Pacific. There is a positive association between the level and the variation in inequality. In general dispersion in inequality is declining over time indicating a convergence in inequality but to a higher level.

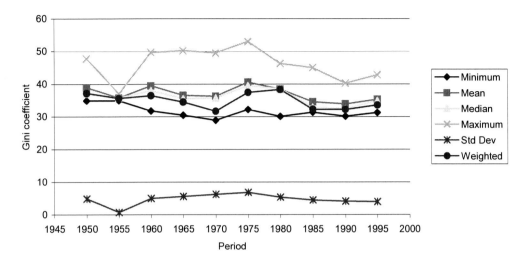

Figure 5.10. Development of Gini coefficient, South Asia.

SUMMARY

Intra-regional inequality refers to disparity in the income distribution within a region consisting of a number of countries possibly members of an economic union. The poverty and inequality has increased in the transition economies of Central and Eastern Europe and the former Soviet Union. The increasing rate is inhomogeneous and might be even higher in countries involved in military conflicts. This is in conflict with the expected positive relationship between democracy and inequality. Several market related determinants of inequality are identified some of which are country specific. The role of transitory events and measurement error in the rising inequality should not be neglected. The inequality in the Scandinavian countries is low and has been relatively stable over time. The Western European countries differ by type of social policy and in their effectiveness in reducing poverty and inequality. The high quality data indicates opposite development for gross and disposable incomes.

The between demographic groups within each member country's inequality is significant. The range of income inequality is wide within the OECD. Its development has been affected greatly by the changes in households, demographic shifts and the labour market situation. Individual studies show that inequality is high among the African countries. The rate varies among countries by various sub-groups, regional location, income sources and over time. The inequality among the Latin American countries also is large and increasing over time. The level and patterns has been affected by labour market, trade and inflation factors. The East Asian countries have been successful in coupling growth and equality. However, the 1997 economic crisis deteriorated these prospects. The conflicting results from the two regions are explained by the entry of China into the world market and the advent of new technology biased against unskilled workers.

Chapter 6

REGIONAL INCOME INEQUALITY
IN SELECTED LARGE COUNTRIES

ABSTRACT

Income inequality can be measured at different levels of aggregation such as global, continental, international and national levels. Here we consider income inequality at the national level but the focus is on the within country regional inequality. Regional inequality in income distribution in a selection of large countries measured by the size of their population and land area with regional, provincial or federation division is examined. The empirical results reported are based on the second half of the 20th century. The countries considered here cover large transition, developing and industrialised countries. The review cover a whole range of measures and methods frequently employed in empirical analysis of income inequality and income distribution. Different determinant factors and their impacts from different studies are presented. Empirical results from the literature is compared with those obtained based on the WIID data covering the period post 1950.

Keywords: Income inequality, income distribution, regions, provinces, federations.

INTRODUCTION

The increased interest in the level, causes and development of global income inequality has been considerable in the 1990s. This has resulted in an extensive literature emerging in recent years that has focused on measurement, decomposition and on the study of how the distribution of incomes across countries has globally developed over time. In several cases the empirical results suggest the tendency for income per capita to converge, and also an increase in inequality in the distribution of personal income in many countries. The increased interest in income inequality is due to cause and effect of the availability of income distribution data and increased awareness about income inequality, poverty and their linkage to non-income inequalities. Availability of household surveys covering many developing countries has been improved and a number of standardised databases have been created. This allows the analysis of income distribution at the most disaggregate individual or per capita household levels, as well as at an intermediate aggregation level such as at sub-groups or regional levels.

Income distribution is often analysed at three levels of aggregation, namely global, international and intra-national (see Chapter 4). Global or world income inequality refers to inequality differences between all individuals in the world (Milanovic 2002a; Schultz 1998; Quah 1999; Bourguignon and Morrisson 2002; Sala-i-Martin 2002b), while international income inequality refers to the economic disparity between countries (Acemoglu 2002; Cornia and Kiiski 2001; Gottschalk and Smeeding 1997; Milanovic 2001). At the intra-national level inequality refers to the distribution of income among people within individual countries (Cameron 2000b; Cowell, Ferreira and Lichtfield 1998; Gustafsson and Shi 2002; Liebbrandt, Woolard and Woolard 2000). Income inequality, in addition to the extreme level of global and international, it can be measured at continental and sub-continental level consisting of geographic or economic regions (see Chapter 5). There are evidences that poverty and inequality have developed differently among transition economies (Milanovic and Ytzhaki 2001; Ivaschenko 2002; Ram 1995; Wan 2002b), East Asian countries (Kakwani and Krogkaew 2000; You 1998) the European Union (Ritakallio 2001; Belbo and Knaus 2001; Gottschalk and Smeeding 2000; Iacoviello 1998; Lindert and Williamson 2001; Mahler 2001), Latin American (LondoNo and Szekely 2000; Wood 1997) and sub-Saharan African (Milanovic and Yitzhaki 2001; Canagarajah, Newman and Bhattamishra 2001; Svedborg 2002) countries.

A discussion of the benefit and limitations of each approach in the measurement of world income inequality is important for a number of reasons, including the increased awareness of the problem, its measurement and quantification, identification of causal factors and for policy measures to affect inequality. Many of these studies show that inequality and poverty are related to a number of determinant factors. Depending on the availability of data, the empirical results are mainly based on the second half of the twentieth century. Here our aim is to cover a range of measures and methods which are frequently employed in empirical analysis of global and regional income inequality and income distribution. Different determinant factors, quantification of their impacts and empirical results from different case studies are discussed. These results are further contrasted to those obtained for the World Income Inequality Database (WIID) which embodies almost the same period as well as the same group of countries.

In addition to the levels listed above the income inequality can be measured at a within-country regional level. Here the focus is on inequality in income distribution in a selection of large countries measured in terms of the population size and land area, where regions include states, provinces, federations or distinct geographic locations within a country. Such studies focus on large countries like China (Tsui 1993; Xu and Zou 2000; Lee 2000; Gustafsson and Shi 2002), Russia (Commander, Tolstopiatenko and Yemtsov 1999; Yemtsov 2002; Luttmer 2001; Shorrocks and Kolenikov 2001; Fedorov 2002), India (Mishra and Parikh 1997; Jha 2000; Datt and Ravallion 1992) and the USA (Patridge, Rickman and Levernier 1996; Black and Dowd 1997; Zandvakili 1999; Moffitt and Gottschalk 2002), as well as a number of smaller developing and transition countries with major impacts on global inequality and poverty.

China and India experienced rapid economic growth after economic reform, accompanied by increased inequality and the reduction in poverty. The level and development of inequality has varied by location and sector. This inequality can further be decomposed into various components associated with inter- and intra-sector and provincial components and their determinants in turn identified (see also Chapter 4). Analysis of within-country regional inequality can reveal the effects of openness, marketisation, convergence due to factor mobility, and may also indicate regional polarisation, or disintegration and widening inequality driven by structural differences between regions. Furthermore it is important to consider heterogeneity in income inequality in both level and development over time, as well as different characteristics of sub-group dimensions. Empirical evidence suggests that inequality and poverty alter following structural adjustment programmes affecting the welfare of sub-groups of a population differently.

In this chapter we review income inequality within country but at the regional level. Regional inequality in income distribution in a selection of large countries with regional division is examined. In some cases region is equivalent of states like in India and USA, provinces in China, or members of a Federation in Russia. In certain cases it can also be defined as more aggregated geographical coastal, central and western regions in China or geographic regions in Russia. The empirical results reported here are based on the second half of the 20th century. The countries considered here covers transition (China and Russia), developing (India) and industrialised (USA) countries. Empirical results from the literature is further complemented and compared with those obtained from the WIID data covering post 1950s.

Rest of the chapter is organised as follows. The next section presents inequality in China. Here we discuss the issues of provincial, regional and sectoral income inequality and its decomposition, policy measure to reduce inequality as well as convergence and polarisation. In section 3 we investigate inequality in Russia. We discuss inequality and transition, inequality and regional polarisation, wage inequality, and inequality decomposition. Regional inequality in India is discussed in Section 3. The focus is on state and sectoral inequality and polarisation. Great emphasis is put on the inequality-poverty-growth relationship. Section 4 is on regional inequality in USA. The focus is on South, Non-South, and interstate income inequality and factors affecting inequality. Inequality in a selection of smaller countries is discussed in Section 5. The WIID data is described in Section 6. Results based on WIID are presented in Section 7. The final Section summarises.

REGIONAL GROWTH, INEQUALITY AND POLARIZATION IN CHINA

Empirical studies on inequality and poverty in China is often based on two household surveys conducted by the Institute of Economics, Chinese Academy of Social Sciences, with the assistance of the State Statistical Bureau (SSB) in Beijing. The first survey of household income for 1988 was implemented in 1989 and the second for 1995 in 1996. Sample households are visited every month by an enumerator for 5 years. The sample size in the first survey was about 20,000 households and about 15,000 in the second. The rural sample cover 109 counties located in 19 provinces and the urban sample cover cities located in 11 provinces. The provinces are chosen such as to reflect the geographical differences in China. The data allow studies of inequality and poverty by sub-groups, income sources, various household characteristics, sectors and locations. For a short description of the data see Gustafsson and Zhong (2000) and Gustafsson and Shi (2001a).

Provincial Inequality and Growth

China has experienced rapid economic growth with major impact on inequality during the recent decade. Xu and Zou (2000) using a new panel data set about Chinese provincial urban level income inequality show that the Gini coefficient increased from 0.17 in 1985 to 0.23 in 1995. The period average varies in the interval 0.17 and 0.25 by provinces and 0.13 and 0.34 by years of observation. The data is obtained from urban household surveys in each of the 29 provinces and various provincial statistical yearbooks covering the period of 1985-1995 (except 1987 and 1988). Based on average incomes for each 5 percentiles, Xu and Zou compute the Gini coefficients, percentage of income of bottom, top and the third and fourth quintiles and the ratio of top to bottom quintiles for each province.

Since the beginning of the economic reforms initiated in 1978, Xu and Zou find that aggregate output growth has been on the average 9.9 per cent per year while the average growth in GDP per capita was 8.8 per cent during the period of 1978-1994. The difference must be explained by changes in the population. The growth rates differ by the location between 4.8 per cent for inland and 14.2 per cent for coastal provinces. The correlation between the growth rate and Gini coefficient is 0.27 and seem to support the Kuznet's (1955) inverted U-curve. This contradict the Alesina and Rodrik (1994) and Person and Tabellini (1994) findings based on cross-section of international data who observed a negative association between income growth and inequality. In analysing the causal mechanism relating inequality and growth in India and China, Quah (2002) pointed out that there is no single evidence about such relation. Many other factors like macroeconomic, technological, political or institutional beyond inequality influence economic growth. Ravallion (1998) suggests that the aggregation can bias tests of whether inequality impedes growth. Ravallion empirically evaluated the effects of asset inequality on consumption growth for rural household in China. The effect is lost in regional growth models.

Determinants of Provincial Inequality

In above we reviewed research identifying factors beyond inequality that influence economic growth. Xu and Zou (2000) looks at the reverse link, i.e. the role played by output growth, increasing exposure to international trade, urbanisation, taxation, government spending, inflation, human capital formation, geography, and the sectoral structure of the economy in determining the changes in income inequality. The relation is specified as:

$$
\begin{aligned}
INEQ_{it} = {} & \beta_0 + \beta_{SOE} SOE_{it} + \beta_{INF} INF_{it} + \beta_{DIS} DIS_{it} + \beta_{SCH} SCH_{it} + \beta_{GDP} GDP_{it} \\
& + \beta_{TRA} TRA_{it} + \beta_{EXP} EXP_{it} + \beta_{URB} URB_{it} + \phi_i + \varepsilon_{it}
\end{aligned}
$$
(6.1)

where $INEQ_{it}$ is Gini coefficient or it can alternatively be measured as the (ratios of) quintile income shares Q5/Q1, Q5, Q1, or Q34. The ϕ_i captures unobserved province-specific effects. The explanatory variables are: the share of state-owned enterprises (SOE), the inflation rate (INF), distance of a province's capital to the nearest port by railroad (DIS), the share of residents with more than secondary schooling (SCH), GDP growth rate (GDP), trade measured as the ratio of value of import and export to GDP (*TRA*), the share of government expenditure as a share of GDP (*EXP*), and the change of urbanisation level of a province measured as the growth rate of the share of non-agricultural population in the province (*URB*). The results show that income distribution has been affected by the changing structure of the economy, the role of the state, and increasing urbanisation. Inequality and Q5 increased (and Q1 decreased) with reduction of SOE share of output, higher inflation, higher growth rate, and foreign trade. Government spending tends to shift resources from the rich and the poor to the middle class. Provinces farther from coast had larger inequality probably reflecting greater imperfection of capital market. Schooling and increasing urbanisation did not affect income inequality. It has not been possible to identify determinants of (unobserved) level differences in inequality across different provinces.

Regional and Sectoral Inequality Decomposition

Since the impacts of economic reform are regionally dissimilar in China not only inter-provincial but also intra-provincial, intra-rural, intra-urban, and rural-urban inequality are crucial in analysing China's regional inequality. Tsui (1993) decompose China's regional inequality into the five components mentioned above using per capita gross value of industrial and agricultural outputs for 1982. The decomposition is based a simple principle where the overall inequality (*I*) of each attribute is the sum of within-group (*WG*) and between-group (*BG*) inequalities expressed as:

(6.2) $I(X_i) = WG_i + BG_i$

where the terms within-group and between-groups are then equivalent to intra-provincial and inter-provincial inequalities. The results show that both intra-provincial and inter-provincial inequalities are the important sources of China's regional inequality. Disparity among the coastal, central and western regions is insignificant but the variance within the coast is substantial. Inter-rural and inter-urban inequality accounts for a large share of intra-provincial and overall inequality but neither of intra-rural and intra-urban are crucial factors to the development of inequality. Eastwood and Lipton (2000) discuss the changes in the focus of reforms in China post 1983. The focus shifted from rural agricultural liberalisation to the urban sector industrial liberalisation with wages more tied to labour productivity. During 1983-1995 substantial rises in total, intra- and inter-sectoral inequalities have been observed. However, inequality was rising faster in the urban sector. Unlike expectations adjustments and liberalisations have not resulted in narrowing the urban-rural gap. Gustafsson et al. (2001) find strong relationship between age and wage indicating that seniority plays a strong role in determining earnings in urban China.

Lee (2000) reinvestigates the Tsui's (1993) findings using recent and more disaggregate data from China's 2165 cities and counties in 1994 but applying the same decomposition method. Per capita consumption[1] and gross value of industrial and agricultural outputs are

---

[1] Tsui (1993) used per capita gross value of industrial and agricultural outputs as measures of income.

used as a measure of income. For the decomposition of inequality index, the Theil's entropy measure is defined as:

$$(6.3) \qquad I(y) = \sum_{i=1}^{n} f_i \log\left(\frac{\mu}{y_i}\right) = \sum_{g=1}^{G} w_g I(y_g) + i(\mu_1 e_1, \mu_2 e_2, ..., \mu_G e_G)$$

where y is per capita consumption, μ_g is the population weighted mean of observation for subgroup g, G is the number of subgroups, $f_i = P_i / P$ is the ith county's population share, $w_g = (n_g / n)$ is population weight, and e_g is an n_g vector of ones capturing unobserved subgroup effects. The weighted sum, $I(y_1), I(y_2), I(y_3)$, are the inequality within coastal, central and western regions, $w_1 I(y_1), w_2 I(y_2), w_3 I(y_3)$ is intra-regional inequality, while $I(\mu_1 e_1, \mu_2 e_2, \mu_3 e_3)$ is the inter-regional inequality and $(w_1 I(y_1) / I(y)) \times 100$ or $(\mu_1 e_1) / I(y)) \times 100$ are the percentage contribution of coastal region intra-regional and inter-regional inequality to the overall inequality.

The results in Lee show that: rural-urban disparity has been reduced in turn reducing the intra-provincial inequality. The dominant sources of overall inequality in output have shifted from the intra-provincial to inter-provincial inequality, from rural-urban to intra-rural inequality, from disparity within the coastal region to the gap between coastal and interior regions. Disparity among coastal, central and western regions has increased while the gap between rural and urban within each region has narrowed. Disparity among the three regions is a dominant source of regional inequality. Output and consumption measures produce different inequality levels and rankings, 0.39 and 0.33. The share of intra (inter)provincial inequality of the overall inequality is 48.5 (51.5 per cent) for output and 63.2 (36.8 per cent) for consumption measures. In the case of consumption, the intra-provincial inequality, rural-urban inequality, and disparity within the coastal region are crucial factors of the overall regional inequality. The role of intra-urban income inequality is currently significant. The coastal and rural-industry-led growth aggravates the intra-rural output inequality. Kanbur and Zhang (1999) also conclude that the contribution of rural-urban disparities to regional inequality far exceeds the contribution of increasing inland-coastal disparities. Difference in the ease of migration provides a partial explanation for the phenomenon.

Gustafsson and Shi (2002) investigates how income inequality varies within and across counties in rural China. Household data covering 18 provinces in 1988 and 1995 is used. Results show that income inequality in rural China has increased rapidly. Differences in mean income between counties within provinces, between provinces as well as diverging means by regions are major contributors to rural inequality. Part of the income inequality within Chinas provinces is spatial. However, Ravallion and Chen (1999) argued that the structural changes in the rural economy are not reflected in the methods used for processing the raw data. Two third of the increase in inequality vanishes when market-based valuation methods are used and allowances are made for regional cost-of-living differences. Using the same data as in Gustafsson and Shi (2002) Gustafsson and Zhong (2000) found that despite impressive economic growth poverty has decreased only slightly due to the changed demographic composition of the population. Based on a common poverty line the poverty is characterised to be a rural and also a geographical problem. The effectiveness of regional targeting in China's poverty alleviation program for the period 1981-1995 is evaluated by Park, Wang and Wu (2002). They find modest positive effects on rural income growth. Perfect targeting may not be optimal due to tradeoffs between targeting and other social objectives.

Income source is the important component in inequality. In a regression-based approach Morduch and Sicular (2002) examined inequality decomposition by income sources. The method is illustrated based on a small farm level data from rural China and compared to Theil-T, CV and Gini decomposition methods. The role of regional segmentation, education, age and political variables is emphasised. The results are found to be sensitive to the choice of decomposition method. Wan (2001) also decomposed changes in regional income inequality in rural China into structural, real inequality and interactive effects by decomposing Gini index by income (wage, farming and residual) sources. Structural effects found to be the driving force underlying increased regional inequality in rural China. The pitfalls in regression-based inequality decomposition are discussed by Wan (2002a). A simple procedure is suggested to rectify these pitfalls. Based on results from data on 30 Chinese regions during 1992-1995 Wan argues that the root of problems relating to constant and residuals are not caused by inequality, rather than lie in the construction of proposed decomposition methodologies.

Convergence in Per Capita Income

China's experience with trade liberalisation after 1978 and with rapid growth in the coastal provinces, give indication of widening inequality among China's diverse regions. Jian, Sachs and Warner (1996) examine the tendency towards convergence in real per-capita income among the provinces of China during the period 1952-1993. No strong convergence or divergence during the initial phase of central planning (1952-1965) was observed. There is a strong evidence of divergence during the cultural revolution (1965-1978) with social planning in favour of richer industrial regions widened the inter-regional inequality. Regional inequality equalised with the extent of marketization and openness that begun in 1978. Convergence is due to factor mobility, flow of labour, capital and technology, increased productivity among the rural regions and convergence within the coastal provinces. A policy to further liberalisation of interior will also promote convergence. Variance decomposition of the log of real GDP (x_i) in each province i is obtained by using the formula:

$$(6.4) \qquad Var(x) = a_1 Var(x_{1i}) + a_2 Var(x_{2i}) + a_{12} (\bar{x}_1 - \bar{x}_2)^2$$

where 1 and 2 refers to the coastal and interior regions, a_1 and a_2 are weights that depend on the number of provinces in each of the two regions, and $\bar{x}_1$ and $\bar{x}_2$ denote means of log of real GDP by region. Zhang, Liu and Yao (2001) investigate the time-series properties of per capita income in China's regions during 1952 to 1997 and compare the consistency of results with cross-sectional methods. The innovation outlier model of the log of relative per capita income (RI) of Perron (1989) is estimated as:

(6.5)

$$\Delta RI_t = \beta_0 + \beta_t t + \beta_{DT} D(T_B)_t + \beta_{DU} DU_t + \beta_{DT} DT_t + \beta_{RI} RI_{t-1} + \sum_{k=1}^{K} \beta_k \Delta RI_{t-k} + \varepsilon_t$$

where T_B is the break year, K is maximum of lag length, $D(T_B)_t = 1$ if $t = T_B + 1$, otherwise 0, $DU_t = 1$ if $t > T_B$, otherwise 0, and $DT_t = t - T_B$ if $t > T_B$, otherwise 0. The specification allows to test changes in intercept $(\beta_{DU} = 0)$ and/or slope $(\beta_{DT} = 0)$. The results based on Gini coefficient, the ratio of per capita income between regions and the coefficient of variation suggests that eastern and western regions have converged to their own specific steady states over the past 40 years. The regional gap between the east and other regions widened before the reforms but economic reforms has worsened the gap further.

Policy Measure to Reduce Inequality

Khan and Riskin (2001) provide a comprehensive analysis of inequality and poverty in China in the age of globalisation. Based on the 1988 and 1995 survey data they observe major changes in the composition of income between the two survey dates. Rural household income mainly from farming has declined from 74 per cent to 56 per cent, while non-farming wages increased from 9 per cent to 22 per cent resulting in increasing income inequality. The Gini ratio for rural income grew by 23 per cent from 0.34 to 0.42 due to unequal distribution of faster-growing wage components of rural income. The corresponding increases in inequality in the urban areas is 43 per cent in seven years from 0.23 to 0.33. The increasing inequality of distribution of income caused rise in urban income inequality. The wage share of income grew from 44 per cent to 61 per cent. Other components of income like income of retirees and housing rental were subject to fast growth as well. Subsidies declined from 20 per cent of urban income to 1 per cent.

Demurger et al. (2002) examined the growth in GDP per capita for the period 1952-1998 and decomposed the location and policy growth rates in the provincial growth regressions to quantify the contribution of each factor in 1996-1999. Their respective contribution varies with the interval of 0-2.8 and 1.6-3.5 per cent. The highest and lowest rates are associated with the coastal and northwestern provinces respectively. The authors list a number of policy measures to solve the unbalanced growth and to reduce the regional disparity. The policy measures include: extension of the deregulation from coastal to include other provinces, introduction of a registration system to prevent movements from the rural poor to prosperous areas, changes in the policy of the monopoly state bank system to allocate more resources to the western provinces, improvement in the infrastructure to overcome geographical barriers, and to increase the human capital formation. Shi (2001) estimated that the growing inequality of income distribution in both rural and urban areas has created more difficulties in reducing poverty since the mid-1980s.

Income Factor Decomposition of Inequality

Previous studies have suggested that non-agricultural activities have been the major cause of rural income inequality. Increase in agricultural income was considered as a policy measure to reduce rural inequality in China. Cheng (1996) used household data from 5 grain producing Chinese regions in 1994 and Lerman and Yitzhaki (1985) decomposition approach showed that Gini coefficient of total income can be expressed as:

$$(6.6) \qquad G = \sum_{k=1}^{K} R_k G_k S_k$$

The above expression shows that inequality within the grain producing areas was also very high, with differences in crop income as the major source of inequality. The decomposition of inequality indicates that 61 per cent of the income inequality of peasant households is due to intra-provincial while remaining 39 per cent from the inter-provincial inequality components. The R_k, G_k and S_k are Gini correlation between the income component k and the rank of total income, the Gini coefficient for income component k, and the share of k in the total income consisting of K components. The inequality contribution of component $k (C_k)$ and marginal effect (M_k) of a percentage change in income source k (e_k) are obtained from:

$$(6.7) \qquad C_k = R_k G_k S_k / G \quad \text{and} \quad M_k = \frac{\partial G / \partial e_k}{G}.$$

We have already described an example of a decomposition of Gini by income source. In a second study which is based on different approach the Gini coefficient of household income is decomposed according to type of income. This method has been used by Gustafsson and Shi (2001b) to analyse the reasons for the rapid increase of income inequality. They investigated the effect of the processes of economic and social transition on the distribution of income in China. The Gini coefficient and the differences of the Gini coefficient between two years, 1 and 0, is written as:

$$(6.8) \qquad \begin{aligned} G &= \sum_{k=1}^{K} \frac{\mu_k}{\mu} C_k \\ \Delta G &= G_1 - G_0 = \sum_{k=1}^{K} (S_{1k} C_{1k} - S_{0k} C_{0k}) \end{aligned}$$

where S_k is the share of income type k, C_k is the concentration coefficient of income type k measuring the association between income type k and total income, and μ_k and μ are means of income type k and total income respectively. Results based on samples of 1988 and 1995 household surveys shows that the changes in relative size of money income due to the distribution of land by household size and its changed profile are found to be the major processes behind the rapid increase of income inequality in rural China. Changes in the urban housing allocation and an increased number of retirees in combination with higher benefits have increased inequality. Using the same data Gustafsson and Shi (2001a) in analysing the Chinese labour market to investigate how earnings[2] inequality and relative earnings have changed between 1988 and 1995. The mean logarithmic deviation (*MLD*) index and the changes in the *MLD* between two periods are written as:

$$L = \sum_{k=1}^{K} \log\left(\frac{\mu}{y_k}\right) / N$$

(6.9) $$\Delta L = L_{t+\tau} - L_t \approx A + B + C + D$$

$$\approx \sum_{k=1}^{K} \bar{v}_k \Delta L_k + \sum_{k=1}^{K} \bar{L}_k \Delta v_k + \sum_{k=1}^{K} (\bar{\lambda}_k - \ln \bar{\lambda}_k) \Delta v_k + \sum_{k=1}^{K} (\bar{\theta}_k - \bar{v}_k) \Delta \ln \mu_k$$

where Δ represents changes, μ_k is the mean value, v_k is the share of group observations in total, $\lambda_k = (\mu_k / \mu)$, $\theta_k = (v_k \lambda_k)$ and τ is incremental time period. The total change is decomposed into 4 components. These are interpreted as: the effect of intertemporal changes in inequality within groups (*A*), the effect of changes in population shares on the within-group inequality (*B*), the effect of changes in population shares on the relative mean earnings of the population group (*C*), and the relative mean earnings of the population groups (*D*). The overall effects of demographic changes are equal to the sum of *B* and *C*. Results show that earnings inequality has increased rapidly affecting all categories of labour as defined by ownership sector, region and education. The contribution of basic wages and subsidies to inequality increase is positive, while those of bonus and other earnings are negative.

Polarization vs Inequality Indices

To overcome the limitation of the two inequality (Gini and Generalized Entropy) indices and three polarisation (Esteban and Ray 1994; Wolfson 1994; and Tsui and Wang 1998) indices in establishing along which dimension polarisation occurs, Kanbur and Zhang (1999) developed a polarisation index (*KZ*) by specifying clusters and measuring the extent of inequality decomposed into within-group and between-group inequality components. Polarisation refers to clustering of the income distribution along with some key dimensions. The indices of Zhang and Kanbur (2001) are written as:

(6.10) $$ER = A \sum_{i=1}^{K} \sum_{j=1}^{K} \pi_i \pi_j \pi_i^{a} |y_i - y_j|$$

(6.11) $$W = \frac{2(2T - G)}{(m/\mu)} = \frac{2(\mu^* - \mu^L)}{m}$$

---

[2] Total earning is decomposed into basic wages, bonus, subsidies and other earnings.

$$(6.12) \qquad TW = \frac{\theta}{N} \sum_{i=1}^{K} \pi_i \left| \frac{y_i - m}{m} \right|^r$$

$$(6.13) \qquad KZ = \frac{I^B(y)}{I^W(y)} = \frac{\sum_{k=1}^{K} w_k I_k}{I(\mu_1 e_1, \mu_2 e_2, ..., \mu_K e_K)}$$

where G is the Gini coefficient, I is inequality index, the subscript k indicates income group, the superscripts B, W, a, and r denote between, within, and sensitivity parameters, π_i is the population frequency in every class, A is used for population normalisation, $\mu^* = (1 - G)$ and μ^L is the distribution of corrected mean income and mean income of the bottom half of the population. The KZ index is expressed as the ratio of between inequality and within inequality. The index is then calculated for each of the four dimensions: West-East, National status, Capital city size and Export share by using income and expenditure definitions. In testing the behaviour of the four indices, it is found that the polarisation indices do not produce different results from the inequality indices. The KZ index seems to offer more insights into changes in China's income distribution. The results show that while polarisation along West-East and national status dimensions remained constant, polarisation along capital city size and export share dimensions increased during 1983-1995. The conclusion is that regional polarisation is driven by structural differences between regions rather than geography or political. In terms of levels, rural-urban polarisation is more serious than inland-cost, while in terms of trend, the inland-coast polarisation has increased much more than rural-urban. Birchenall (2001) used the following modified formulation of the Esteban and Ray as a measure of polarisation:

$$(6.14) \qquad B = A \sum_{i=1}^{K} \sum_{j=1}^{K} \pi_i^{1+\alpha} \pi_j \left| y_i - y_j \right|$$

where $A = \left[\sum_{i=1}^{K} \pi_i \right]^{-(2+\alpha)}$ is used for population normalisation. This measure is applied to Colombian income distribution. Human capital accumulation reduced the dispersion of income distribution leading to a period of stagnation when mobility declined. The structural reforms made the economy less equal with increased mobility.

Summary of Regional Inequality in China

China has experienced rapid economic growth in the post economic reform initiated in 1978 with the implications for inequality. Research analysing income inequality in China is often based on household surveys collected in late 80s and 90s or published statistics at regional level. The surveys are of good coverage when regional, provincial and sectoral dimensions are considered. There is a general agreement among research presented above that

Gini coefficient increased over time and heterogeneously across provinces. The dissimilar impact of growth on inequality is not limited to inter-provincial, but also intra-provincial, intra-urban, intra-rural and rural-urban inequality. Intra-provincial, intra-rural and intra-urban inequality components contribute significantly to the overall inequality. The growing inequality has created more difficulties in reducing poverty. Income sources are important differently to the sectoral inequality. The correlation between the growth and inequality support the Kuznet's inverted U-curve relationship. In analyzing the causal mechanism relating inequality and growth many other factors like macroeconomic, technological, political and institutional factors beyond the inequality influence of economic growth. Output growth, increasing exposure to international trade, urbanisation, taxation, government spending, inflation, human capital, geography and the sectoral structure of the economy determine the extent and direction of changes in inequality. The regional polarisation is driven by the structural differences between regions.

REGIONAL INEQUALITY IN RUSSIA

The Russian Household Budget Survey (HBS) conducted since 1952 by Goskomstat and the Russian Longitudinal Monitoring Survey are the main data source used in analysis of income inequality, income distribution and poverty in Russia. The Soviet style family budget nature of the survey was revamped in 1997. The new sample covers around 49,000 families observed in a quarterly basis. It is representative of each region (89 territorial units or Federations) of Russia for urban/rural subgroups. For a brief description of the HBS data see Yemtsov (2002).

Inequality and Transition

Unlike other transition economies, the level of inequality defined as Gini coefficient and Theil mean log deviation index was quite high when Russia entered transition. Using the Russian Longitudinal Monitoring Survey dataset Commander, Tolstopiatenko and Yemtsov (1999) demonstrate that inequality rose further. A number of factors are identified as the driving forces behind the increases. The factors are the wealth transfers through privatisation programme, changes in government expenditure, growth in earning dispersion, and shifts in the structure of income. Yemtsov (2002) also analyses inequality and poverty in the Russian regions over the period 1992-2000. Yemtsov uses household budget survey (HBS) data to construct regional level data. Results show significant between and within regional inequality with increasing trend. The dynamics of poverty depend on inter-regional differences in the average incomes. The observed regional differences in inequality are related to endowments and initial conditions, transfers, restructuring policies, and economic shocks.

Regarding the incidence and the depth of poverty during 1992-1996, Commander, Tolstopiatenko and Yemtsov (1999) indicates that at the start of transition about half of the population of households fell below the region-specific poverty lines. Poverty is measured as headcount, poverty gap and the squared poverty gap. The share declined to 40 per cent at the end of 1996, but a large fraction of households were locked in chronic poverty. Luttmer

(2001) also suggests that after accounting for transitory shocks around 80 per cent of the poor in Russia and Poland remains in poverty for at least one year. Results in Shorrocks and Kolenikov (2001) covering the period 1985-1999 suggest that falling real per capita income and growing inequality each contributed to raising poverty rate in Russia by about 20 per cent, while lowering poverty line reduced poverty by 13 per cent. Measurement errors in the data might have lead to an overestimation of the poverty rate. The data errors can be due to unregistered incomes from the growing informal economic activities and home production activities.

None of the factors listed above is concerned with the human capital. Human capital is found to be important for economic growth. Russia, despite its high level of human capital is having a living standard of a middle income developing country. Furthermore, Russia has experienced sharply negative growth rates for more than a decade. In finding explanations to the above patterns Fan, Overland and Spagat (1999) presented a model, using a two-sector overlapping generations framework, dealing with transition economics from a theoretical perspective placing emphasis on the importance of human capital. The model captures the characteristics of the Russian economy with both human capital and education system that produces the wrong skills for the market economy. The authors propose a rule for the timing of restructuring the education system and simultaneously reducing inequality. It is suggested that a late implementation of restructuring early in the transition process will reduce the Russian's investment in human capital and skills. Early education restructuring as part of the transition strategy and continuous subsidisation of the education system is recommended. An early restructuring is expected to reduce inequality by providing underprivileged youth with an upward mobility.

Inequality and Regional Polarisation

Increasing regional inequality and regional polarisation has become serious policy concerns of the Russian Federation. The heterogeneous economic development, size, ethnic and natural diversity of regions might cause disintegration and widening regional differences as the standard of living continues to grow. Fedorov (2002) documents the changes in regional inequality during 1990-1999 in per capita monetary income and expenditures and employ several measures of polarisation to analyse empirically dimensions of regional polarisation in Russia. The Generalised Entropy (GE) measure and Esteban and Ray (ER), Wolfson (W) and Kanbur and Zhang (KZ) indices of polarisation are used. The Generalised Entropy class of inequality measures in Kanbur and Zhang (1999) is written as:

$$(6.15) \quad GE = \begin{cases} \sum_{k=1}^{K} f(y_i)((y_i/\mu)^c - 1), & c \neq 0,1 \\ \sum_{k=1}^{K} f(y_i)(y_i/\mu)\log(y_i/\mu), & c = 1 \\ \sum_{k=1}^{K} f(y_i)\log(\mu/y_i), & c = 0. \end{cases}$$

The remaining three polarisation indices are previously defined. The *KZ* polarisation index is derived from the *GE* index measurement. Polarisation has to do with clustering of the income distribution along key dimensions, while inequality concerns the overall distribution. The dimensions here include West vs. East, national republics vs. ethnically Russian regions, region with large capitals vs. region with smaller capitals, exporting regions vs. other regions. The household survey data used cover 77 out of a total of 89 in theory politically equal members of the Federation which are economically distinct regions.[3]

Trends in regional inequality and polarisation are analysed in Fedorov (2002) by calculating Gini coefficient and the Generalised Entropy inequality measures. The Gini coefficient for income rose from 0.11 in 1991 to 0.29 in 1999 and for expenditure from 0.12 to 0.37. Inequality is increasing before 1996 and then levels out and is constant at the end of period. The results show that the transition period affected differently not only different groups of the population but also regions. The Esteban-Ray and Wolfson indices of polarisation using Gini and income distribution parameters show that regional polarisation has been increasing since the beginning of transition with similar trends as in the inequality.[4] The index is calculated for each of the four dimensions: West-East, national status, capital city size and export share by using income and expenditure definitions. The polarisation measures do not provide a better insight into the pattern of regional polarisation than Gini and Generalised Entropy measures. Polarisation is found to be increasing along the capital city size and export share dimensions while it is decreasing along the West-East and national status dimensions over the course of economic transition. Based on the above observations Fedorov concludes that regional polarisation in Russia is driven by structural differences between regional rather than geographic or political.

Inequality Decomposition

Yemtsov (2002) analyses inequality and poverty in the Russian regions over the period 1992-2000. Household budget survey (HBS) data is used to construct regional level data. Inequality is decomposed into inter-regional and intra-regional inequalities. The between regional inequality accounts for one third of the overall inequality and it is trended towards an internationally high level. The dynamics of poverty will increasingly depend on inter-regional differences in the average incomes. The observed differences in inequality are found to be related to a number of determinants such as endowments and initial conditions, transfers, restructuring policies and economic shocks.

Wage Inequality

Wage inequality in Russia following the end of the central planning has risen more than in Central and Eastern European (CEE) countries undergoing transition. Flemming and Micklewright (2000) investigate differences in income distribution (defined as earnings of

---

[3]   Regions with domestic conflicts are excluded from the study.
[4]   Similarity in trends between regional inequality and the two polarization indices is found in Zhang and Kanbur (2001) for China using data from 1983 to 1995.

full-time employees, per capita household incomes, and transfers) between market and planned economies. The latter are considered both during socialist and transition periods. They estimate that the Gini coefficient for per capita income in Russia rose from 0.22 before transition to 0.41 in 1994 and fell to 0.37 in 1997. Despite considerable heterogeneity, the corresponding rise in Gini for CEE was from 0.20 to 0.25. The level was relatively high for some countries like Czech Republic, Hungary and Poland. The increase has been much higher when wage inequality in Russia is considered. Rising earnings dispersion seems to have been the major factor behind rising inequality in personal incomes. At the household level dispersion is however lower.

Due to the lack of data Flemming and Micklewright indicate that it has not been possible to account for important features of the transition like the impact of housing privatisation and the relative price effects of liberalisation on income distribution. It is worth mentioning that the comparison among countries in above is based on data that are not strictly comparable. Luttmer (2001) analysed the impact transitory shocks and measurement errors on inequality and mobility in Poland and Russia. There is a positive association between noise in the data and increased inequality. Economic insecurity is estimated to be substantial. The high levels of economic mobility, foremost in Russia, largely are driven by transitory events and noisy data.

In addition to high level of wage inequality and increasing wage dispersion unlike other CEE transition countries Russia also has an extremely large incidence of wage arrears (withholding wages) affecting the wage distribution and wage inequality. Results from Russian Longitudinal Monitoring Survey (RLMS) data for 1994, 1996 and 1998 presented by Lehman and Wadsworth (2001) shows that the conventional measure of earnings dispersion would be 20 to 30 per cent lower in the absence of wage arrears. In 1998 about 70 per cent of employees did not receive a wage complete or on time. Lehman and Wadsworth discuss the pay distribution by gender, education, region and industry and quantify the wage gaps between counterfactual and observed wage distributions by these characteristics.[5] The counterfactual group represent those not in the arrears.

Summary of Regional Inequality in Russia

The level of inequality in the Russia Federation has been higher than in other transition economies when Russia entered its process of transition. The factors causing the increase in inequality are wealth transfer, changes in government expenditure, growth in earnings dispersion, shifts in the structure of income and also disruption in production. Several studies point to significant between and within regional inequality with increasing trend. The regional inequality differences found to be related to endowments and initial conditions, transfers, restructuring policies and economic shocks. Measurement errors due to unregistered income, growth of the informal economic activities and home production do not allow estimation of the negative growth rate and increasing incidence of poverty with accuracy. A restructuring of the education system is suggested as an important step to avoid continuous production of wrong skills and to reduce inequality. However, increasing regional inequality, regional

---

[5] For extensive discussion of the issues of wage arrears in Russia see also: Earle and Sabirianova (2001) and Lehman, Wadsworth and Aquisti (1999).

polarisation and heterogeneous economic development together with size, ethnic and natural diversity of regions may cause further disintegration and widening regional differences in living standards in Russia. Regional polarisation is driven by structural differences between regions rather than geography or political. Rising income dispersion is a major factor behind rising inequality in personal income. It is to be noted that measures of inequality and poverty might be biased. The bias is a result of the fact that the effects of housing privatisation, relative price effects of liberalisation and wage arrears on income distribution are not accounted for.

REGIONAL INEQUALITY IN INDIA

Nearly all of the empirical studies of poverty, inequality, human development and labour studies in India are based on the National Sample Survey (NSS) data covering the India's 24 states in the post 1944. The NSS database includes details on consumer expenditure, demographic characteristics, and labour market statistics. The data consists of annual stratified sample household surveys collected and processed by the Indian bureau of statistics. The household sample size varies greatly between the surveys. For the short description and examples of the use of the data see Jha (2000) and Datt and Ravallion (1992).

State and Sectoral Inequality

Inequality in regional economic policies is often discussed at the inter-regional level.[6] But regions differ with regard to the intra-regional patterns of distributions. Mishra and Parikh (1997) focus on the measurement and use of Gini coefficient for the distribution of income per capita of household consumption expenditure in 17 major Indian states in 1983. They examined the inter-regional inequality variations. Regional inequality is decomposed into urban and rural components. They estimate the measure of inequality by approximating the observed distribution using linear interpolation and fitting a hypothetical function like log-normal distribution to calculate the inequality measure from it. Inequality can also be measured nonparametrically without imposing any functional form of statistical distribution by specifying Lorenz curve.

The parametric and non-parametric methods used by Mishra and Parikh resulted in Gini in the range of 0.24-0.37 and 0.24-0.36 respectively. Various tests using state level regressions indicate evidence of heterogeneity among the Lorenz curves of the states. This confirms the importance of decomposition of inequality into interstate and intrastate

---

[6] An interesting study examining the performance of Indian regions in the areas of health and education and the role of government expenditure in promoting non-income objectives during 1970-1990 is by Dutta, Panda and Wadhwa (1997). Regions are found to differ in performance. The correlation between per capita incomes and performance levels in health (measured as infant and child mortality achievement) or education (measured as achievement in primary to high school) indices is low. The relative position of the states indicates stagnant patterns of human development at the interstate level. Regression analysis indicates that expenditure is an important determinant of level of achievement in health and education sectors. Poverty alleviation programs are found to target often only at the level of the state. For mapping of poverty at more disaggregate level like the districts level see Bigman and Srinivasan (2002). This improves their coverage and reduces the leakage to non-poor sub-groups and the program costs.

components. The between state component contribute 50 per cent of the total inequality. The within component is large and can be further decomposed into rural and urban components. The rural and urban Gini measures vary in the interval 0.17-0.35 and 0.28-0.38, respectively. The residual component consists of about 9 per cent to 37 per cent of the overall inequality. Mishra and Parikh suggest that policies to reduce inequalities should be concentrated on reducing the within state urban and rural inequalities simultaneously.

Inequality-poverty-growth Relationship

There has been a great interest in quantifying the relative contribution of economic growth and redistribution to changes in poverty. The objective is to know whether the growth and shift in income distribution helped or hurt the poor population during period of economic expansion or contraction. For this reason Datt and Ravallion (1992) decomposed changes in poverty *(P)* measures into three components:

(6.16)
$$P_{t+n} - P_t = G(t, t+n; r) + D(t, t+n; r) + R(t, t+n; r)$$
$$\equiv \left[P(z/\mu_{t+n}, L_r) - P(z/\mu_t, L_r) \right] + \left[P(z/\mu_r, L_{t+n}) - P(z/\mu_r, L_t) \right] + R(t, t+n; r)$$

where *G(.)*, *D(.)* and *R(.)* are growth, redistribution and residual components, *t*, *t+n* and *r* refer to the initial, terminal and reference dates, *z* is poverty line, μ mean income and *L* is the Lorenz curve. The growth component is defined as the change in poverty due to a change in the mean income holding the Lorenz curve constant at some reference level. The redistribution component is defined as the change in the Lorenz curve while keeping the mean income constant at the reference level. The residual vanishes if the mean income and Lorenz curve remain constant over the decomposition period. The method is illustrated with analysis of poverty alleviation in India and Brazil during 1977-1988. Results show that growth and redistributional effects on poverty (measured as head count, poverty gap and Foster-Greer-Thorbecke (FGT) index) were different and uneven across sectors and over time in both countries. India's urban sector contributed to a rising share of aggregate poverty. The distributional shifts and economic growth have aided poverty alleviation in India.

The inequality-poverty-growth relationship can be studied by using other methods rather than decomposition method described above. To mention an example, Jha (2000) examines the empirical relationship between inequality, poverty and growth in India using data on consumption from the 13th to the 53rd (1957-1997) rounds of the national Sample Survey. He computes Gini coefficient and measures of poverty for urban/rural and over time. Inequality is increased over time but poverty has declined only marginally post the reform period, 1990-1991. The rise in inequality is explained by increased capital intensity in production, drop in the rate of labour absorption, and the rapid growth of the service sector. Changes in the capital intensity have resulted in a shift in the distribution of income from wages to profits. The rise in inequality has reduced the poverty-reducing effects of higher growth. The macroeconomic stabilisation and structural adjustment reforms[7] which begins in 1990-1991 have also been characterised as widening regional inequality. To study the behaviour of inequality over time in separate urban and rural regression the Gini coefficient is regressed on a number of determinants as follows:

$$(6.17) \qquad GINI_{it} = \beta_i + \beta_{HCR}HCR_{it} + \beta_{MC}MC_{it} + \beta_{MC2}MC_{it}^2 + \varepsilon_{it}$$

where the subscript i and t denote state and time periods, HCR and MC are head count ratio and real mean consumption. Inequality at the urban is higher than rural and economic growth implies a shift in the population from rural to urban. The gradual nature of the reform process combined with high job security has reduced the negative impact of inequality. Statistical convergence among states in terms of inequality, poverty and consumption is weak. This is tested using Kendall's index of rank concordance and regression analysis. The coefficient of concordance is written as:

$$(6.18) \qquad CC_j = \left[\sum_j R_j - \overline{R}\right]^2 \Big/ \frac{1}{12}(T^2)N(N^2-1)$$

where R_j is rank of state j, T and N are the number of years and states. The growth has increased inequality with the reform. In some states with poor growth performance inequality has constrained their economic growth. Rapid economic growth combined with a redistributive policy that does not make the distribution of consumption further skewed is found to be an optimal policy measure.

Inequality and Polarisation

Chakravarty and Majumder (2001) explore the possibility of using different ethical indices of inequality to generate alternative indices of polarisation. The index of polarisation measures the extent of decline on the middle class. Their numerical illustration is based on Indian statewise household expenditure data for the period 1987/88 and 1993/94. Monthly per capita total expenditure from 6 states is taken as a proxy for income. Two indices including the Wolfson index and a new general ethical index is suggested and applied to compute polarisation for rural and urban India. The Wolfson index is related to the new general index corresponding to the Gini welfare function. It is established that all inequality indices may be employed to produce alternative indices of polarisation. In several states inequality and polarisation have gone down. In some states polarisation increased in urban sector over the period. In general the equality component of polarisation dominates the inequality component. Inequality and polarisation are found to differ by state, sector and develop differently over time. The relative indices of polarisation which are dependent on income

[7] The economic reform program in India involved fiscal consolidation and stabilisation, industrial policy and foreign investment, trade and exchange rate policies, tax reform, public sector policy, fiscal sector policy, agricultural sector reform, labour market reform, and complementary social measures.

shares are developed in Chakravarty, Majumder and Roy (2002) to form an absolute polarisation index which depends on absolute income differentials. Numerical illustration of the results is based on the Indian data presented above for the period 1993/94. Results suggest that inequality and polarisation are not the same issue in income distribution analysis.

Summary of Regional Inequality in India

The data quality underlying inequality and poverty analysis in India qualitatively seem to be much better than those of the Russia Federation. Many Indian studies discuss both inter-regional and intra-regional inequality. The latter is further decomposed into urban and rural components. Results suggests that policies to reduce inequality should be concentrated on reducing the within state urban and rural inequalities simultaneously. A decomposition of changes in poverty shows that growth and redistribution effects on poverty were different and uneven across sectors and over time. The urban sector contributed to the raising share of aggregate poverty. The distributional shifts and economic growth have aided poverty alleviation. Changes in capital intensity have resulted in a shift in distribution of income and rise in inequality following macroeconomic stabilisation and structural adjustment reforms. This in turn has reduced the poverty reducing effects of economic growth. To make growth more pro-poor the rapid economic growth must be combined with the better redistributive policies. Polarisation differs by states, sectors and it has developed differently over time.

REGIONAL INEQUALITY IN USA

The Panel Study of Income Dynamics (PSID) has intensively been used for the analysis of income inequality and income distribution in US. PSID is a nationally representative longitudinal study of about 8,000 families in US. The same families and individuals are followed over time since its introduction in 1968. On an annual basis information is collected on economic, health and social behaviour. More information about the data is found at http://psidonline.isr.umich.edu/.

South, Non-South and Regional Income Distribution

Piketty and Saez (2003) studied the long-run dynamics of income inequality in US during 1913-1998 with reference to wages, income and capital gain shares. Progressive taxation on capital prevented the recovery of top capital incomes following the depression and wars. Top share of wages recovered in late 60s. Declines in progressive taxation could result in high wealth concentration.

The US South has historically had both lower incomes and greater inequality than the Non-South. Migration of skilled and highly educated manpower and industrial relocation has narrowed the regional differences and reduced the persistence in income disparity. Bishop, Formby and Thistle (1992) present evidences that reveal convergence of the South and Non-South income distributions taken place following the changes in the income distributions in

1969-1979. The basic income measure is household income from all sources in 1969 and 1979. It is adjusted for regional price differences by using constructed regional cost-of-living estimates. Results show that in 1969 Non-South rank-dominates the South but in 1970s household income distribution in the South and Non-South converges at all deciles points except the very bottom one in 1979. Tests of South versus Non-South mean income equality are performed.

At a somewhat disaggregate regional level Loewy and Papell (1996) further developed the Carlini and Mills (1993) stochastic convergence formulation of a time series notion of convergence to investigate the convergence among eight US regions during the 1929-1990 period. Loewy and Papell incorporate endogenously determined break points. Regions represent a set of economies where conditions underlying convergence in per capita income are satisfied. The negative relationship between initial log per capita income and the rate of growth conditioning on the factors determining the steady state is the evidence of convergence. By using US regional data conditional convergence is tested.[8] In seven out of eight regions the unit root hypothesis is rejected. The results indicate that regional incomes are stochastically converging to that of the nation as predicted by the neoclassical growth model.

Inter-state Income Inequality

Trends in interstate income inequality using a panel of the 48 US states for the 1960-1990 period is examined by Partridge, Rickman and Levernier (1996). The focus is on the estimation of a multitude of potential causes of the sharp increase in US income inequality. The following empirical model for family income inequality in state i at time period t written as:

$$(6.19) \qquad GINI_{it} = f(ECON_{it}, DEMOG_{it}, INST_{it}) + \mu_r + \lambda_t + \varepsilon_{it}$$

is estimated. Where *ECON*, *DEMOG* and *INST* are vectors of economic, demographic, and institutional variables that vary cross states and over time, μ, λ and ε are regional-specific, time-specific (skill-biased technological change and common trend component) and a random error term. Partridge, Rickman and Levernier find that greater international migration, greater metropolitan share of population, increased per cent households headed by females, greater female labour market participation affected reducing low-skilled wages and advanced stages of economic development increase income inequality while greater labour-force participation rate decreases inequality. Unionisation did not affect state level income inequality. There is little evidence that technological change increases income inequality. The estimated fixed state effects suggest that the other institutional and cultural differences and their changes over time may be partly responsible for the increase in income inequality.

Price levels differ among regions within a country for many reasons such as transportation distance. Using constructed state-level price data Black and Dowd (1997)

---

[8] The condition is often made on human capital, physical capital and population growth as determinants (see Mankiw, Romer and Weil, 1992).

examined real interstate personal income inequality in US. The real income inequality index for the U.S. states is:

$$(6.20) \qquad I = \sum_{i=1}^{n} p_i \ln(p_i / y_i) = \sum_{i=1}^{n} \left(\frac{POP_i}{POP_{US}} \right) \ln \left(\frac{(POP_i / POP_{US})}{(y_i / PI_i)/(y_{US} / PI_{US})} \right)$$

where p_i and y_i are the shares of state i in the total population and total personal income, and PI_i is state level price deflator. The data cover 48 continental states and the District of Colombia for the period 1963-1989. The results show that real income inequality is 53 per cent larger than its nominal counterpart. Regression of real and nominal income inequalities (I) on a trend and squared trends:

$$(6.21) \qquad I_t^R = \beta_0 + \beta_1 T + \beta_2 T^2 + u_t^R \quad \text{and} \quad I_t^N = \alpha_0 + \alpha_1 T + \alpha_2 T^2 + u_t^N .$$

The above equation shows that both income inequalities have steadily increased over time among the states.

Factors Influencing Inequality across States of USA

Several factors which affect inequality are discussed above. Income inequality affects the welfare of individuals and households in different ways. A survey of the debate over the association between health (measured as mortality), inequality and economic development is given by Deaton (2001). Deaton and Lubotsky (2002) argue that the (positive) correlation between mortality and income inequality across the cities and states of the US is confounded by the effects of racial composition. Empirical results based on Compressed Mortality Files (CMF) from 1968 to 1994 show that conditional on the fraction of black, neither city nor state mortality rates are correlated with income inequality. The high rate of mortality where the fraction of black is higher is because white mortality is higher in such place, not because of higher mortality rate or lower black incomes. The results are robust to conditioning on income, education and unobservable state effects.

Availability of microdata has resulted in better investigation of determinants of inequality. Zandvakili (1999 and 2000) investigates the effects of race in conjunction with age, education and marital status on income inequality among female heads of household. Results using PSID data for the period 1978-1986 show that short-run inequality has generally increased influenced by the existence of transitory components. The long-run inequality is declining due to smoothing of the transitory component. Race and education are found to explain over one-third of observed inequality. Age and marital status also were possible factors influencing inequality. Most movements occur within each group and there is an indication of permanent inequality among female heads of household. Moffitt and Gottschalk (2002) find that the variance of permanent component of male earnings in US increased in the late 1970s and in the 1980s, while the variance of transitory component rose in the 1980s but declined in the 1990s. Zandvakili and Mills (2001) find that social security income and income taxes reduce income inequality in a given year, but there are no significant changes over time. Income transfers have minimal impact in reducing inequality.

Conventional inference procedures like those above assume independent samples. Inference tests are conducted based on calculated standard errors for estimates of inequality indices. Zheng and Cushing (2001) propose a method for correction of sample dependency in testing inequality indices. Simulations and applications to the Current Population Surveys (CPS) and PSID data indicate that failure to correct for sample dependency may increase the standard error by 3.3 to 17.1 per cent. Recently Maasoumi and Heshmati (2003) employed the extended Kolmogorov-Smirnov tests of first and second order stochastic dominance to examine the dynamic evolution of disposable and gross incomes for several household groups[9] in the PSID panel data at several points from 1968 to 1997. They find a surprising number of strong rankings, both between groups and over time, and in both gross and disposable incomes.

Summary of Regional Inequality in USA

Access to high quality household data covering long period for US allows analysis of dynamics of income inequality and distribution. Analysis of income is performed at different levels. US South historically had both lower incomes and greater inequality than the Non-South. The income per capita is however converging over time. At the regional level, incomes are stochastically converging to the level of the nation. There is significant interstate income inequality. Greater international migration, increased metropolitan share of population, changes in family structure, increased share of female headed households, increased female labour participation and institutional and cultural differences increased income inequality, while greater labour force participation reduced inequality. Race, education, age and marital status are key factors affecting inequality in the US. It is important to distinguish between transitory and permanent components of inequality. Short-run inequality is influenced by the transitory shocks, while long-run inequality is declining due to the smoothing of transitory component.

REGIONAL INEQUALITY IN A SELECTION OF SMALLER COUNTRIES

It has not been possible to trace regional studies of income distribution and inequality covering smaller but yet populated developing and transition countries. In the absence of such few single country studies covering different regions and levels of development including Colombia, Indonesia, Philippines, South Africa, Zambia, and Poland are presented below. By looking at various dimensions, several of these studies can serve as examples of applications of regional inequality studies to data from smaller developing and transition countries.

---

[9]   The household head characteristics that Maasoumi and Heshmati (2003) condition on include: age, marital status, working status, race, gender, occupation, number of children, level of education, length of unemployment, and geographical mobility.

Colombia

Birchenall (2001) discuss the recent increase in income inequality and dynamic aspects of income and educational mobility in Colombia for 1976 to 1996. Human capital accumulation reduced the dispersion of income distribution leading to a declining mobility in 1983 to 1990. Trade liberalisation increased the wage differential of skilled workers. It increased inequality, induced polarisation and lead to high mobility. The relationship between inequality and polarisation is dynamically mutual, and in long-run bi-directional. Fixed investment growth has little impact on polarisation. This indicates that the deterioration of income distribution being attributed to the trade liberalisation process. The results suggest that the polarisation of income measured as a modified version of the Esteban-Ray index (see equation 6.10). This variable most strongly and dynamically correlated with income inequality and GDP growth.

Indonesian Java

Cameron (2000) uses the method of DiNardo et al. (1996) modified to decompose changes in distribution of per capita household income of 20,000 households in Java between 1984 and 1990. The changes are related to the ageing population, higher educational attainment, movement out of agriculture, changes in income within industry and age/education categories. The results indicate that the welfare cost of increasing income inequality was more than offset by the social welfare gain from higher incomes. Poverty reduction measures have caused inequality to increase. Inequality increased from 0.40 in 1984 to 0.42 in 1990. Increase in non-agricultural incomes, movement out of agriculture and increased educational attainment increases inequality. However, the growth in income has partially compensated for growing inequality.

Philippines

The ultimate objective of concern for economic policy is the well-being of individuals. However, in practice the significance of intra-household inequality and distribution of resources within a household has been neglected. There is little experience on the impact of intra-household inequality on the conventional measures of inequality and poverty. Haddad and Kanbur (1997) present a framework where the inequality is decomposed into intra-household and inter-household inequality components. In the illustration it accounts for intra-household inequality in nutritional status and applied it to food consumption data from Philippines. There are three variables of interest: individual calorie adequacy (ICA_i), mean ICA within the household $(MICA_i)$, and household calorie adequacy (HCA_h) defined as:

$$(6.22) \qquad MICA_i = \frac{1}{n_h}\sum_{i=1}^{n_h} ICA_i \quad \text{and} \quad HCA_h = \sum_{i=1}^{n_h} CI_i \Big/ \sum_{i=1}^{n_h} CR_i$$

where CI_i is calorie intake, CR_i is calorie requirement of individual i, and n_h is number of individuals in household h. The data covers a sixteen month period in 1984-1985 and 448 households comprising 2,880 individuals. The results based on the three variables of interest and five commonly used measures of inequality[10] suggest that the neglect of intra-household inequality might result in an understatement of inequality and poverty. The errors are of the order of 30 per cent or more but it might not reverse the rankings of policy-relevant socio-economic groups ranked by inequality and poverty.

South Africa

From a policy perspective the relative importance of income sources is crucial in analysing the inter-household inequality and poverty. Recent advances in decomposition of Gini coefficient by income components (Duro and Esteban 1998; Zandvakili 1999; Cameron 2000; Goerlich-Gisbert 2001; Biewen 2002a) allows for assessment of changes in income components on the Gini coefficient. Liebbrandt, Woolard and Woolard (2000) following Lerman and Yitzhaki (1985) applied such a decomposition technique to 8,691 South African household's data for the rural former homeland areas observed in 1993. Here the income sources include remittances, wage income, capital income, state transfers, agriculture and self-employment. Wage income is found to be the most important income component and source of inequality. Hence, policies increases average income and reduces unemployment can have major impact on the distribution of income with positive net welfare effect. This method could be useful tool in the assessment of the South African government's post-apartheid economic and social policies.

The high inequality of South Africa has been often explained by the racial legacy. Liebbrandt and Woolard (2001) show that between race contributions to inequality have declined, although the within each race group inequality widened during 1975 and 1996. Income is measured as per adult equivalent. The overall inequality using the same method as mentioned above is decomposed into sectors, different sub-groups and income sources. The results suggest the existence of complex patterns of inequality generation.

Zambia

Determinants of poverty, inequality and growth in Zambia during the 1990s are examined by McCulloch, Baulch and Cherel-Robson (2003). Five different measures of inequality (coefficient of variation, Gini coefficient, standard deviation of logs, Theil's entropy measure and Theil's mean log deviation) and three measure of poverty (headcount, poverty gap and squared poverty gap) are used. Poverty line is locally defined based on the cost of basic needs approach and also based on the World Banks US\$1/per day. The empirical results are based on three nationally representative household surveys from 1991, 1996 and 1998. During this period Zambia implemented radical programmes of structural adjustment to boost long-term growth and poverty reduction. Income is defined as the total consumption expenditure.

---

[10] The five inequality measures are: coefficient of variation, log variance, Gini coefficient, the Theil's second measure, and the Atkinson equally distributed equivalent measure with inequality aversion parameter equal to 2.

Poverty rate, changes in poverty and inequality is reported over time by various measures and each decomposed into urban, rural and nine provinces. Results show that growth has been weak and poverty has increased dramatically in the urban areas in 1991-1996. There was a reduction in poverty concentration in rural areas between 1996 and 1998. Rural Gini coefficient declined from 0.62 to 0.48 and the urban from 0.47 to 0.43. The authors outline four policy lessons to be learned from the 1990s: (i) reforms should be adjusted to account for external shocks, (ii) internal liberalisation can have a poverty impact as external liberalisation, (iii) protection of social expenditure during stabilisation and adjustment be combined with maintaining high level of expenditure, and (iv) development of social safety net to protect sub-groups suffering from price changes.

Poland

The impact of transition on earnings inequality by using data across 49 Polish regions during 1994-1997 is estimated by Sibley and Walsh (2002). The regions are divided into 6 groups based on the taxonomy of the inherited public infrastructure.[11] Nine measures of earnings inequality are used.[12] Results indicate that earnings inequality is higher in regions that are advanced in restructuring. At the national level there is evidence of a relationship between rapid growth and rise in earnings inequality. Aggregate inequality is not changing much over time, but the between region inequality is widening over time. The range of regional inequality is 0.21-0.25 and 0.19-0.27 in 1994 and 1997 respectively.

Keane and Prasad (2002) analyse the evolution of inequality in Poland during the economic transition 1990-1997 by using household budget survey data. The results indicate that income and consumption inequality in 1997 is lower than in 1990-1992. Social transfer mechanism including pensions played an important role in dampening the increase in overall inequality. Cross country evidence from the transition economies suggest that the redistribution reduces income inequality which can also enhance economic growth.

Summary of Regional Inequality in a Selection of Smaller Countries

Variations in income inequality in a selection of smaller countries mainly by other dimensions than regional were reviewed. In the case of Colombia the deterioration of income distribution is attributed to the process of trade liberalisation. Polarisation of income is correlated with income inequality and GDP growth. The changes in the distribution of income in Java is related to the ageing population, higher educational attainment, industrial structure, changes in income within industry and age/education categories. Growth in income partially compensated for growing inequality. Evaluation of economic policy in Philippines show that in practice the significance of intra-household inequality and distribution of resources within

---

[11] Four indicators are used in ranking the regions: (i) number of Telephones and (ii) number of Fax Machines in a region per 1000 inhabitants, (iii) Number of Railways and (iv) Number of Public Roads in a region per 100km squared.

[12] The nine earnings inequality measures include: relative mean deviation, coefficient of variation, standard deviation of logs, Gini index, Mehran index, Piesch index, Kakwani index, Theil entropy index, and mean log deviation.

a household has been neglected resulting in understatement of inequality and poverty. Research analysing inter-household inequality and poverty in South Africa point to the importance of source of income as determinant of income inequality. The between racial group inequality has declined but the within racial group has increased. Stabilisation and adjustment programmes in Zambia resulted in reduction in concentration of poverty and declining inequality. An examination of the impact of transition on income inequality in Poland indicates a positive relationship between rapid economic growth, advances in restructuring and rise in earnings inequality. The social transfer mechanism including pensions dampened increases in overall inequality. Redistribution that enhances inequality can enhance growth.

THE WIID DATA

The data underlying analysis in the next section are obtained from the WIDER World Income Inequality Database (WIID). WIID contains information on income inequality, income shares, and a number of variables indicating the source and coverage of data for 146 countries. The countries are observed on an irregular basis mainly covering the period post 1950 until 1998. Here we focus on the inequality among selected large countries. At the absence of data at the within country regional level, we use time series data, although countries are not observed consecutively over time.

Table 6.1 Mean Gini coefficient by country, based on WIID

Country/ Region	Min	Max	N	Range	Minimum	Mean	Median	Maximum	StdDev	Range	Wgini
China	1953	1998	26	45	18.60	29.35	29.34	55.80	7.18	37.20	28.59
East Asia	1953	1998	93	45	18.60	33.67	31.20	55.80	7.65	37.20	28.81
India	1950	1997	41	47	28.86	34.55	34.94	46.25	3.63	17.39	34.12
South Asia	1950	1997	106	47	28.86	36.94	35.75	53.00	5.37	24.14	34.49
Russian Fed.	1981	1998	13	17	25.10	34.14	36.55	44.81	7.64	19.71	39.35
East Europe	1955	1998	191	43	15.90	25.14	25.04	44.81	5.06	28.91	31.57
US	1944	1997	53	53	35.18	38.65	37.93	44.78	2.35	9.60	38.85
Industrialized	1867	1998	495	131	19.87	34.79	33.83	67.20	7.90	47.33	36.08
All regions	1867	1999	1631	132	15.90	41.12	40.24	79.50	9.61	27.91	35.65

Min	First year of observation
Max	Last year of observation
N	Number of years observed
Range	The difference between the last and first years of observation
Minimum	Minimum Gini value
Mean	Mean Gini value
Median	Median Gini value
Maximum	Maximum Gini value
StdDev	Standard deviation of the Gini
Range	The difference between maximum and minimum Gini values
Wgini	Population weighted mean Gini

The Gini coefficient is measured in percentage points. It is mean of multiple observations for a country in a given year. The multiplicity of observations is due to differences in income definitions, data sources, reference units, and population coverage. Gini coefficient was also calculated adjusted for share of population. Such adjustment is most relevant when aggregating inequality to the global level. However, the population adjusted Gini measure is very sensitive to the exit and entry of countries with large population like China and India.

In order to provide a picture of the distribution of income and inequality we report the first, the last, the period range and the number of years a country is observed. In addition to the mean Gini coefficient, median, minimum, maximum, standard deviation, range and annual changes in Gini are provided in Table 6.1 for large countries together with mean values for the region where they are located. In Table 6.2 we report Gini coefficient and population weighted Gini together with distribution of income. The deciles observations are transformed to quintile income shares with the objective to make the income distribution comparable across countries and over time. As a second measure of inequality the ratio of the highest to the lowest quintiles are calculated and reported in Table 6.2.

Table 6.2 Mean Gini coefficient and quintile shares by country, based on WIID

Country/ Region	Min	Max	N	Range	Gini	WGini	Q1	Q2	Q3	Q4	Q5	Q5/Q1
China	1953	1998	26	45	29.35	28.59	0.08	0.12	0.16	0.25	0.39	5.21
East Asia	1953	1998	93	45	33.67	28.81	0.07	0.12	0.16	0.23	0.41	5.55
India	1950	1997	41	47	34.55	34.12	0.09	0.12	0.16	0.21	0.41	4.83
South Asia	1950	1997	106	47	36.94	34.49	0.08	0.12	0.16	0.21	0.42	5.13
Russian Fed.	1981	1998	13	17	34.14	39.35	0.09	0.12	0.16	0.22	0.41	4.56
East Europe	1955	1998	191	43	26.14	31.57	0.10	0.14	0.18	0.22	0.35	3.54
US	1944	1997	53	53	38.65	38.85	0.05	0.11	0.17	0.24	0.43	9.17
Industrialized	1867	1998	495	131	34.79	36.08	0.07	0.12	0.17	0.24	0.40	5.72
All regions	1867	1999	1392	132	38.06	38.26	0.07	0.11	0.16	0.22	0.44	6.88

Min   First year of observation
Max   Last year of observation
N   Number of years observed
Range   The difference between the last and first years of observation
Gini   Mean Gini value
WGini   Population weighted mean Gini value
Q1-Q5   Income shares of the first-fifth quintiles of population
Q5/Q1   the ration of the fifth quintile share to the first quintile income share

It should be noted that the point observations are not comparable across countries or for the same country over the entire time period. The data incomparability is due to differences in unit of measurement, area and population coverage, and income definitions. There is a trade off between the number of observations and the consistency of the data. Long time series is required to investigate trends in inequality. This is the motivation for our preferences for a maximisation of the number of observations rather than a search for maintaining data consistency.

RESULTS BASED ON THE WIID

The comparison of income inequality among the four large countries reported in Table 6.1 show that mean Gini coefficient in China (29.35) and India (34.55) is lower than the regional mean values where the countries are located, while those of Russia (34.14) and US (39.65) are higher than their respective regional means. It is to be noted that the country mean values are based on observations covering different sub-periods.

With the exception of Russia the mean and median values are quite close. However, the standard deviation and range between minimum and maximum Gini values differ greatly among the countries. India (3.63) and US (2.35) shows less dispersion in Gini coefficient over time. The lowest quintile income share in US (0.05) shown in Table 6.2 is lowest compared to the 0.08-0.09 among the other countries. The low Q1 combined with the high Q5 share (0.43) compared with those of the results of the other countries (0.39-0.43) result in a high Q5/Q1 ratio for US (9.17). The corresponding for other countries is 4.56 (Russia), 4.83 (India) and 5.21 (China).

In Table 6.3 in addition to Gini coefficient and quintile income shares we report the percentage changes in Gini coefficient as well as the population and per capita incomes over time for the sample of four large countries. The quintile income shares are not reported in some years due to missing observations. The annual changes with the exception of US can vary greatly for China, India and Russia reflecting effects of economic crises or shocks to the economy. In case of Russia the large changes are always leading to increasing inequality, while in the cases of China and India large reductions in inequality can be observed in certain periods. The US annual income inequality change with the exception of 1991/92 and 1996/97 is small and not exceeding 10 per cent. The growth in population is highest in India, while the growth in GDP per capita is highest in China followed by US. Worth to mention is that the 1997 level of per capita income in US (30,573) unadjusted for PPP is more than 9.5 times of that of China (3,192) in 1997. Distinction should be made between relative and absolute values in comparing the four countries with respect to per capita GDP and populations.

Table 6.3 Development of Gini coefficient and quintile income shares by country

Year	Gini	DGini	Q1	Q2	Q3	Q4	Q5	Q5/Q1	Popul	GDP
A. China:										
1953	55.8	.	.	.	.	.	.	.	.	.
1964	30.5	-4.1	.	.	.	.	.	.	698355	960
1970	27.9	-1.4	.	.	.	.	.	.	818315	1008
1975	26.6	-0.9	.	.	.	.	.	.	916395	1041
1977	18.6	-15.0	.	.	.	.	.	.	943455	1050
1978	22.5	21.2	.	.	.	.	.	.	956165	1111
1979	23.7	5.0	.	.	.	.	.	.	969005	1165
1980	29.4	24.3	0.08	0.12	0.18	0.25	0.37	4.6	981235	1204
1981	19.7	-32.9	.	.	.	.	.	.	993861	1231
1982	23.6	19.6	0.08	0.14	0.18	0.22	0.38	4.4	1008599	1285
1983	24.4	3.6	0.09	0.15	0.17	0.24	0.36	4.1	1023288	1348
1984	23.4	-4.3	0.10	0.14	0.19	0.23	0.34	3.4	1036803	1479
1985	29.8	27.5	0.08	0.12	0.16	0.23	0.40	4.8	1051013	1622
1986	27.3	-8.7	0.08	0.12	0.16	0.26	0.39	5.1	1066758	1706

**Table 6.3 Development of Gini coefficient and quintile income shares
by country (Continued)**

Year	Gini	DGini	Q1	Q2	Q3	Q4	Q5	Q5/Q1	Popul	GDP
1987	28.0	2.6	0.07	0.11	0.16	0.28	0.38	5.4	1083998	1776
1988	31.9	14.1	0.07	0.11	0.16	0.29	0.38	5.7	1101596	1864
1989	29.8	-6.6	0.06	0.12	0.16	0.24	0.42	6.5	1118623	1860
1990	32.0	7.3	0.07	0.11	0.16	0.24	0.41	6.2	1135160	1912
1991	31.0	-3.2	0.06	0.11	0.15	0.31	0.36	5.6	1150756	2064
1992	33.0	6.5	0.06	0.11	0.16	0.26	0.42	6.9	1164951	2264
1993	29.5	-10.6	.	.	.	.	.	.	1178402	2470
1994	31.5	6.8	.	.	.	.	.	.	1190918	2672
1995	35.4	12.3	0.08	0.10	0.15	0.22	0.47	6.2	1203324	2894
1996	28.3	-19.9	.	.	.	.	.	.	1215414	3062
1997	29.3	3.3	.	.	.	.	.	.	1227177	3192
1998	40.3	37.7	0.08	0.10	0.15	0.22	0.46	5.6	1238599	3282
B. India:										
1950	41.0	.	.	.	.	.	.	.	368633	740
1951	36.0	-12.2	0.07	0.12	0.16	0.22	0.43	6.1	374563	762
1952	35.8	-0.6	0.07	0.12	0.16	0.22	0.42	6.0	380493	773
1953	34.9	-2.4	0.07	0.12	0.17	0.22	0.42	5.8	386423	802
1954	38.1	9.0	0.07	0.11	0.16	0.22	0.44	6.4	392352	816
1955	35.8	-6.1	0.08	0.12	0.16	0.22	0.43	5.8	398282	817
1956	35.0	-2.2	0.08	0.12	0.16	0.21	0.43	5.2	406188	840
1957	35.8	2.4	0.08	0.12	0.16	0.22	0.43	5.4	415083	830
1958	35.3	-1.5	0.08	0.12	0.16	0.22	0.42	5.7	422989	870
1959	36.0	2.0	0.08	0.12	0.16	0.22	0.43	5.5	431884	863
1960	35.6	-1.0	0.08	0.12	0.16	0.22	0.41	4.9	434849	917
1961	36.7	2.9	0.08	0.12	0.16	0.22	0.42	5.1	444470	925
1962	40.4	10.2	0.08	0.12	0.16	0.22	0.41	4.9	454585	941
1963	31.7	-21.4	0.09	0.13	0.17	0.22	0.40	4.5	465133	984
1964	35.2	11.0	0.09	0.13	0.17	0.22	0.40	4.5	476061	1033
1965	35.9	1.9	0.09	0.13	0.17	0.22	0.40	4.5	487324	992
1966	31.7	-11.7	0.08	0.13	0.17	0.22	0.40	4.7	498884	964
1967	34.0	7.2	0.09	0.13	0.17	0.22	0.39	4.6	510709	1016
1968	36.9	8.7	0.09	0.13	0.16	0.22	0.41	4.8	522775	1040
1969	31.8	-13.7	0.09	0.13	0.17	0.22	0.40	4.7	535065	1125
1970	31.3	-1.6	0.09	0.13	0.17	0.22	0.39	4.5	547569	1116
1972	32.3	1.5	0.09	0.13	0.16	0.22	0.41	4.8	573130	1092
1973	28.9	-10.6	0.09	0.13	0.17	0.23	0.38	4.2	586220	1091
1974	29.9	3.6	.	.	.	.	.	.	599643	1059
1975	40.5	35.5	.	.	.	.	.	.	613459	1127
1976	41.6	2.7	.	.	.	.	.	.	627632	1116
1977	32.1	-22.7	0.09	0.12	0.16	0.22	0.41	4.8	642134	1188
1978	35.6	10.8	.	.	.	.	.	.	656941	1218
1981	46.3	10.0	.	.	.	.	.	.	702821	1262
1983	31.3	-16.1	0.08	0.12	0.16	0.17	0.46	5.5	734072	1364
1986	32.2	0.9	0.09	0.12	0.16	0.21	0.41	4.8	781893	1512
1987	32.5	0.9	0.09	0.12	0.16	0.21	0.41	4.6	798680	1549
1988	32.0	-1.5	0.09	0.13	0.16	0.21	0.40	4.5	815590	1656
1989	31.3	-2.2	0.09	0.13	0.17	0.22	0.40	4.4	832535	1716
1990	30.7	-2.0	0.09	0.13	0.17	0.22	0.39	4.3	849515	1755

**Table 6.3 Development of Gini coefficient and quintile income shares
by country (Continued)**

Year	Gini	DGini	Q1	Q2	Q3	Q4	Q5	Q5/Q1	Popul	GDP
1991	32.5	5.8	0.09	0.12	0.16	0.21	0.42	4.7	866530	1716
1992	32.4	-0.3	0.09	0.13	0.16	0.21	0.41	4.7	882300	1773
1994	30.6	-2.7	0.13	0.12	0.16	0.21	0.38	3.0	913600	1954
1995	31.3	2.3	.	.	.	.	.	.	929358	2064
1996	32.2	2.7	.	.	.	.	.	.	945612	2217
1997	35.5	10.2	0.11	0.11	0.14	0.19	0.45	4.0	962378	2359
C. Russian Federation:										
1981	25.1	.	.	.	.	.	.	.	.	.
1986	26.1	0.8	.	.	.	.	.	.	.	.
1988	25.2	-1.7	.	.	.	.	.	.	.	.
1989	26.5	5.3	.	.	.	.	.	.	.	.
1990	26.0	-2.1	.	.	.	.	.	.	.	.
1991	30.7	18.2	.	.	.	.	.	.	148624	9434
1992	39.7	29.2	.	.	.	.	.	.	148689	8806
1993	36.5	-7.9	0.10	0.12	0.17	0.23	0.37	3.7	148520	8685
1994	44.8	22.6	.	.	.	.	.	.	148336	7619
1995	41.9	-6.5	0.05	0.10	0.15	0.22	0.47	8.7	148141	7093
1996	42.9	2.4	0.08	0.11	0.16	0.23	0.41	5.0	147739	7032
1997	38.8	-9.4	0.11	0.14	0.17	0.21	0.37	3.4	147304	7305
1998	39.6	1.9	0.10	0.13	0.16	0.20	0.41	4.2	146909	6951
D. USA:										
1944	43.6	.	.	.	.	.	.	.	.	.
1945	41.1	-5.7	.	.	.	.	.	.	.	.
1947	37.3	-4.6	0.05	0.12	0.19	0.23	0.41	8.2	.	.
1948	37.5	0.4	0.04	0.12	0.19	0.23	0.41	10.3	.	.
1949	37.8	0.9	0.04	0.12	0.19	0.24	0.41	10.3	.	.
1950	37.5	-0.7	0.05	0.12	0.17	0.23	0.43	9.5	152567	11095
1951	36.8	-1.9	0.05	0.12	0.18	0.23	0.42	8.3	155578	11656
1952	37.1	0.9	0.05	0.12	0.17	0.23	0.42	8.6	158589	11817
1953	35.2	-5.3	0.05	0.13	0.18	0.24	0.41	8.7	160596	12186
1954	37.6	7.0	0.05	0.12	0.18	0.23	0.42	9.4	163608	11851
1955	36.5	-3.0	0.05	0.12	0.18	0.24	0.41	8.6	166619	12464
1956	36.4	-0.2	0.05	0.12	0.18	0.24	0.41	8.2	169630	12464
1957	36.0	-1.1	0.05	0.13	0.18	0.24	0.40	7.9	172641	12454
1958	36.2	0.5	0.05	0.13	0.18	0.24	0.41	7.8	175652	12145
1959	36.8	1.8	0.05	0.12	0.18	0.24	0.41	8.4	177660	12724
1960	36.7	-0.4	0.05	0.12	0.18	0.24	0.41	8.6	180671	12817
1961	38.0	3.5	0.05	0.12	0.17	0.24	0.42	9.0	183691	12881
1962	37.0	-2.6	0.05	0.12	0.18	0.24	0.41	8.3	186538	13445
1963	36.9	-0.3	0.05	0.12	0.18	0.24	0.41	8.2	189242	13836
1964	36.9	-0.0	0.05	0.12	0.18	0.24	0.41	8.1	191889	14455
1965	36.6	-0.7	0.05	0.12	0.18	0.23	0.42	8.0	194303	15221
1966	36.7	0.4	0.05	0.12	0.18	0.23	0.42	8.4	196560	16005
1967	38.6	5.1	0.05	0.11	0.17	0.24	0.43	9.1	198712	16184
1968	37.1	-3.9	0.05	0.12	0.18	0.24	0.42	8.4	200706	16790
1969	37.7	1.6	0.05	0.12	0.18	0.24	0.41	7.9	202677	17175
1970	36.7	-2.8	0.05	0.11	0.17	0.24	0.42	8.8	205052	17011

**Table 6.3 Development of Gini coefficient and quintile income shares
by country (Continued)**

Year	Gini	DGini	Q1	Q2	Q3	Q4	Q5	Q5/Q1	Popul	GDP
1971	38.6	5.3	0.05	0.11	0.17	0.24	0.42	8.8	207661	17383
1972	38.1	-1.3	0.05	0.11	0.17	0.24	0.43	8.9	209896	18159
1973	38.8	1.7	0.05	0.11	0.17	0.24	0.42	8.7	211909	19039
1974	35.6	-8.0	0.05	0.12	0.18	0.24	0.41	7.8	213854	18733
1975	38.1	6.9	0.05	0.11	0.17	0.24	0.42	8.5	215973	18417
1976	37.4	-1.7	0.05	0.11	0.17	0.24	0.42	8.5	218035	19313
1977	39.1	4.6	0.05	0.11	0.17	0.24	0.42	8.8	220239	20068
1978	37.9	-3.1	0.05	0.11	0.17	0.24	0.43	8.9	222585	21002
1979	36.6	-3.5	0.05	0.12	0.18	0.25	0.41	8.1	225055	21447
1980	37.8	3.1	0.05	0.11	0.17	0.25	0.43	9.0	227225	21099
1981	39.5	4.7	0.05	0.11	0.17	0.25	0.43	9.2	229466	21443
1982	39.2	-0.8	0.04	0.11	0.17	0.24	0.44	9.8	231664	20838
1983	40.4	3.0	0.04	0.11	0.17	0.25	0.44	9.9	233792	21609
1984	39.6	-2.1	0.04	0.10	0.17	0.25	0.44	10.0	235825	23143
1985	39.7	0.4	0.04	0.11	0.17	0.25	0.43	9.7	237924	23800
1986	38.9	-2.1	0.05	0.11	0.17	0.24	0.43	9.4	240133	24363
1987	40.5	4.2	0.04	0.10	0.16	0.24	0.45	10.7	242289	24985
1988	40.7	0.4	0.04	0.10	0.16	0.24	0.45	10.7	244499	25799
1989	41.1	1.1	0.04	0.10	0.16	0.24	0.46	10.9	246819	26423
1990	40.5	-1.5	0.04	0.10	0.16	0.24	0.45	10.7	249440	26542
1991	38.6	-4.7	0.05	0.11	0.17	0.24	0.43	8.8	252124	26123
1992	42.7	10.5	0.04	0.09	0.16	0.24	0.47	12.3	254995	26755
1993	44.8	5.0	0.04	0.09	0.15	0.23	0.49	13.6	257746	27182
1994	42.4	-5.3	0.05	0.10	0.15	0.23	0.47	9.6	260289	28110
1995	44.3	4.5	0.04	0.09	0.15	0.23	0.49	13.2	262765	28629
1996	44.8	1.1	0.04	0.09	0.15	0.23	0.49	13.2	265190	29463
1997	40.4	-9.7	0.04	0.10	0.15	0.23	0.47	13.2	267744	30573
E. WIID mean:										
Mean	38.1	0.83	0.07	0.11	0.16	0.22	0.44	6.88	70676	8418

Year   Year of observation
Gini   Mean Gini coefficient
DGini   Change in Gini coefficient
Q1-Q5   First to Fifth quintile income shares
Q5/Q1   Ratio of the fifth to the first quintile income shares
Popul   Population in 1000
GDP   Read GDP per capita

The development of Gini coefficient together with quintile income shares and the Q5/Q1 ratio for individual countries are presented in Figures 6.1 to 6.4. In order to make the data levels comparable the Q5/Q1 ratio is divided by 10 and Gini coefficients are reported in decimal form in the 0-1 interval. Furthermore, the years where quintile income shares are missing are excluded from the graphs. Only years where all information is available are used in drawing the graphs. However, complete set of data including excluded observations can be viewed in Table 6.3.

Figure 6.1 shows that income share of the second and third quintiles in China are declining over time. Shifts in income are taken place mainly among the fourth and fifth quintiles. Inequality show increasing trend post 1985. The Q5/Q1 ratio is increasing sharply between 1984 and 1989 but it declines from 1992. Inequality in India has declined before 1972 and remained constant until 1994 then increased (see Figure 6.2). The income share of the first quintile in India has increase during 1950-1967 and 1992 onward. The Gini coefficient follows same temporal patterns as that of the fifth quintile. The Q5/Q1 ratio is declining over time before 1993. The corresponding numbers for Russia (see Figure 6.3) during 1993-98 are quite stable with the exception of 1995 when major shift in the quintile income shares is observed. In similarity with India the US Gini coefficient develops in the same way as income share of the fourth quintile (see Figure 6.4). Shifts in the income shares are from the second and third quintiles to the fifth quintile. The Q5/Q1 ratio fluctuates greatly in post 1980. Finally, development of Gini coefficient for all four countries is shown in Figure 6.5. The trend in inequality in US, China and Russia is positive, while that of India is negative but variable.

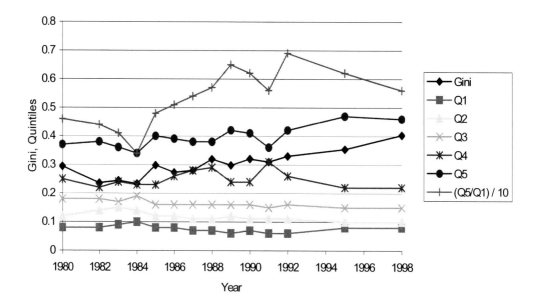

Figure 6.1. Development of Gini coefficient and income shares in China

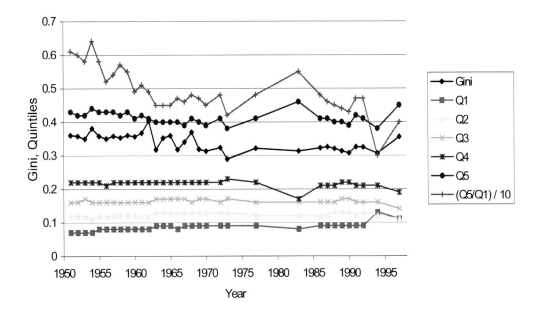

Figure 6.2. Development of Gini coefficient and income shares in India.

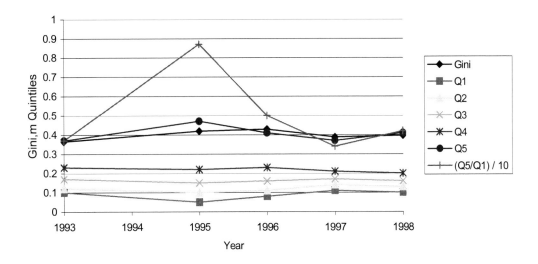

Figure 6.3. Development of Gini coefficient and income shares in Russian Federation.

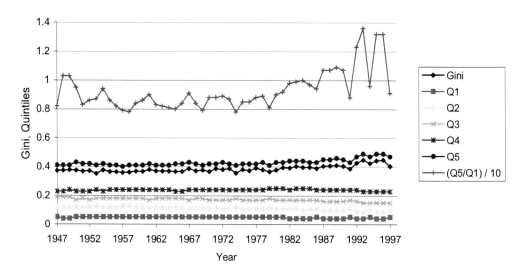

Figure 6.4. Development of Gini coefficient and income shares in USA

SUMMARY

Income inequality can be measured at different dimensions and levels of aggregation. In this chapter the within-country income inequality at the regional level was reviewed. Regional inequality in a selection of large countries with regional division is also examined. Here region is equivalent of states, provinces, federation or geographic regions within a country. The empirical results reported here are mainly based on the second half of the 20th century and four large countries including China, Russia, India and USA, as well as a number of smaller developing and transition countries.

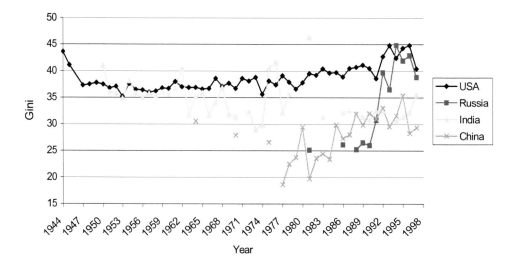

Figure 6.5. Development of Gini coefficient by country.

China has experienced a rapid economic growth post the economic reform accompanied by an increased inequality. The positive correlation between growth and inequality is in support of Kuznet's U-shaped curve. The level and development of inequality has been different by geographical location and economic sectors. In a number of studies attempts has been made to identify determinants of inequality across different provinces. The inequality is decomposed into components associated with inter-sector and intra-sector and inter-provincial and intra-provincial components. Regional equality has improved following openness, marketisation and convergence due to factor mobility. There is an indication of regional polarisation driven by structural differences between regions and provinces.

Regional inequality and polarisation is of a more serious policy concern in the Russian Federation. Heterogeneous economic development, size, ethnic and natural diversity of regions, restructuring policies and economic shocks caused disintegration and widening regional inequality and poverty. Data quality and measurement error also causes biased estimation of inequality and poverty. A restructuring of the education system is suggested to reduce inequality and to increase mobility.

The study of empirical relationship between growth, inequality and poverty in India shows that inequality is increased but poverty has declined marginally during the post reform period. Both inter-regional and intra-regional inequalities are equally emphasised. Policies that target reduction of inequality should be concentrated on reducing the within state urban and rural inequalities simultaneously. Economic growth and redistribution have aided poverty. However raising capital intensity in production have resulted in the shift in income distribution reducing the effects of economic growth. Rapid economic growth must be combined with pro-poor redistributive policies.

The US South has historically had lower income but higher inequality than the Non-South. Migration, skill, technology, gender and changing household characteristics affected increased income inequality. State level income per capita is stochastically converging over time to that of the nation. There is significant inter-state and intra-state inequality. Race, education, age and marital status are the key factors affecting household income inequalities. Distinction between transitory and permanent components of inequality matters.

Variations in income inequality in the selection of smaller countries show significant degree of heterogeneity in both level and development over time, as well as other sub-group characteristics dimensions. Empirical results suggest that inequality and poverty alter following various structural adjustment programs affecting the welfare of sub-groups differently.

The results of WIID show that inequality in US has increased slightly over time. The trend in inequality in India is negative but variable. There is a positive trend in inequality in China and Russian Federation following their economic reforms.

Chapter 7

DATA ISSUES AND DATABASES USED IN ANALYSIS OF GROWTH, POVERTY AND ECONOMIC INEQUALITY

ABSTRACT

This chapter focuses on the importance of data issues to the analysis of growth, poverty and economic inequality. We introduce a number of major databases frequently used in applied research on growth, poverty and global and international income inequality. A discussion of data quality, data consistency, variable definitions and measurement, changing population and household size leading to various necessary scale and price adjustment procedures will follow. The sampling design and various dimensions of sample dependency are also discussed. Based on the existing experience we identify a number of factors that are important in applied research. The focus is on these factors which impacts on reliability, precision, sensitivity and consistency of the results and conclusions drawn.

Keywords: Income inequality, poverty, growth, decomposition, databases, adjustment, Gini coefficient

INTRODUCTION

Availability of more and better quality data on income distribution plays a major role to the ongoing and increasing interest in measuring and understanding the level, causes and development of income inequality and poverty. The 1990s was signified by a shift in research previously focused on economic growth, identification of the determinants of economic growth and convergence in per capita incomes across countries to analysis of distribution of income, its development over time and identification of factors determining the distribution of income and poverty reductions. This shift among others reflects the increased availability of data and awareness of the growing disparity and the importance of redistribution and poverty reductions. The growing disparity calls for the analysis of various aspects of income inequality and poverty including their measurement, decomposition, causal factors and issues related to data underlying such analysis.

Literature on income inequality refers to the inequality of the distribution of individuals, household or some per capita measure of income. The most widely used index of inequality is the Gini coefficient (for reviews of economic inequality see Subramanian 1997a, Cowell 2000 and Chapter 2 of this monograph). The other notable measures of inequality are: the range, the variance, the squared coefficient of variation, the variance of log incomes, the absolute and relative mean deviations and Theil's two inequality indices. Inequality can have many dimensions. Economists are concerned specifically with the monetarily measurable dimension related to individual or household incomes. However, this is just one perspective and inequality can be linked to inequality in skills, education, opportunity, happiness, health, life expectancy, welfare, assets and social mobility. There are several studies focusing on the analysis of the interrelationship between inequality in earnings, poverty, education, growth and health. The measurement of inequalities is beyond the scope of this chapter. In Chapter 2 we presented reviews the recent advances in the measurement of inequality and gives attention to the interrelationship between income and non-income dimensions of inequality.

The extensive literature emerging in recent years are focused on the study of how the distribution of incomes across countries and globally has developed over time. The increased interest in income inequality may be both cause and effect of the availability of data. Availability of household surveys has been improved and several standardized databases have been created. These allow analysis of income distribution at the most disaggregate individual or per capita household levels. Income distribution is otherwise often analyzed at four levels of aggregation, namely global, continental or regional, international and intra-national levels. Income inequality can also be measured at a within-country regional level. Here the focus is on inequality in income distribution in large countries like China, India, Russia and US where regions include states, provinces, federations or distinct geographic locations within a country. Empirical studies at each level are extremely data intensive and which are based on the second half of the twentieth century.

A number of databases are frequently used in applied global, international, regional, intra-national growth, poverty and income inequality research. The descriptions of such databases are found in Summers and Heston (1991), Barro and Lee (1996), Deininger and Squire (1996) and Atkinson and Brandolini (2001). Despite the differences in objectives, country coverage, sources, units of measurement and income definitions each plays an important and complementary role in growth and inequality studies. Each set of data has both benefits and limitations. The choice of data seems to affect the conclusions drawn about trends in inequality. Quality, consistency, income definition and measurement, changing population, household size and various variable adjustment procedures are among important issues that are discussed. Consistency across countries and over time is a key issue to the reliability of results. The measurement of income, its decomposition by source and sub-groups with satisfactory coverage, sampling and representation of population are important in the generation of consistent information about the state of income inequality. An absence of such properties it might result in misleading or spurious results.

This paper is on the importance of data to the analysis of growth, poverty and economic inequality. We introduce a number of major databases frequently used in applied research. A systematic discussion of various aspects of each of these data follows. Based on existing experience we identify a number of factors that impacts on reliability, precision, sensitivity and consistency of the results and conclusions drawn. This review of its comprehensive analyses of various issues of data makes an important contribution to the literature of economic inequality.

Rest of the chapter is organised as follows. First we introduce a number of major databases frequently used in applied growth, poverty and global and international inequality research. In Section 3 a discussion of data quality and data consistency is given. Section 4 is on variable definitions and measurement. The issues of changing population and household size leading to various necessary scale and price deflator adjustment procedures, adjustment for unit characteristics and price regimes are discussed in Section 5 to 7. Sampling design and various dimensions of sample dependency are explored in Section 8. The last Section summarises the findings.

MAJOR DATABASES

Secondary cross-national data sets play an important role in empirical economic research offering cross-country panel data analysis. The Summers and Heston (1991), Barro and Lee (1996), Deininger and Squire (1996), World Income Inequality Database, and other by World Bank, United Nations and Luxembourg Income Study (LIS) are among the widely used secondary data sets containing information on education, population, trade, finance, health, politics and income distribution. The premise and pitfalls in the use of such data-sets and how they can be best assembled and used in income inequality (in OECD countries as a case study) are discussed by Atkinson and Brandolini (2001). The primary concern of Atkinson and Brandolini is with data quality and data consistency. These are two important but in their view neglected issues in most applied research. In the following we provide a brief description of each of the important data sets listed above. It extends the Atkinson and Brandolini (2001) by using up-to-date relevant references and available data sources.

The Barro and Lee Data Set

Many researchers have attempted to construct measure of educational attainment for international comparison. Education, as measure of human capital, has been a major variable used intensively in the specification of growth models and in explaining the variations in countries and regions growth rates. Most widely used such data is given by Barro and Lee (1996). This data has been updated to cover 109 countries with complete information observed at five years intervals for the years 1960-1995 and projections for 2000. The data set provides the estimates of age groups over age 15 and 25 and also the break-up by sex. It also includes the number of years of schooling achieved by the average person at the various levels and at all levels of schooling combined. A full description of the updates and implications together with the discussion about the estimation methods for the measurement of educational attainment is found in Barro and Lee (2000). These estimated values are also related to alternative international measures of human capital stocks (international test scores by students, international adult literacy test, estimates of market value of human capital, and OECD estimates of educational attainment). The complete data is available and freely downloadable from the web-site of the Center for International Development at Harvard University (http://www.ksg.harvard.edu/CID).

The Penn World Tables

The Penn World Tables (PWT) is probably the data set that most frequently used in Growth and income studies. It is also known as the Summers and Heston (1991) data. The PWT (http://www.nber.org/pwt56.html) provides statistical information in form of a set of national accounts economic time series covering 152 countries and 29 subjects including macro, industry, international trade, patent and others. The National Bureau for Economic Research (NBER) provides interface for retrieving subsets of data from the tables. A menu guides researchers through the process of selecting countries, data types, and date ranges.

The PWT database is particularly valuable for it historical depth. Another value is the relatively high quality and comparability of the data across countries. It follows the International Comparison Programme (ICP) effort to make cross-country comparisons possible on a consistent basis. Available data includes national income account statistics, balance of payments, populations, exchange rates, transportation, and standard of living indices. One important aspect of PWT is that it is based on ICP benchmark studies which provide expenditure data in a common set of parity prices including an overall purchasing power parity (PPP). An ICP benchmark study starts with a price survey of an identical set of goods and services in many countries. Drawing on the survey results, price parities for about 150 categories covering all of GDP are computed. These are used as weights in a complicated aggregation procedure to get country-specific price parties for various components and the overall PPP. The price parities and PPPs are used to convert individual countries' national currency expenditures to a common currency unit (most commonly US dollar) to make real quantity comparisons both between countries and over time. The estimates of capital stock like the human capital, factor inputs prices and price parties for each country's currency are seen as an invaluable contribution to the researchers round the world.

Potentials and pitfalls in international price and quality comparisons with reference to PWT are discussed in Heston and Summers (1996). The ICP benchmark pitfalls are summarized as a number of difficulties. First, the quality of the benchmark comparisons is determined by the quality of surveys and the national accounts of the country. Second, heterogeneity in price comparisons of identical or equivalent goods across countries creates substantial matching problems. Third, the choice of an aggregation method for putting together the benchmark prices is based on consumption and national accounts data. Finally, the benchmark estimates are limited to the expenditure side of national accounts which does not allow for sectoral (value added based) productivity comparisons. Despite the pitfalls, PWT provides a unique platform for working with both economic and non-economic variables to study development. Among important potentials of the PWT is that it allows real inter-country comparisons at different time periods. For a few applications based on PWT see Duro and Esteban (1998) in the context of decomposition of cross-country income inequality, Bhargava, Jamison, Lau and Murray (2001) who modelled the effects of health on economic growth, and Park (2001) analyzes the trends in global distribution of income.

The Luxembourg Income Study

The Luxembourg Income Study (LIS) was created in 1983 under the joint sponsorship of the government of Luxembourg and the Center for Population and Policy Studies. The primary goal of this project is to promote comparative research on the economic status of populations in different countries. LIS is a compilation of large, national microdata on a broad array of employment income, taxes, transfers, demographic, expenditure, and occupation data. There are now more than 20 OECD countries that are supplying data to the LIS. Work on adding data from more developed countries is in progress. However, the member countries do not supply data on an annual basis, as survey data are not collected consecutively every year. These data are therefore arranged in a number of five years waves, 1979-1983, 1984-1988, 1989-1994, and 1995-1999. It permits both cross sectional and cross temporal analysis. The LIS data are available (http://www.lisproject.org/). User support files are available via an anonymous FTP site to acquire data information. For the use of LIS data and description of various dimensions of the data see several recent studies such as: Jäntti and Danziger (2000) who studied income poverty in advanced countries, Atkinson and Brandolini (2001) evaluating the use of secondary data in the study of income inequality, Iacoviello (1998) on income dynamics, Mahler (2001) on income inequality and Ritakallio (2001) on trends of poverty and inequality among OECD countries.

The World Income Inequality Database

The WIDER-UNDP World Income Inequality Database (WIID) is an expanded version of the Klaus Deininger and Lyn Squire 1997 World Bank database.[1] The full description of the data is found in Deininger and Squire (1996). The expanded version contains information on income inequality, income shares, and a number of variables indicating the source of data, and quality classification for 151 developed, developing and transition countries observed on an irregular basis mainly covering the period post 1950 until 1998. The current version of the database, Version 1.0 released on September 2000, is in an easily retrievable, exportable, and analyzable format. It is publicly available in the WIDER web-site (http://www. wider.unu.edu/wiid/wiid.htm) for browsing and free downloads to facilitate further analysis and debate on global income inequality. The document fully describes the data, background information, quality guidance and instructions is available for download on the above web-site.

For a limited number of applications for using this data set and its earlier versions are: Deininger and Squire (1996 and 1998) for description of the data, Cornia and Kiiski (2001) on inequality, growth and poverty in the era of liberalization and globalization, Cornia and Court (2001) who studied trends in income distribution in the post World War II period, Atkinson and Brandolini (2001) on the use of secondary data sets, Wan (2002b) on income inequality and growth in transition economies, Biancotti (2003) on polarisation of distribution of income, and Li, Squire and Zou (1998) on variations in income inequality. The later data has drawn on Deininger and Squire (1996) was also used by Ravallion (2003a) to test

---

[1] The data sources distributed by their share of total number of observations are as follows: WIDER (42.7%), Deininger and Squire (44.8%), and remaining sources (UNICEF/ICDC, LIS and WB HEIDE) 12.5%.

inequality convergence. The WIID data has recently been utilised by Heshmati (2003 and 2004a) to study the impact of globalizations on income inequality and poverty and by Heshmati (2004b) to analyse the relationship between growth, inequality and poverty. Other cases of application based on WIID are analysis of the world distribution of income and income inequality (Chapter 4 of this monograph), analysis of continental and sub-continental income inequality (Chapter 5), and analysis of regional inequality in selected large countries (Chapter 6).

Galbraith and Kum (2003) suggest the data published by the University of Texas on Inequality Project (UTIP) which is based on the Industrial Statistics database published annually by the United Nations Industrial Development Organization (UNIDO) as an alternative global inequality dataset. Deininger and Squire (2002) present an update of their 1996 dataset. The new data cover more observations with increase coverage for developing and transition countries and is based on micro level surveys.

The World Development Indicators

World Development Indicators (WDI) is the premier data source of World Bank available on global economy from 1960 onwards. However, several series of large number of developing countries are missing prior to 1970. WDI is annual compilation of data about global development. WDI 2002 includes approximately 800 indicators in 87 tables, organized in six sections: World View, People, Environment, Economy, States and Markets, and Global Links. The tables cover 152 economies and 14 country groups with basic indicators for another 55 economies. The Economy data part contains statistical data for over 550 development indicators and time series data from 1960-2001 for 207 countries and 18 country groups. The data includes social, economic, financial, natural resources, and environmental indicators. More details on the data and annual subscription to access WDI are found in the World Bank web site (http://www.worldbank.org/data/). For a few applications using WDI see: Anand and Kanbur (1997) in the context of inequality and development, Bhargava (2001) who examine stochastic specification of the international GDP series, and Addison and Heshmati (2004) who studied the global determinants of FDI flows to the developing countries.

The Human Development Indicators

Recently World Bank also produces tables on Poverty and Hunger for countries which included in the HDI database (http://www.developmentgoals.org/Data.htm). The tables provides information about people living on below $1 a day, poverty gap at $1 a day, percentage share of income or consumption held by 20% of the poorest and prevalence of child malnutrition. Description of sample survey data from 91 countries that has been used by Milanovic (2002a) is also found on the World Bank web-site on available Research Data sets (http://econ.worldbank.org/). Studies based on the World Bank World Tables include income mobility by Parker and Gardner (2002), Ravallion (1997) on economic growth and human development, and Noorbakhsh (1998) who computed human development index.

The Millennium Development Goals Indicators Database

On an annual basis the United Nations Development Program (UNDP) in its Human Development Report (HDR) also publishes Tables on various issues like poverty, income inequality, education, health, etc. The 2003 UNDP HDR (2003) published Tables on Millennium Development Goals (MDG) indicators.[2] The United Nations Statistics Division maintains the recently created global Millennium Indicators Database (http://millenniumindicators.un.org). The data is compiled from international data series provided by international data agencies. The database forms the statistical basis for annual report to the UN General Assembly on global and regional progress towards the Millennium Development Goals and their targets. The database provides updated data to the UN system organizations, various research institutes and individual researchers to be used in research related to the MDGs. For a recent study of the progress towards the MDG in Africa see Sahn and Stifel (2003).

DATA QUALITY AND DATA CONSISTENCY

The original sources of data described above are often found in the national household surveys, administrative income tax record data, social security and labour market agency records. Each source has its benefits and limitations. For instance, income tax record is often limited to incomes exceeding a certain level, while household surveys may not be representative of the population studied.

Some data sources like the LIS data is related to standardised and internationally comparable micro-data-sets. Despite an increased data availability and improved data quality, there is a gap between theoretical advancement on determinants of income and wealth and their distribution and the empirical investigations due to lack of sufficiently detailed high quality data on distribution. To mention an example, Elbers, Lanjouw and Lanjouw (2003) provides micro-level estimation of poverty and inequality based on expenditure per capita using Ecuadorian data that have levels of precision comparable to those of commonly used survey based welfare estimates. This is an improvement over survey based estimates which are only consistent for very large number of households.

In the following section we focus on secondary data sources. A comparison of different data sources show that the choice of data affects the conclusions drawn about trends in income inequality for a single country over time. For instance, differences in income concept, income source, measurement unit and methodology may affect not just the level but also the trend in income inequality. In an attempt to link secondary data sets Atkinson and Brandolini (2001) compare four secondary data sets including the studies of United Nations in the 1950s and 1960s, the World Bank compilation in the 1970s, the Deininger and Squire data-set, and

---

[2] In the 2000 UN Millennium Declaration, countries committed to work together to meet concrete 8 goals consisting of 18 targets for advancing development and reduction of poverty by 2015 or earlier. The MDGs are: (i) to eradicate extreme poverty and hunger, (ii) to achieve universal primary education, (iii) to promote gender equality and empower woman, (iv) to reduce child mortality, (v) to improve maternal health, (vi) to combat HIV/AIDS, malaria and other disease, (vii) to ensure environmental sustainability, and (viii) to develop a global partnership for development.

the WIID data-set for the period 1945 to 1970 but limiting their attention to the (European) OECD countries.

Atkinson and Brandolini (2001) analyzed the secondary data sets on income distribution which make a number of suggestions regarding the construction, development and the use of secondary data sets. They conclude among others that such data should be a fully documented commutation of earlier work and provide a complete picture of available information to their users. Guidelines are given regarding the choices to be made in defining the distribution under consideration, sources of the data and ways to deal with differences in definition across countries or over time. The authors find the differences in definitions quantitatively important, but doubt whether simple adjustments are satisfactory solution to the heterogeneity of the available statistics.

Country heterogeneity is an important issues that analyst should account for. Estimation of unobservable country heterogeneity may not be a satisfactory measure in pooling data. Lloyd, Morrissey and Osei (2001) in testing validity of pooling countries in large panel in empirical analysis of the aid and trade relationship find significant differences in results for distinct panels. If the nature of the time series relationship underlying specific observation differs, these should not be pooled into one panel. Results from such data might be misleading if not spurious. Going back to micro-data authors highly recommended the use of data sets where the observations are as fully consistent as possible. Several arguments for the use of consistent micro-data can be found in for instance: Heady, Mitrakos and Tsakloglou (2001) who analyse the comparative effects of cash transfers on inequality and poverty by using consistent household data, Foster and Shorrocks (1991) on subgroup consistent measures of poverty, and Salas (1998) on welfare-consistent inequality indices in changing populations.

Many secondary data sets contain multiple observations. The presence of multiple observations for the same country and at the same period might be due to the differences in definition, levels, coverage, weights or methods of calculation. The definition of income may differ by source across country and time. The problem of consistency across country and over time is a key issue to the reliability of results in country comparison studies based on panel data. The issue of consistency is in particular emphasised in the WIID database. However, accounting for consistency in a very strict way leave researchers with a very small sample of countries and observations inadequate for analysis of income inequality at the global, regional or international levels.

VARIABLE DEFINITIONS AND MEASUREMENT

In this section the focus is mainly on key variable containing the WIID database. The choice is motivated by the fact that WIID embodies several other data sources. The WIID database contains information on Gini coefficient (measured in percentage points), income shares (accruing to the specified part of the population), and the number of variables indicating the source of data including area coverage, population coverage, income definition, source of the data,[3] and quality classification. Some of the Gini estimates originated from the

---

[3] A bibliography on the original sources of each data point is provided on the WIDER web-site. For time-series or cross-sectional analysis based on WIID, one should verify the consistency of the data sources for chosen

source, while others have been computed from grouped data at UNU/WIDER using mainly POVCAL software.[4]

Different concepts of income are used in the WIID database. For instance, income is measured as: (i) gross/factor/market income, (ii) net income including/excluding non-taxable transfers, (iii) gross/net monetary income, (iv) gross/net taxable income, (iv) gross/net earnings, (v) gross/net expenditure, (vi) disposable income, and (vi) pre/post tax and transfer income.[5] The concepts of multidimensionality and complexity of the income is a good indicator of the many consistency and quality problems associated with the use of such databases. Lack of consistent and high quality micro data across countries does not leave a better choice to the researchers.

Income can be decomposed into different income sources used in income inequality measurement by income sources (for examples, such decomposition and comparison see Shorrocks (1982), Lerman and Yitzhaki (1985), Cheng (1996), Liebbrandt, Woolard and Woolard (2000), Milanovic (2000), Wan (2001), Morduch and Sicular (2002), and Podder and Chatterjee (2002)). Understanding the key sources of inequality is important. The inequality can be linked to the cause of income sources. Blacklow and Ray (2000) in their comparison of income and expenditure inequality used Australian unit record data and found inconsistencies between the two inequality movements. The within household groups inequality dominated the between groups component.

A decomposition analysis by income sources throws new lights on the identification and the process of generating income inequality. Lerman and Yitzhaki decomposed income into: head wages and salaries, head self-employment earnings, spouse earnings, other family earnings, transfers and property income sources. Cheng used household survey data from 1994 collected from 5 grain producing provinces in China to study the impacts of agricultural activities on inequality in non-agricultural cases by province and various sources of household income. Wan studied changes in regional inequality in rural china by the measures of decomposing inequality change by the Gini index. He divided the Gini index into: structural effects, real inequality effects, interactive effects and aggregate full contribution from wages, farming and residual income components. Milanovic in testing the median-voter hypothesis, income inequality and income redistribution used household budget survey data on factor, gross and disposable income definitions. Results showed that different concepts highlight different aspects of distribution.

Liebbrandt, Woolard and Woolard (2000), in their analysis of the contribution of various income (remittances, wage, capital, state transfers, agriculture and self-employment) components to income inequality in the rural former homelands of South Africa found that wage income is both the main income component and also the most important source of inequality for the African population. To improve wage earnings the policy induced change is

---

countries across time and make necessary corrections to make the national data comparable across countries in terms of income concepts and reference units. However, it should be noted that Atkinson and Brandolini (2001) in their review of the secondary data sets doubt whether simple adjustments are satisfactory solution to the heterogeneity of the available statistics.

[4] POVCAL is a statistical program designed by Shaohua Chen, Gaurav Datt, and Martin Ravallion at DEC-RG, World Bank. It is an easy to use and reliable tool for routine poverty assessment work. It uses sound and accurate methods for calculating poverty and inequality measures with only a basic PC and grouped distributional data. For an overview of the program, data requirement, and free downloads see the web-site: http://www.worldbank.org/html/prdph/lsms/tools/povcal/

that they should target the rural labour market and wages. The linkage between the labour market and inequality are analysed by using a panel of African households in Kwazulu-Natal studied by Liebbrandt and Woolard (2001) showed that the contribution of wage income is uneven across different levels of aggregation and across time suggesting complex patterns of inequality generation.

The reference unit when referring to an income distribution, often labelled as unit of measurement or income recipients can be different from one data set to another. It is often defined as: (i) household or family, (ii) household or family equivalent (scale squared, social assistance, OECD, Oxford and HBAI), (iii) person, household per capita, head of household, or simply the tax unit. Here family is defined as family plus unrelated individual family excluding non-dependent.

The sampling unit can be a person, household or family. The enumerated unit determining the inequality are ranked by person, household, family, or head of household. In some cases the person is both sampling and enumeration units, while in other the household is the sampling unit, but following per capita equalisation procedure the person is enumeration unit. The distribution in the former is the true person distribution, while in the later inconsistency may appear as a result of the fact that the distribution consists of multiple observations within a household.

The area coverage is another key factor affecting the sample representativeness of the population. It refers to the land area included in the original sample surveys: (i) total land, (ii) urban, capital, cities, metropolitan, (iii) rural, rural interior or regions.

The population coverage refers to the population covered in the sample surveys in the chosen land area. It include: (i) all, (ii) different shares of all, all excluding different sub-groups, (iii) different sub-sectors, (iv) income recipients, (v), taxpayers, or other sub-groups of the population. Inequality can be decomposed by different subgroups (Shorrocks 1984) where the overall inequality can always be calculated from the size, mean and inequality value of each population subgroup. For instance Li (2001) examined changes in poverty profile in China by localities and population sub-groups. Chakravarty (2001) studied the variance of a subgroup decomposable measure of inequality. At more aggregate level inequality decomposition can be made by rural-urban or agriculture-non-agricultural industrial and service sectors.

In order to improve the reliability of results from secondary data sets, the WIDER data points have been assigned to two broad categories 'Reliable' and 'Less Reliable' data observations. The assignments were based on various sources of information obtained from the primary information. The primary information concerns: survey composition, sampling methods, time period, non-response, weighting methods, income definitions, coding and various statistical adjustments. The Reliable earnings, income or expenditure data refer to entire national, rural or urban populations of a country. It further refers to the employed, economically active, or other such subsets of the entire, rural or urban populations of a country. Labelling an observation as Less reliable data reflects the presence of missing information, inconsistencies, errors in grouping or estimation methods, small population coverage, or other factors limiting the data quality.[6]

---

[5] Market income includes the earnings of all household members and all incomes from interest, dividends, rents and other market sources. Disposable income is equal to market income plus transfers minus taxes.

[6] Detailed information on micro data collection, sampling, data quality, documentation and various aspects of data sources can be found for instance at: http://psidonline.isr.umich.edu/ on Panel Study of Income Dynamics, at

The variable describing the data source is a variable indicating the source from which the observation value has been obtained. It is divided into primary and secondary sources. Most databases used in cross-country comparisons belong to the second class of data sources.

EQUIVALENCE SCALES

Households differ in many respects other than income like the size and the composition which affect the well being of the household members. Heterogeneity in actual and estimated consumption needs by age of the member of household and the presence of economies of scale due to the household size, makes it necessary that some equivalence methods of scales be used. The method allows comparison of households of different sizes and age compositions and calculation of effective household size by assigning the household members a weight. The assigned weight is based on representative consumption amounts. The Gini coefficient will differ by the applied equivalized households or scale methods of individual household members. In addition to the data comparability, the equivalence scale reflects the cost of additional members for a household by comparing the inequality before and after household size increases.

There is a number ways to construct an equivalence scale. The first measure is an overestimated extreme equivalence scale, where income equal to the total amount of household income assigned to each household member, i.e. a weight of 1 is given to all members. A second extreme measures is an underestimated scale obtained by dividing the aggregate income by the number of households members (n), i.e. giving a weight of 1/n to each member. In the later case in the estimation of the income distribution adjustment is made for the household size. Several other but intermediate scale measures are possible to use. One smooth measure is the square-root-scale where the weight assigned is $1/\sqrt{n}$. Another intermediate possibility is to assign heterogeneous weights, $\sum_{i=1}^{n} w_i$, to different household members (i) by age and gender. For instance, to assign the first adult in a household a weight of 1, the second (or other) adults 0.7 and each child a weight of 0.5, or alternatively a range of weights according to the ages and needs of the children. Blacklow and Ray (2000) using Australian data finds income and expenditure inequality estimates sensitive to the equivalence scale used as the household size deflator.

There is a desire that the differences among individuals ability and needs be reflected in the designing of tax-and-transfer systems. As a measure Atkinson and Bourguignon (1987) and Jenkins and Lambert (1993) developed sequential Lorenz dominance in multi-dimensional framework to rank income distributions when needs differ. Mayshar and Yitzhaki (1995) suggested a method for identifying indirect tax reforms that adhere to uni-dimensional criterion for a Dalton's principle of transfers, approving a small enough transfer from rich to the poor. Mayshar and Yitzhaki (1996) extended the approach to a two-dimensional criterion for a Dalton-improving tax reform, when there is social approval for transfers from the more able to the less able and from the less needy to the more needy households. Households' size, age composition, or health status are the indications of

http://www.diw.de/english/sop/index.html on The German Socio-Economic Panel Study, and at the World Bank data-site http://www.worldbank.org/poverty/data/index.htm for various data sources and from different countries.

heterogeneous needs and are distinct from heterogeneous abilities. The later approach and its application and comparison with other criteria is carried out by using the UK household expenditure and tax data. Cowell (2000) in his analysis of income distribution as a multivariate problem, proposes that the households or families should be distinguished by characteristics other than income referring to income sources and needs. Recently, Ebert and Moyes (2003) proposes a new and normative approach for adjusting household income by introducing an equivalent income and size adjusting functions in order to compare the living standards of households with different needs.

Despite various adjustments and modification of household data like those discussed above, few researchers explore motivations for measurement of inequality. Kaplow (2002) criticises the large body of literature devoted to various measures or indices of income inequality, in which little attention is given to the question to measure inequality. The reasons for measurement will determine whether and how measurement should be done. Descriptive measures (used for instance in the regression analysis of relationship between inequality and growth) and Normative measures (designed to have direct policy relevance) are examined by Kaplow. The latter depending on the economic theory and field of empirical application may be useful and an appropriate measure of inequality. Kaplow emphasis that more attention to be devoted to the purposes of measurement, which affects how the practice of measurement should be undertaken.

ADJUSTMENTS FOR UNIT CHARACTERISTICS

At the micro level changes in the composition of families are important factors that must be accounted for in the analysis of distribution of income of households. Recently, US income inequality by sub-groups like gender, marital status, full/part-time employment, over time, and contribution of growing wage disparities and changing family composition on the overall income inequality between 1979 and 1996 estimated by Burtless (1999). Burtless examines the trend in overall inequality using the concept of adjusted equivalent personal income. The definition of equivalent income used is written as: $Y_A = Y_U / (F/H) \times H^\theta$ where Y_A is the adjusted money income per person, Y_U is the unadjusted total family income, F is the number of persons in nuclear family unit, H is the number of persons in household, and θ is the assumed adjustment parameter for family size. It can also, as previously mentioned, to reflect the needs of individual family members. If family and household sizes are equal, $F=H$, then $Y_A = Y_U / H^\theta$ and in a single-person household, $F=1$, $Y_A = Y_U$. The adjustment resulted in a rise in the Gini coefficient of family income inequality from 0.365 to 0.425 or about 16.4% increases. While growing pay disparities especially among the men is the direct contributor to the trend in overall inequality, much of the rise is found to be due to the shifts in family composition and other causes. The impact of growing correlation of husband and wife earned income and the increasing percentage of persons who live in single-adult families and with more unequal incomes on overall inequality are found to be significant. Burtless used US Current Population Survey (CPS) files show that the higher gender earnings disparity, growing positive correlation of income within families, and growing proportion of families with single adults explains 33-44%, 13% and 21-25% of the increase in overall inequality respectively.

There are numerous empirical cases of adjustment procedures to incomes. One such case is Biewen (2002a) on dynamics of equivalent incomes in Germany. Another is Jäntti and Danziger (2000) on equivalent scale for aggregate and different population sub-groups in industrialized countries. Paraje (2002) adjusted income for adult equivalent and economies of scale to compute polarisation measures in the Greater Buenos Aires. Finally, Schmidt (2002) analyzed income polarisation using cross-national equivalent files.

In earlier discussion we showed that the age composition in a household resulted in heterogeneity in the needs by households requiring adjustments and scales. In addition to the heterogeneity impacts of the within household age composition, the distribution of age at the aggregate level has implications for cross-country studies. Based on micro data on self-assessment of health status Gerdtham and Johannesson (2000) estimated income-related inequality in Sweden with respect to life-years, health status and quality-adjusted life-years (QALYs). Survival and quality-adjusted survival years in different income groups is estimated. Results indicate that inequalities in health favouring the higher income groups. Health inequality increases with age. Income affects health and the other way around. Income is correlated with other factors that affect health such as education and unemployment. Gerdham and Johannesson's results show that the inequality comparisons between countries may be affected by differences in the countries age distribution.

At the macro level changing population and its impacts on the performance of inequality indices in a single dynamic analysis and in cross-country static welfare analysis explored by Salas (1998). The standard welfare-consistent inequality indices satisfy the marginal population replication axiom or marginal entrants. These indices are found to perform well when comparing inequality over different population distributions. As a further line of research Salas recommends analyses of the performance of population subgroup decomposable inequality indices under changing subgroup populations.

Various studies have found large differences and conflicting results in terms of how income distribution in the world has changed. Svedborg (2002) attributes the differences to the fact that those studies employ: (i) different measurements of income, (ii) different measurement of income distribution, and that (iii) they weight/select countries and populations differently. In comparison of countries many studies as measurement of income have used: national per capita GNP converted to US dollars according to current official exchange rates or national GNP per capita adjusted for differences in purchasing power across countries. The later is more reliable by taking into consideration for the differences in the relative prices of goods and services sold locally or internationally by the poor or rich countries.

The most frequently used alternative measurement of income distribution are: the ratios of the per capita incomes in the richest and poorest countries at certain times called Kuznets ratios, and the income distribution over the entire range of countries, such as Gini coefficient. None of the two measures in Svedborg's view however, capture transitions or changes in position of countries in per capita income ranking over time. Estimation of changes in world income distribution must be taken into consideration for countries population size and its variations over time. Then the Gini coefficient will reflect changes in per capita incomes across countries, as well as changes in respective countries' share of the world's population.

Most studies have used different measurement of the relative distribution neglecting how the absolute differences (gap) in income between countries have developed over time.

As mentioned previously, data sources and income definitions may result into different and conflicting inferences. Capeau and Decoster (2003) explain the driving forces behind the differences in the two extreme positions on rise (Sala-i-Martin 2002a and 2002b) and fall (Milanovic 2002a and 2002b) of inequality by income measures, population weighted inequality measures and inequality among citizens irrespective of location. See also Atkinson and Brandolini (2001) for discussion of the use of several different databases and their implications for inferences about the level and temporal patterns of income inequality.

In regression analysis a typical way to deal with differences in definition across countries or over time is by introducing dummy variables to adjust (additively or multiplicatively) for differences in, say, income definitions. There is a risk that selection of countries and years may bias the result. The Deininger and Squire (1996) propose comparison of paired estimates, i.e. comparison of gross and net incomes for the same country at the same period as preferred method. Furthermore, the dummy adjustment may also be unsatisfactory for demographic factors. Atkinson and Brandolini (2001) conclude that simple dummy variable adjustments mentioned above are unsatisfactory solutions to capture the country, income definition and time period heterogeneity in the existing data. They prefer the use of data sets where observations are as fully consistent as possible.

ADJUSTMENTS FOR PRICES REGIMES

The cost of living varies across regions which has implications for comparisons of welfare levels of households situated in different regions within a country. Such cost heterogeneity has been neglected in welfare programs. Construction of bilateral and multilateral spatial cost of living and welfare indices developed by Kakwani and Hill (2002) is applied to construct urban and rural cost of living and welfare indices for five regions of Thailand. This price adjustment has implications for poverty and inequality measurement. Maasoumi, Diamond, Nieswiadomy and Slottje (1994) also studied the effects of relative price changes and cost of living adjustment on welfare indices.

Among other examples of empirical cases of price adjustment to mention are Ravallion and Chen (1999) who used Chinese provinces micro data to find that two-thirds of the conventionally measured increases in the post reform inequality vanishes when market-based valuation methods are used and allowances are made for regional cost-of-living differences and structural changes in the rural economy. Non-farm income, grain production and higher returns to farmland increased inequality, while lower returns to physical capital and private transfers reduced inequality. Declich and Polin (2002), in analysing absolute poverty in Italy have taken into account for possible effects of different costs of living in the northern and southern areas. The regional variation in the cost of living is accounted for in the price adjustment to regional inequality.

Pendakur (2002) finds the standard adjustment for price regimes by using expenditure-independent price deflators and price-independent equivalence scale not fully adequate adjustment measures. Pendakur shows that more flexible expenditure-dependent price deflators and price-dependent equivalence scale affects both the level and trend in measuring family expenditure inequality in Canada over 1969-1997. In the later rich and poor and large and small families are allowed to respond to price changes differently. The price deflators vary across regions and overtime. Unlike the cases described above Blacklow and Ray (2000) using Australian data did find income and expenditure inequality estimates sensitive to the equivalence scale used as the household size deflator, but not to the cost of living index which used as the price deflator.

SAMPLING DESIGN AND SAMPLE DEPENDENCY

The techniques of simple random sampling are seldom appropriate in the empirical analysis of income distribution. Cowell and Jenkins (2000) in this relation has draw attention to potential problems and proposes various types of weighting schemes required from the point view of welfare-economics, sampling design or estimation problem considerations. The different types of weights can have different implications for the sampling distribution of estimated welfare indices. The weights reflect endogenous and exogenous attributes that may affect the way in which we choose to aggregate the information about the income distribution. The attributes here refer to the household size and partitioning households into internally homogenous subgroups. The extent of bias on the estimated welfare index will thus depend on the degree of heterogeneity of population by size, asymmetry in the composition of sample and the sample variance.

Conventional inference procedures assume independent samples when testing for inequality changes over time. The issue of inference for testing the interpolated Gini coefficient and the generalised entropy class indices with dependent samples is examined by Zheng and Cushing (2001). They establish inference tests for changes in inequality indices with completely independent samples (PSID), and then generalise it to cases with partially dependent samples (CPS). The effects of sample dependency on standard errors of inequality changes are examined through simulation studies and applications to the CPS and PSID data.[7] An inspection of the results suggests that sample dependency has substantial effects, in the range of 3.3 to 17.1 per cent, on the standard errors if the samples are strongly correlated/or have significant overlap requiring a method to correct for sample dependency. Yitzhaki (1991), Karagiannis and Kovacevic (2000), Ogwang (2000) and Giles (2002) are a few recent examples of proposing methods to compute the Gini index and to calculate the (Jackknife) variance estimator for the Gini coefficient. In the latter case the Gini measure is obtained from an artificial OLS or seemingly unrelated regressions. For the empirical part the Penn World Tables five-year interval data on 133 countries in the years 1970-1985 is used.

The issue of statistical inference for inequality and poverty measurement with dependent data is also discussed by Schluter and Trede (2002). This concerns another dimension of dependency, namely data contemporaneously dependent across members of the same household. Much empirical research is based on methods assuming that income is an independent and identically distributed random variable. Application of such methods to contemporaneously dependent data produces biased results. Monte Carlo results show that

---

[7] For recent examples of sample dependency and block bootstrapping in testing for first and second order stochastic dominance based on balanced panel of PSID and Swedish household data-sets see Maasoumi and Heshmati (2003).

standard errors in the presence of dependence are larger regardless of the nature of the intra-household correlation. The authors develop distribution-free non-parametric methods of statistical inference when there are contemporaneous dependencies and consider Generalized Entropy index of inequality, Gini coefficient, Lorenz curves and common poverty indices FGT (Foster, Geer and Thorbecke (1984)). In comparison of the performance of the proposed method to the standard ones assuming various degree of dependency, the conclusion is that there is a large gain in precision if one takes dependencies into account without any loss at the absence of dependencies. The sample size also matter for the biasedness of the Gini coefficient. Deltas (2003) finds a negative relationship between Gini coefficient and populations size. The Gini coefficient is downward biased in small populations when income is generated by common distributions like log normal and exponential. This is relevant especially when comparing Gini coefficient across sub-populations of small sizes.

SUMMARY

There exists a number of databases that frequently are being used in applied global, international and regional growth and income inequality and poverty research. Although, these databases differ by objectives, country coverage, sources, unit of measurement and income definitions, yet each one play an important role in inequality studies and by serving as complement to each other. Each data have of course their benefits and limitations and the choice of data affects the conclusions drawn about trends in inequality for a single or groups of countries and over time.

Quality, consistency, income definition and measurement, changing population and household size and various variable adjustment procedures are among important data issues discussed here. Consistency across countries and over time is a key issue to the reliability of results in panel data studies. However, an invalid pooling due to differences in the nature of the time series relationship underlying the data might result in misleading or spurious results.

Measurement of income, its decomposition by source and sub-group with satisfactory coverage, sampling and enumeration units and representative of population is important in generation of consistent information about the state of income inequality. Heterogeneity in ability, in actual consumption and consumption needs by age, gender and size of households and presence of economies of scale requires calculation of representative consumption amounts by using some measures of equivalence methods of scales. The cost of living varies by location primarily divided into urban, rural or regions. Empirical results show that estimates of income and consumption inequalities are sensitive to the cost of living index_as the price deflator.

Higher gender earnings disparity, growing positive correlation of income within families, and growing proportion of families with single adults explains large parts of the increase in overall inequality. An incorrect assumption about independent and identically distributed income over time and contemporaneous dependent across members of household produces biased results. Few existing studies show that there is a large gain in precision if one takes dependencies into account.

Chapter 8

SUMMARY AND CONCLUSIONS

There has been an increased interest in the 1990s in the measurement of the level and searches for the causes and the development of global income inequality. This period signifies also by a shift in focus from the issues of convergence of per capita income to the distribution of income and its development over time across regions and countries of the world. This shift in focus is a reflection of increased awareness of the importance of growth, redistribution and poverty reduction, as well as availability of more and better data. Various internal and external factors have resulted in growing disparities within and foremost between countries of the world. The growing disparity motivates the analysis of the trends in global income inequality.

This manuscript addressed a number of issues crucial to the measurement and analysis of global income inequality. The issues include the concepts, measurement and decomposition of inequality, and the analysis of the world distribution of income and inequality measured at different ranges of aggregation. Other areas of interest are brief investigation of the relationship between macroeconomic variables, inequality, poverty and globalization. The gained experiences from the above analyses are then reflected in the discussion of the data underlying the literature and their role in the generation of the differences in conclusions drawn regarding the direction of changes in global income inequality. Remaining part of this chapter summarises the results from the review of literature and the author's findings based on the WIID database.

Inequality have different dimensions both income and non-income. Here the focus is centred on income and consumption dimensions. Although several non-income dimensions like inequalities in skill, education, opportunities, happiness, health, life-years, welfare and assets were briefly addressed as well. Several inequality indices can be derived from Lorenz diagram. These indices are presented and basic properties that each index satisfy or violate are discussed. The properties are to be used in their ranking and evaluation of performances. The most widely used index of inequality is the Gini coefficient. Gini has been generalized to accommodate differing aversions of inequality. Income inequality can be decomposed at different levels of aggregation. At the national and international levels it can be decomposed into within-subgroup and between-subgroup and within-country and between-country components respectively. If possible it is highly desirable that in measurement of world income inequality the preferences should be given to the citizens of the world as a unit of analysis. Here representative individuals based on micro household data preferred to those based on constructed individuals of representing countries.

Regarding non-income inequality there is evidence that inequality in education explains a minor fraction of the differences in cross-country earnings inequality. The impact depends on the countries' economic development and skill-intensive nature of their production technologies. There is no direct link from income inequality to ill health measured as mortality, but a range of mechanism and social arrangement indicates the presence of an indirect link. Employment in addition of being a source of income, it is also a provider of social relationships and identity the individuals in a society. Joblessness has direct cost to both the employee and employers and also social costs. The additional burden of unemployment on the individual wellbeing, the non-pecuniary costs of joblessness are much larger than the pecuniary effect that stems from the loss of income.

A literature on inequality decomposition is developing to measure variations in inequality and associate it with underlying causal factors. Inequality can be decomposed at different levels of aggregation. Methods have been developed to decompose inequality by sub-groups, income sources, causal factors and by other unit of observational characteristics. At the national level it is decomposed into within-subgroup and between-subgroups components, while at the international it is decomposed into within-country and between-country components. Different methods of decomposing the changes in poverty into growth, redistribution and poverty standard components are also suggested. Poverty changes can be decomposed across regions and over time to estimate the magnitude of heterogeneity and dynamics. Such information can be very useful in affecting redistributive policies. Here the aim is to study the effect of growth on poverty accounting for the changes in the distribution of income and poverty standards.

Regression-based methods of decomposition of inequality by income sources have been proposed. Compared with unconditional approach, the latter provides possibilities to quantify the conditional roles of various characteristics in a multivariate context and confidence intervals for disaggregated contributions to the inequality index constructed. In particular one distinguishes between the transitory and permanent components of earnings. Economic policy aiming at changes in earnings and its inequality should distinguish shocks that household are able to smooth out and target those that they are not. The main disadvantage of the latter method is the assumption of functional forms of the relationships and its specification. Statistical inferences for inequality measurement to provide estimates of the sampling distribution of inequality are discussed. The bootstrap is used to calculate confidence intervals of inequality within and between sub-groups, by income sources, to compare inequality over time, and before and after tax and transfers. Jackknife and regression methods are employed to report Gini standard errors.

A number of ways to construct world indices of income distribution and to measure global income inequality are reviewed. Few of them compare the world's distribution of income at the individual level. A combined micro and macro approach where mean income per capita complemented with some measures of income dispersion or income share from household surveys is often used. Economic growth, population growth, life expectancy, and the changes in the structure of income inequality are important factors determining the evolution of world income distribution. Empirical results show that the world inequality measured as Gini coefficient increased and poverty measured as headcount decreased. Inequality within individual countries is not increasing but inequality between countries and regions is increasing affecting the evolution of world income inequality. The temporal patterns of international inequality differ by whether Gini is weighted by the population or not. The results from a weighted Gini shows that world inequality has declined due to the faster growth in India and China than the world economy but at the cost of an increased within-country inequality. In general, the between country contribution is much higher then the within country contribution to the world inequality. Results based on the WIID database show no convincing sign of a significant global trend in income inequality over the last 50 years. Inequality was volatile prior to 1970 but more stable and slowly increasing in the post 1986.

It is much easier to influence the within-country inequality by policy decisions than the dominating between-country inequality. Empirical results show that growth increases inequality. The inequality effects of growth can however be reduced by making the growth and its distribution pro-poor. The traditional common factors causing within-country inequality are land concentration, urban biased development, ageing population, inequality in education, and more recently wealth transfers through privatization programme during transition. Land reform, expanding education and active regional policy are found to be the effective policy measures to reduce within-country inequality. The social security reforms in EU show evidence of the positive impacts of taxes and targeting transfers on distribution of income and inequality within the region. The major new external causes of inequality in developing countries are trade and financial liberalisation, technological change, stabilisation and adjustment programmes. Geographic factors, institutional structure and democracy also play role to the development and inequality. Political and capital market factors have more impacts on inequality across countries. The current level of world redistribution in form of cross border transfers is very small and not optimal relative to world inequality and poverty and to achievement of the Millennium Development Goals.

In addition to global, international and national levels we considered income inequality at regional level defined as continents or sub-continents. The same decomposition of inequality within and between regions applies. Intra-regional inequality refers to disparity in income distribution within a region consisting of a number of countries. Regardless of chosen measure as in the case of inter-national comparisons a transformation of income to PPP and its adjustment for population size are important factors affecting the development of inter-regional inequality in the world. Several studies suggest that poverty and inequality has increased in the transition economies. The increasing rate is however not homogeneous and in conflict with the expected positive relationship between democracy and inequality. In this context several markets related and sometimes country-specific determinants of inequality are identified. For instance transitory events and measurement error might have played a role to the rising inequality.

Inequality in the Scandinavian countries is low and relatively stable over time. The Western European countries differ by the type of social policy and in their effectiveness in reducing inequality. Results from the studies of limited individual country shows that inequality is high among the African countries. Inequality varies among countries by sub-groups, regional location, income sources and over time. Inequality among the Latin American countries is also large and increasing over time. The level and patterns has been affected by labour market, and foremost by trade and inflation factors. The East Asian countries have been successful in coupling growth and equality prior to the 1997 economic crisis. The entry of China into the world market and the advent of new technology biased against unskilled workers did have major impacts on the inter-regional development of inequality. Finally, results based on WIID database show large inter-regional heterogeneity in both the level and the development of income distribution and income inequality over time. Inequality in Latin America, East Europe and Former Soviet Republics showed increasing trends in the post 1970s.

The within-country income inequality at the regional level in a selection of large countries with regional division was examined. The results are mainly based on the second half of the 20th century and four large countries including China, Russia, India and USA. China has experienced a rapid economic growth post the economic reform accompanied by an increased inequality. Empirical results suggest that the level and development of inequality has been greatly different by geographical locations and economic sectors. In a number of studies attempts have been made to identify the determinants of inequality across different provinces. There is indication that regional polarization been driven by structural differences between regions. Regional inequality and polarization is of a more serious policy concern in Russia. Heterogeneous economic development, size, ethnic and natural diversity of regions together with restructuring policies and economic shocks caused widening regional inequality and poverty in Russia. The results might however be biased due to data quality and measurement error. Restructuring of the education system in Russia is suggested to enhance growth and to reduce inequality.

Studies of the relationship between growth, inequality and poverty in India suggest that inequality increased while poverty declined but only marginally during the post reform period. Economic growth and redistribution have aided poverty to a limited extent. Raising capital intensity in production has however resulted in the shift in income distribution reducing the positive effects of economic growth to the low skilled workers. Several studies suggest that rapid economic growth must be combined with pro-poor redistributive policies. The US South has historically had lower income but higher inequality than the Non-South. Several factors like migration, skill, technology, gender and changing household characteristics have affected increased income inequality. State level income per capita is however stochastically converging over time to the national level. There exists a significant inter-state and intra-state inequality. Race, education, age and marital status are key factors affecting household income inequalities. Results based on the WIID database show that inequality in US has increased slightly over time. The trend in inequality in India is negative but variable. There is a positive trend in inequality in China and Russia during their post economic reform periods.

The literature on the relationship between openness, growth, inequality and poverty is comprehensive. The findings suggest a positive relationship between openness and growth, but its impact on the distribution of income is found to be different. There is no indication of a systematic relationship between trade and inequality, but a conflicting viewpoint about the effects of inequality on growth. The existing empirical results indicate the presence of convergence in per capita income, but also divergence in income inequality. For instance, there is evidence of strong convergence among more homogenous and integrated advanced countries but also divergence among less developed countries or even among regions of the world. The process of democratisation in Western countries has led to institutional changes and improved taxation and redistribution system reducing their inequality and poverty. The East and South East Asian countries have also been successful in coupling low inequality and high growth, while on the contrary Sub-Saharan Africa has experienced the reverse relationship with a high inequality and low growth. One major limitation of the literature is that the simultaneous and direction of causal relationship between these key macroeconomic variables has to a large extent been neglected.

The empirical results on the relationship between growth, inequality and poverty reviewed, showed that the outcomes of policy measures are quite heterogeneous in their impacts. In general it is rather difficult to measure the effects of inequality and growth on the developing countries' efforts to reduce poverty in the course of economic development. Economic growth benefits the poor but in the absence of effective redistribution policies in these countries it might deteriorate further the income distribution. The countries' initial conditions, institutions, their specific structures, and time horizons each play a significant role in their targeting policies to make economic growth pro-poor. Globalization, openness and technical change have been biased to skilled labour in industrialized countries widening wage differentials suggesting positive association between openness and wage inequality. For developing countries these changes due to the differing nature of the skilled bias are expected to reduce wage inequality by narrowing the wage gap between skilled and unskilled workers. Regression results based on the WIID database covering a large number of countries a whole range of development suggest that income inequality is declining over time. Inequality is also declining with the growth of income. There is significant regional heterogeneity in the levels of inequality and its development over time.

In an attempt to analyse the link between inequality and poverty and globalization alternative composite indices of globalizations are constructed. The indices quantify the level and development of globalization to rank countries. They are decomposed into four main components: economic integration, personal contact, technology, and political engagements. Such a breakdown provides possibilities to identify the sources of globalization and associate it with policy measures to bring about changes in desirable directions. Internal and external conflicts are found to reduce the countries' globalization prospects. The low rank is often associated with political and personal factors, while high rank with economic and technology development. In particular the mean globalization by region show that technology factors play an important role in the ranking of the regions. Simple unconditional correlation among the inequality, poverty and globalization indices show that the Gini coefficients negatively correlated with personal, technology and political components, but not correlated with the economic component. The same negative relationship holds between income inequality and the aggregate globalization indices. Globalization reduces poverty and increases the poorest share of income and thereby reducing inequality. The reduction in poverty is mostly associated with technology component of globalization.

The conditional results from the regression analysis of the relationship between inequality, poverty and globalization show that the globalization index explains 7-11 per cent of the variations in income inequality, and 9 per cent of variations in poverty among the sample countries. More specific personal contacts and technology transfers reduce inequality, while economic integration increases inequality. Political engagement is found to have no effects on income inequality. Economic globalization increases poverty, while personal contact reduces poverty. In controlling for heterogeneity by geographic location, we find that the regional variable plays an important role in explaining the variations in inequality and poverty. Despite the limitations of the data and the composite index these preliminary results shed lights on the link between globalization, inequality and poverty.

There are a number of databases that are frequently used in applied global, international, regional and also in national growth and inequality research. Despite their benefits, limitations and differences by objectives, composition of countries, country coverage, sources, unit of measurement and income definitions, each play an important and complementary role in inequality studies. The choice of data affects the conclusion drawn about the trends in inequality for a single or groups of countries and over time. Quality, consistency, income definition and measurement, changing population and household size and various adjustment procedures are among important data issues discussed here. The existing empirical results are found to be quite sensitive to these factors. Consistency across countries and over time is the key issue to the reliability of the results in panel studies. For instance, in international or global income studies an invalid pooling of data might lead to misleading or spurious results.

Measurement of income, its decomposition by source and sub-group with satisfactory coverage, sampling units and representative of population is important in generation of consistent information about the state of income inequality. It is important that heterogeneity in ability, in actual consumption and consumption needs by various household characteristics is accounted for in the calculation of representative consumption amounts by using appropriate measures of equivalence scales. Estimates of income and consumption inequalities are found to be sensitive to the regional variations in the cost of living index as the price deflator.

SOME FINAL WORDS

In sum the results in the literature points to conflicting and unsatisfactory results regarding the level and development of inequality and its relationship with openness, growth, poverty and globalization. The differences are to be found in the use of different or sub-set of same databases underlying studies of international and global income inequality. A major limitation of these studies is in the short time period and in the lack of income surveys with satisfactory coverage. The optimal long-term solution would be to create a new database consisting in part of information from existing household surveys and in part based on new surveys to be collected. The Luxembourg Income Study (LIS) database could serve as an example in the creation of a World Income Study (WIS) database. Similar attempts have been done but at smaller scale covering the transition and a number of developing countries.

The creation of WIS will in similarity with Penn World Tables and Luxembourg Income Study break down effectively the current monopoly situation where the access to data during a critical period is limited to few individuals or groups of researchers. Collection, storage and data management at the WIS scale, of course, require a large amount of resources. A centralisation of the activities does not necessarily make the process more expensive than currently one. On the contrary, the same data with homogenous quality can be delivered to researcher on an equal basis and indiscriminately and at a much lower cost. The researchers focus will then be on the analysis of data rather than the creation of semi-private datasets.

It is important that the data level extracted for research purpose should be at a medium level of aggregation. It should be something between the extreme case of household survey and aggregate nationally representative household levels and manageable by the users. The disaggregation ideally should incorporate representative individuals for various sub-groups. These are identified based on internationally standardized common time-invariant household characteristics like age, gender, marital status, family size, skills, regions and sectors. WIS would improve the possibilities to use the results not only in measuring international and global inequality but also in the design of fair and effective taxes, transfers and redistributive policies at both within country and cross-border levels.

This chapter tended more towards presenting the summary of this monograph and also added some evaluative observations of general character on each part. There was both notable presence and also absence of stress in different studies on the very fundamental fact that the extent of global income inequality is vast, given the amount of country-specific poverty that accompanies such large inequality. The human predicament of large numbers of people in sub-Saharan Africa is something that merits underlining but very much been neglected for the reasons of data and local knowledge. This should have lead to some evaluative appraisal of the stance of the North toward the South, as well as of the quality of internal governance in the countries of the South and their lacking serious efforts to create necessary and sufficient conditions and bring about desired changes.

In my view researchers from South and in particular those positioned in many influential international, continental, regional and national organizations carry a heavy responsibility and key role in the creation of infrastructure in the form of databases, making data available, providing accurate and competent analysis and suggesting suitable solutions to their problem. These are issues on which silence in many studies including this study must be expected to intrigue most readers. The researchers with origin from South, their large numbers, their influence and skills should serve as an effective tool in providing a clear picture of the poverty and inequality, causal factors and to propose appropriate measures to reduce their magnitudes.

Given the enormous emphasis on empirical findings in the book and many other work, one would expect that the often inconclusive and even contradictory findings of different studies, for example, with respect to the relationship between growth, inequality and poverty, must at least prompt some critics on the dogmatic sorts of prescriptions for development such as those emanating from the Washington Consensus. The strength of such for the inoptimal prescriptions for every specific case in South is a reflection of the weakness of the analysts from the South. There may also be a case for cautioning against extreme Right and Left positions on, e.g., globalization, by pointing to the need for a case by case analysis that takes into account the specificity of situations as they present themselves in the real world.

The rising global or national inequality, although undesirable, is not inevitable, as individuals, regions and countries are different by initial conditions, goals and in productivity. It is evident that the wealthy and advanced nations in the capacity of technology leaders and deriving force of development are the main beneficiaries of economic development. Despite such persisting difference, the current world's social situation argues that although living standards have improved in many places the poverty remains entrenched. This and as a result of existing technology gap the gap between the rich and the poor will widen further calling for immediate actions. Growth is considered as effective mean of reducing poverty. However, focusing only on economic growth is an ineffective way of achieving development and equality. Redistribution is often a neglected measure in the debate. The multidimensionality of inequality and its overall impacts on the poor in form of inequality in income, wealth, opportunity, health and education should not be neglected.

Although China and India have made considerable progress, there is evidence that income gap at different levels has in parallel increased. The development agenda could not be advanced without addressing inequality, such as the gender gap, the gap between skilled and unskilled workers, urban and rural sectors, and the formal and informal sectors in developing countries. Expanding opportunities for productive employment and forces enhances competitiveness and better living standard, but these must be combined with measures to bring marginalized groups into society and working force to distribute the benefits of the increasingly open world economy and to lift the poor out of poverty. Many of these measures are internal and the negative development is a result of mismanagement, corruption, weak and unable governance in the developing countries.

REFERENCES

Aaberge R., Björklund A., Jäntti M., Palme M., Pedersen P.J., Smith N. and T. Wennemo (2002), Income inequality and income mobility in the Scandinavian countries compared to the United Sates, *The Review of Income and Wealth* 48(4), 443-470.

Acemoglu D. (2002), Cross-country inequality trends, NBER Working Paper No. 8832.

Acemoglu D., S. Johnson and J.A. Robinson (2002), Reversal of fortune: geography and institutions in the making of the modern world income distribution, *Quarterly Journal of Economics* 117(4), 1231-1294.

Acemoglu D. and J.A. Robinson (2000), Why did the west extended the franchise? Democracy, inequality, and growth in historical perspective, *The Quarterly Journal of Economics* CXV, 1167-1199.

Acemoglu D. and J. Ventura (2002), The world income distribution, *Quarterly Journal of Economics* CXVII(2), 659-694.

Addison T. and A. Heshmati (2004), The new global determinants of FDI to developing countries, *Research in Banking and Finance* 4, 151-186.

Agénor P.R. (2003), *Does globalization hurt the poor?,* World Bank, Unpublished manuscript.

Aghion P. (2002), Schumpeterian growth theory and the dynamics of income inequality, *Econometrica* 70(3), 855-882.

Aghion P. and S. Commander (1999), On the dynamics of inequality in the transition, *Economics of Transition* 7(2), 275-298.

Alexeev M. and J. Leitzel (2001), Income distribution and price controls: targeting a social safety net during economic transition, *European Economic Review* 45, 1647-1663.

Alesina A., R. DiTella and R. MacCulloch (2001), Inequality and happiness: are Europeans and Americans different?, NBER Working Paper 8189.

Alesina A. and D. Rodrik (1994), Distributive politics and economic growth, *Quarterly Journal of Economics* 109, 465-490.

Anand S. (1997), The measurement of income inequality, in: S. Subramanian (ed) *Measurement of inequality and poverty,* Oxford University Press, pp. 81-105.

Anand S. and S.M.R. Kanbur (1997), Inequality and development: a critique, in S. Subramanian (ed) *Measurement of inequality and poverty,* Oxford University Press, pp. 128-158.

Andersen T.M. and T.T. Herbertsson (2003), Measuring globalization, IZA Discussion Paper 2003:817.

Aronsson T. and M. Palme (1998), A decade of tax and benefit reforms in Sweden: effects on labour supply, welfare and inequality, *Economica* 65, 39-67.

Assadzadeh A. and S. Paul (2003), Poverty, growth and redistribution: A case-study of Iran, in Rolph van der Hoeven and Anthony Shorrocks (eds), Perspectives on Growth and Poverty, United Nations University Press.

Atkinson A.B. (1997), Bringing income distribution in from the cold, *The Economic Journal* 107, 297-321.

Atkinson A.B. (1999), Is rising inequality inevitable? A critique of the transatlantic consensus, The United Nations University, WIDER Annual Lectures 3, Helsinki: UNU/WIDER.

Atkinson A.B. (2000), Increased income inequality in OECD countries and the redistributive impact of the Government budget, WIDER Working Papers 2000/202, Helsinki: UNU/WIDER.

Atkinson A.B. and F. Bourguignon (1987), Income distribution and differences in needs, In: Feiwel G.R. (ed.), *Arrow and Foundations of the Theory of Economic Policy,* Macmillan, London.

Atkinson A.B. and A. Brandolini (2001), Promise and pitfalls in the use of "secondary" data-sets: income inequality in OECD countries as a case study, *Journal Economic Literature* 39, 771-799.

Attanasio O., G. Berloffa, R. Blundell and I. Preston (2002), From earnings inequality to consumption inequality, *The Economic Journal* 112, March C52-C59.

Babones S.J. (2002), Population and sample selection effects in measuring international income inequality, *Journal of World-System Research* 8(1), 7-28.

Babones S. J. and J. H. Turner (2003), Global Inequality, in Ritzer G. (ed.), *Handbook of Social Problems, A Comparative International Perspective,* Chapter 7, SAGE Publications.

Baker M. (1997), Growth-rate heterogeneity and the covariance structure of life-cycle earnings, *Journal of Labor Economics* 15(2), 338-375.

Baker M. and G. Solone (1998), Earnings dynamics and inequality among Canadian men, 1976-1992: evidence from longitudinal income tax records, Institute for Policy Analysis, University of Toronto, mimeo.

Barrett G.F. and K. Pendakur (1995), The asymptotic distribution of the generalized Gini indices of ineqyaluty, *Canadian Journal of Economics* 28, 1042-1055.

Barro R.J. (1991), Economic growth in a cross section of countries, *Quarterly Journal of Economics* 106, 406-443.

Barro R.J. (1997), Determinants of economic growth: a cross-country empirical study, MIT press, Cambridge, MA.

Barro R.J. (2000), Inequality and growth in a panel of countries, *Journal of Economic Growth* 5(1), 5-32.

Barro R.J. and J-W Lee (1996), International measures of schooling years and schooling quality, *American Economic Review* 86(2), 218-223.

Barro R.J. and J-W. Lee (2000), International data on educational attainment: updates and implications, Centre for International Development at Harvard University, CID Working Paper 2000:42.

Barro R.J. and X. Sala-i-Martin (1995), *Economic Growth*, McGraw-Hill Inc.

Bartholomew D.J. (1982), Stochastic models for social processes, Third edition, Wiley, Chichester, UK.

Bata M. and A.J. Bergesen (2002a), Global inequality: an introduction, *Journal of World-System Research* 8(1), 2-6.

Bata M. and A.J. Bergesen (2002b), Global inequality: an introduction, *Journal of World-System Research* 8(2), 146-148.

Belbo M. and T. Knaus (2001), Measuring income inequality in Euroland, *Review of Income and Wealth* 47(3), 301-320.

Benabou R. (1996), Inequality and growth, in NBER Macroeconomics Annual, B.S. Bernanke and J. Rotemberg, eds., Canbridge MA: MIT Press.

Bergesen A.J. and M. Bata (2002), Global and national inequality: are they connected?, *Journal of World-System Research* 8(1), 129-144.

Bernard A.B. and S.N. Durlauf (1995), Convergence in international output, *Journal of Applied Econometrics* 10, 97-108.

Bernard A.B. and C.I. Jones (1996), Productivity across industries and countries: time series theory and evidence, *Review of Economics & Statistics* 78(1), 135-146.

Berry A., F. Bourguignon and C. Morrisson (1983), Changes in the world distribution of income between 1950 and 1977, *Economic Journal* 93(370), 331-350.

Bhargava A. (2001), Stochastic specification and the international GDP series, *Econometric Journal* 4, 274-287.

Bhargava A., Jamison D.T., Lau L.J. and C.J.L. Murray (2001), Modeling the effects of health on economic growth, *Journal of Health Economics* 20, 423-440.

Biancotti C. (2003), A polarization of polarization? The distribution of inequality 1970-1996, Bank of Italy.

Biewen M. (2002a), Bootstrap inference for inequality, mobility and poverty measurement, *Journal of Econometrics* 108(2), 317-342.

Biewen M. (2002b), Book Review: Handbook of inequality and measurement, by Jacques Silber (ed.), Kluwer 1999, *Journal of Development Economics* 70(2), 543-548.

Biewen M. (2002c), The covariance structure of the East and West German incomes and its implications for the persistence of poverty and inequality, IZA Discussion Papers 2002:459.

Bigman D. and P.V. Srinivasan (2002), Geographical targeting of poverty alleviation programs: methodology and applications in rural India, *Journal of Policy Modeling* 24(3), 237-255.

Bigsten A. and J. Levin (2003), Growth, income distribution and poverty: a review, in Van der Hoeven R. and A. Shorrocks Eds., *Perspectives on growth and poverty,* United Nationa University Press.

Birdsall N. (1998), Inequality and global coordination, Why inequality matters: the developing and transition economies, mimeo, Carnegie Endowment for International Peace, Washington D.C.

Birchenall J.A. (2001), Income distribution, human capital and economic growth in Colombia, *Journal of Development Economics* 66, 271-287.

Bishop J.A., Formby J.P. and P.D. Thistle (1992), Convergence of the South and Non-South income distribution, 1969-1979, *The American Economic Review 82*(1), 262-272.

Björklund A. and M. Palme (1997), Income redistribution within the life cycle versus between individuals: empirical evidence using Swedish panel data, Stockholm School of Economics, Working Paper Series in Economics and Finance 1997:197.

Black D.C. and M.R. Dowd (1997), Measuring real interstate income inequality in the United States, *Economics Letters* 56, 367-370.

Blacklow P. and R. Ray (2000), A comparison of income and expenditure inequality estimates: the Australian evidence, 1975-76 to 1993-94, *Australian Economic Review* 33(4), 317-329.

Borjas G.J. (1994), The economics of immigration, *Journal of Economic Literature* 32 December, 1667-1717.

Borjas G.J. (1999), Economic research on the determinants of immigration: lessons for the European Union, World Bank Technical Paper No. 438.

Bornschier V. (2002), Changing income inequality in the second half of the 20th century: preliminary findings and propositions for explanations, *Journal of World-System Research* 8(1), 99-127.

Bourguignon F. and M. Fournier and M. Gurgand (2001), Fast development with a stable income distribution in Taiwan, 1979-94, *Review of Income and Wealth* 47(2), 139-163.

Bourguignon F. and C. Morrisson (1998), Inequality and development: the role of dualism, *Journal of Development Economics* 57, 233-257.

Bourguignon F. and C. Morrisson (1999), *The size distribution of income among the world citizens*, mimeo, DELTA, Paris.

Bourguignon F. and C. Morrisson (2002), Inequality among world citizens: 1820-1992, *American Economic Reviews* 92(4), 727-747.

Bowles S. and H. Gintis (2002), The inheritance of inequality, *Journal of Economic Perspectives* 6(3), 3-30.

Burtless G. (1999), Effects of growing wage disparities and changing family composition on the U.S. income distribution, *European Economic Review* 43, 853-865.

Cameron J. (2000), Policy arena. Amartya Sen on economic inequality: the need for an explicit critique of opulence, *Journal of International Development* 12, 1031-1045.

Cameron L.A. (2000a), The impact of the Indonesian financial crisis on children: an analysis using the 100 villages data, Innocenti Working Paper 2000:81.

Cameron L.A. (2000b), Poverty and inequality in Java: examining the impact of the changing age, educational and industrial structure, *Journal of Development Economics* 62, 149-180.

Caminada K. and K. Goudswaard (2001), International trends in income inequality and social policy, International Tax and Public Finance 8(4), 395-415.

Canagarajah S., C. Newman and R. Bhattamishra (2001), Non-farm income, gender, and inequality: evidence from rural Ghana and Uganda, *Food Policy* 26, 405-420.

Capeau B. and A. Decoster (2003), The rise or fall of world inequality: big issue or apparent controversy?, Unpublished manuscript.

Cappellari L. (2000), The dynamics and inequality of Italian male earnings: permanent changes or transitory fluctuations?, Institute for Social and Economic Research.

Cappellari L. and S.P. Jenkins (2002), Who stays poor? Who becomes poor? Evidence from the British household panel survey, *The Economic Journal* 112, March C60-C67.

Carlini G.A. and L.O. Mills (1993), Are U.S. regional income converging? A time series analysis, *Journal of Monetary Economics* 32, 335-346.

Caselli F., G. Esquivel and F. Lefort (1996), Reopening the convergence debate: a new look at cross-country growth empirics, *Journal of Economic Growth* 1, 363-389.

Castello A. and R. Domenech (2002), Human capital inequality and economic growth: some new evidence, *The Economic Journal* 112, March C187-C200.

Chakravarty S.R. (2001), The variance of a subgroup decomposable measure of inequality, *Social Indicators Research* 53(1), 79-95.

Chakravarty S.R. and A. Majumder (2001), Inequality, polarisation and welfare: theory and applications, *Australian Economic Papers* 40(1), 1-13.

Chakravarty S.R., A. Majumder and S. Roy (2002), A treatment of absolute indices of polarisation, Unpublished manuscript, Indian Statistical Institute, Calcutta, India, Presented at the International Workshop on Income Distribution and Welfare, Bocconi May 30 to June 2 2002.

Chen S., G. Datt and M. Ravallion (1994), Is poverty increasing in the developing world, *Review of Income and Wealth* 40(2), 359-376.

Cheng Y-S. (1996), A decomposition analysis of income inequality of Chinese rural households, *China Economic Review* 7(2), 155-167.

Chiu W.H. (1998), Income inequality, human capital accumulation and economic performance, *The Economic Journal* 108, 44-59.

Chotikapanich D. and W. Griffiths (2001), On calculation of the extended Gini coefficient, *Review of Income and Wealth* 47(4), 541-547.

Chotikapanich D. and W. Griffiths (2002), Estimating Lorenz curves using a Dirichlet distribution, *Journal of Business and Economic Statistics* 20, 290-295.

Chuang H.L. and W. Huang (1997), Economic and social correlates of regional suicide rates: A pooled cross section and time series analysis, *Journal of Socio-Economics* 26, 277-289.

Clark A.E. and A.J. Oswald (1994), Unhappiness and unemployment, *The Economic Journal* 104, 648-659.

Clark A.E. and A.J. Oswald (1996), Satisfaction and comparison income, *Journal of Public Economics* 61, 359-381.

Commander A., A Tolstopiatenko and R. Yemtsov (1999), Chanells of redistribution: inequality and poverty in the Russian transition, *Economics of Transition* 7(2), 411-447.

Cornia G.A. (1999), Liberalization, globalization and income distribution, WIDER Working Paper 1999/157, Helsinki: UNU/WIDER.

Cornia G.A. and J. Court (2001), Inequality, growth and poverty in the era of liberalization and globalization, Policy Brief No. 4, Helsinki: UNU/WIDER.

Cornia G.A. and S. Kiiski (2001), Trends in income distribution in the post WWII period: evidence and interpretation, WIDER Discussion Paper 2001/89, Helsinki: UNU/WIDER.

Cowell F.A. (2000), Measurement of inequality, in Atkinson A.B. and Bourguignon F. (Eds), *Handbook of Income Distribution,* Volume 1, North Holland, chapter 2, 87-166.

Cowell F.A., F.H.G. Ferreira and J.A. Litchfield (1998), Income distribution in Brazil 1981-1990: parametric and non-parametric approaches, *Journal of Income Distribution* 8(1), 63-76.

Cowell F.A. and S.P. Jenkins (1995), How much inequality can we explain? A methodology and an application to the USA, *Economic Journal* 105(429), 421-430.

Cowell F.A. and S.P. Jenkins (2000), *Estimating welfare indices: household weights and sample design*, London School of Economics

Cowell F.A. and M-P. Victoria-Feser (1996a), Robustness properties of inequality measures, *Econometrica* 64(1), 77-101.

Cowell F.A. and M-P. Victoria-Feser (1996b), Poverty measurement with contaminated data: a robust approach, *European Economic Review* 40, 1761-1771.

Datt G. and M. Ravallion (1992), Growth and redistribution components of changes in poverty measures: A decomposition with applications to Brazil and India in the 1980s, *Journal of Development Economics* 38, 275-295.

Davies J.B. and A.F. Shorrocks (2000), The distribution of wealth, in Atkinson A.B. and Bourguignon F. (Eds), *Handbook of Income Distribution,* Volume 1, North Holland, chapter 11, pp. 605-675.

De Gregorio J. and J-W. Lee (2002), Education and income inequality: New evidence from cross-country data, *Review of Income and Wealth* 48(3), 395-416.

Deaton A. (2001), Health, inequality, and economic development, NBER Working Paper 8318.

Deaton A. and D. Lubotsky (2002), Mortality, inequality and race in American cities and states, *Social Science & Medicine* 55(6), 1139-1153.

Declich C. and V. Polin (2002), Absolute poverty and the cost of living: an experimental analysis for Italian households, ISAE DP.

Deininger K. and L. Squire (1996), A new data set measuring income inequality, *World Bank Economic Review* 10(3), 565-591.

Deininger K. and L. Squire (1998), New ways of looking at old issues: inequality and growth, *Journal of Development Economics* 57, 259-287.

Deininger K. and L. Squire (2002), Revisiting inequality: new data; new results, World Bank and Global Development Network.

Deltas G. (2003), The small-sample bias of the Gini coefficient: results and implications for empirical research, *The Review of Economics and Statistics* 85(1), 226-234.

Demurger S., J.D. Sachs, W.T. Woo, S. Bao, G. Cheng and A. Mellinger (2002), Geography, Economic Policy, and regional development in China, NBER Working Paper 8897.

Devroye D. and R. Freeman (2001), Does inequality in skills explain inequality of earnings across advanced countries? NBER Working Paper 8140.

Dhongde S. (2002), Measuring the impact of growth and income distribution on poverty: an analysis of the States in India, Unpublished manuscript.

Dickens (2000), The evolution of individual male earnings in Great Britain: 1975-95, *The Economic Journal 110*, January 27-49.

Dikhanov Y. and M. Ward (2002), Evolution of the global distribution of income in 1970-99. Unpublished manuscript presented at the International Workshop on Income Distribution and Welfare, Bocconi May 30 to June 2 2002.

DiNardo J., N.M. Fortin and T. Lemieux (1996), Labor market institutions and the distribution of wages, 1973-1992: a semiparametric approach, *Econometrica* 64(5), 1001-1044.

Dollar D. and P. Collier (2001), *Globalization, growth and poverty: Building an inclusive World economy*, Oxford University Press.

Dollar D. and A. Kraay (2001a), Trade growth and poverty, Development Research Group, The World Bank.

Dollar D. and A. Kraay (2001b), Growth is good for the poor, Policy Research Working paper 2001:2199, Development Research Group, The World Bank.

Donaldson D. and J.A. Waymark (1980), A single-parameter generalization of the Gini index of inequality, *Journal of Economic Theory* 22, 67-86.

Dowrick S. and D-T. Nguyen (1989), OECD comparative economic growth 1950-85: catch-up and convergence, *American Economic Review* 79(5), 1010-1030.

Duro J.A. and J. Esteban (1998), Factor decomposition of cross-country income inequality, 1960-1990, *Economics Letters* 60, 269-275.

Dutta B., M. Panda and W. Wadhwa (1997), Human development in India, in S. Subramanian (ed) *Measurement of inequality and poverty,* Oxford University Press, pp. 329-358.

Earle J. and K. Sabirianova (2001), Understanding wage arrears in Russia, *Journal of Labor Economics 20,* 661-707.

Eastwood R. and M. Lipton (2000), Rural-Urban dimensions of inequality change, WIDER Working Papers 2000/200, Helsinki: UNU/WIDER.

Ebert U. and P. Moyes (2003), Equivalence scales reconsidered, *Econometrica* 71(1), 319-343.

Eicher T.S. and C. Garcia-Penalosa (2001), Inequality and growth: the dual role of human capital in development, *Journal of Development Economics 66, 173-*197.

Elbers C., J.O. Lanjouw and P. Lanjouw (2003), Micro-level estimation of poverty and inequality, *Econometrica* 71(1), 355-364.

Epstein G.S. and U. Spiegel (2002), Natural inequality, production and economic growth, *Labour Economics* 8, 463-473.

Esteban J-M. D. Ray (1994), On the measurement of polarization, *Econometrica* 62(4), 819-851.

Fan C.S., J. Overland and M. Spagat (1999), Human capital, growth and inequality in Russia, *Journal of Comparative Economics* 27(4), 618-643.

Fedorov L. (2002), Regional inequality and regional polarisation in Russia, 1990-99, *World Development* 30(3), 443-456.

Fellman J., Jäntti M. and P.J. Lambert (1999), Optimal tax-transfer systems and redistributive policy, *Scandinavian Journal of Economics* 101(1), 115-126.

Fields G.S. (2000), *Measuring Inequality Change in an Economy with Income Growth, The International Library of Critical Writings in Economics: Income Distribution,* (Edward Elgar).

Fields G.S. and E.A. Ok (1996), The meaning and measurement of income mobility, *Journal of Economic Theory* 71(2), 349-377.

Fields G.S. and E.A. Ok (1999), Measuring movement of incomes, *Economica* 66, 455-471.

Firebaugh G. (1999), Empirics of World Income Inequality, *American Journal of Sociology* 104(6), 1597-1630.

Firebaugh G. (2000a), The Trend in Between-Nation Income Inequality, *American Review of Sociology* 26, 323-339.

Firebaugh G. (2000b), Observed Trends in Between-Nation Income Inequality and Two Conjuctures, Commentary and Debate, *American Journal of Sociology* 106(1), 215-221.

Firebaugh G. and B. Goesling (2004), Accounting for the Recent Decline in Global Income Inequality, *American Journal of Sociology* 110(2), 283-312.

Fischer R.D. (2001), The evolution of inequality after trade liberalization, *Journal of Development Economics* 66, 555-579.

Flemming J. and J. Micklewright (2000), Income distribution, economic systems and transition, in Atkinson A.B. and Bourguignon F. (Eds), *Handbook of Income Distribution,* Volume 1, North Holland, chapter 14, pp. 843- 918.

Fordyce M. (1998), A review of research on happiness: A sixty second index of happiness and mental health, *Social Indicator Research* 20, 355-381.

Formby J.P., W.J. Smith and B. Zheng (1999), The coefficient of variation, stochastic dominance and inequality: a new interpretation, *Economics Letters* 62, 319-323.

Foster J.E., Greer J. and E. Thorbecke (1984), Notes and comments: a class of decomposable poverty measures, *Econometrica* 52(3), 761-766.

Foster J.E. and A. Sen (1997), On economic inequality after a quarter century, In: On economic inequality, expanded ed., Clarendon Press, oxford.

Foster J.E. and A.F. Shorrocks (1991), Subgroup consistent poverty indices, *Econometrica* 59(3), 687-709.

Galbraith J.K. and H. Kum (2003), Estimating the inequality of household incomes: filling gaps and fixing problems in Deininger & Squire, UTIP Working Paper 2003:22.

Georlich-Gisbert F.J. (2001), On factor decomposition of cross-country income inequality: some extensions and qualifications, *Economics Letters* 70, 303-309.

Gerdtham U-G. and M. Johannesson (2000), Income-related inequality in life-years and quality-adjusted life-years, *Journal of Health Economics 19*, 1007-1026.

Geweke J. and M. Keane (2000), An empirical analysis of earnings dynamics among men in the PSID: 1968-1989, *Journal of Econometrics* 96, 293-356.

Giles D.E.A. (2002), Calculating a standard error for the Gini coefficient: some further results, University of Victoria, Depart of Economics, Working paper EWP0202.

Giorgi. G.M. (1999), Income inequality measurement: the statistical approach, in Silber J. and A. Sen (eds), *Handbook of income inequality measurement,* chapter 8, pp. 245-267, Kluwer Academic Publishers.

Gottschalk P. (1997), Inequality, income growth, and mobility: the basic facts, *Journal of Economic Perspectives* 11(2), 21-40.

Gottschalk P. and T.M Smeeding (1997), Cross-national comparisons of earnings and income inequality, Journal of Economic *Literature 35, 633-687.*

Gottschalk P. and T.M. Smeeding (2000), Empirical evidence on income inequality in industrialized countries, in Atkinson A.B. and Bourguignon F. (Eds), *Handbook of Income Distribution*, Volume 1, North Holland, chapter 5, pp.261-308.

Goudie A. and P. Ladd (1999), Economic growth, poverty and inequality, *Journal of International Development* 11, 177-195.

Gradstein M. and B. Milanovic (2002), Does liberte=egalite? A survey of the empirical links between democracy and inequality with some evidence on the transition economies, WB PRWP 2002:2875.

Graham C. (2002), Mobility, opportunity and vulnerability: the dynamics of poverty and inequality in a global economy, *Journal of Human Development* 3(1), 57-94.

Gustafsson B. and L. Shi (2001a), The anatomy of rising earnings inequality in Urban China, *Journal of Comparative Economics* 29(1), 118-135.

Gustafsson B. and L. Shi (2001b), The effects of transition on the distribution of income in China: a study decomposing the GINI coefficient for 1988 and 1995*, Economics of Transition* 9(3), 593-617.

Gustafsson B. and L. Shi (2002), Income inequality within and across counties in rural China 1988 and 1995, *Journal of Development Economics* 69(1), 179-204.

Gustafsson B., L. Shi, L. Nivorozhkia and K. Katz (2001), Rubles and Yuan: wage functions for urban Russia and China at the end of the 1980s, *Economic Development and Cultural Change* 50(1), 1-17.

Gustafsson B. and W. Zhong (2000), How and why has poverty in China changed? A study based on microdata for 1988 and 1995, *The China Quarterly* 164, 983-1006.

Haddad L. and R. Kanbur (1997), How serious is the neglect of intra-household inequality?, in S. Subramanian (ed) *Measurement of inequality and poverty*, Oxford University Press, pp. 106-127.

Hartog J. and H. Oosterbeek (1998), Health, wealth and happiness: why pursue a higher education?, *Economics of Education Review* 17(3), 245-256.

Hasegawa H. and H. Kozumi (2003), Estimation of Lorenz curves: a Bayesian nonparametric approach, *Journal of Econometrics* 115, 277-291.

Heady C., T. Mitrakos and P. Tsakloglou (2001), The distributional impact of social transfers in the European Union: evidence from the ECHP, *Fiscal Studies* 22(4), 547-565.

Heshmati A. (2003), Measurement of a multidimentional index of globalization and its impact on income inequality, WIDER Discussion Paper 2003/69, Helsinki: UNU/WIDER.

Heshmati A. (2004a), "Growth, Inequality and Poverty Relationships", IZA Discussion Paper 2004:1338 and MTT Discussion Paper 2004:16, 29 pages.

Heshmati A. (2004b), "The Relationship Between Income Inequality, Poverty and Globalization", IZA Discussion Paper 2004:1277 and MTT Discussion Paper 2004:12, 35 pages.

Heshmati A. (2005), Continental and Sub-continental Income Inequality, *ICFAI Journal of Applied Economics* 5(6), 7-52.

Heshmati A. (2006), The World Distribution of Income and Income Inequality, *Journal of World Systems Research*, forthcoming.

Heston A. and R. Summers (1996), International price and quality comparisons: potentials and pitfalls, *American Economic Review* 86(2), 20-24.

Hossain M.A. (2001), Inter- and intraregional incidence of inequality and poverty in Thailand's Northeast region, including comments by I. Sarntisart, *Regional Development Dialogue* 22(2), 185-197.

Huck S., H-T. Normann and J. Oechssler (2001), Market volatility and inequality in earnings: experimental evidence, *Economics Letters* 70, 363-368.

Hurrell A. (2001), Global inequality and international institutions, *Metaphilosophy* 32(1/2), 34-57.

Iacoviello M. (1998), Inequality Dynamics: evidence from some European countries, Working Paper No. 191, Maxwell School of Citizenship and Public Affairs, Syracuse University.

Islam N. (1995), Growth empirics: a panel data approach, *The Quarterly Journal of Economics* 110, 1127-1170.

Ivaschenko O. (2002), Growth and inequality: evidence from transitional economics, CESIFO Working Paper 2002:746.

Jenkins S.P. (1995), Accounting for inequality trends: decomposition analysis for the UK, *Economica* 62, 29-64.

Jenkins S.P. and P.J. Lambert (1993), Ranking income distributions when needs differ, *Review of Income and Wealth* 39, 337-356.

Jenkins S.P. and P. Van Kerm (2003), Trends in income inequality, prop-poor income growth and income mobility, IZA Discussion Paper 2003:904.

Jha R. (2000), Reducing poverty and inequality in India: Has liberalization helped?, Working Papers 2000/204, Helsinki: UNU/WIDER.

Jian L.R. and Tendulkar (1990), Role of growth and distribution in the observed change of headcount ratio-measure of poverty: a decomposition exercise for India, Technical report no. 9004 (Indian Statistical Institute, Delhi).

Jian T., J.D. Sachs and A.M. Warner (1996), Trends in regional inequality in China, *China Economic Review* Volume 7(1), 1-21.

Jones C.I. (1997), On the evolution of the world income distribution, *Journal of Economic Perspectives* 11(3), 19-36.

Jones C.I. (2002), Introduction to economic growth, Second Edition, W.W. Norton & Compacy.

Judge K., J-A. Mulligan and M. Benzeval (1998), Reply to Richard Wilkinson, *Social Science and Medicine* 46, 567-579.

Jäntti M. (1997), Inequality in five countries in the 1980s: the role of demographic shifts, markets and government policies, *Economica* 64, 415-440.

Jäntti M. and S. Danziger (2000), Income poverty in advanced countries, in Atkinson A.B. and Bourguignon F. (Eds), *Handbook of Income Distribution,* Volume 1, North Holland, chapter 6, pp.309-378.

Kakwani N. (1980), On a class of poverty measures, *Econometrics* 48, 437-446.

Kakwani N. and R.J. Hill (2002), Economic theory of spatial cost of living indices with application to Thailand, *Journal of Public Economics* 86, 71-97.

Kakwani N. and M. Krongkaew (2000), Introduction: Economic growth, poverty and income inequality in the Asia-Pacific region, *Journal of the Asia Pacific Economy* 5(1/2), 9-13.

Kakwani N. and K. Subbarao (1990), Rural Poverty and its alleviation in India, *Economic and Political Weekly,* March 31, 1990.

Kakwani N., A. Wagstaff and E. van Doorslaer (1997), Socioeconomic inequalities in health: measurement, computation, and statistical inference, *Journal of Econometrics* 77, 87-103.

Kanbur R. and X. Zhang (1999), Which regional inequality? The evolution of rural-urban and inland-coastal inequality in China from 1983 to 1995, *Journal of Comparative Economics* 27(4), 686-701.

Kaplow L. (2002), Why measure inequality?, NBER Working Paper Series 2002:9342.

Karagiannis E. and M. Kovacevic (2000), A method to calculate the Jackknife variance estimator for the Gini coefficient, Oxford Bulletin of Economics and Statistics 62, 119-122.

Keane M.P. and E.S Prasad (2002), Inequality, transfers and growth: new evidence from the economic transition in Poland, *The Review of Economics and Statistics* 84(2), 324-341.

Khan A.R. and C. Riskin (2001), Inequality and poverty in China in the age of globalization, Oxford University Press.

King M.A. (1983), An index of inequality: with applications to horizontal equity and social mobility, *Econometrica* 51(1), 99-116.

Kopczuk W., J. Slemrod and S. Yitzhaki (2002), Why world distribution fails, NBER Working Paper Series 2002:9186.

Korzeniewicz R.P. and T.P. Moran (2000), Measuring World Income Inequalities, Commentary and Debate, *American Journal of Sociology* 106(1), 209-214.

Kuznets S. (1955), Economic growth and income inequality, *American Economic Review* 45, 1-28.

La Porta R., F. Lopez-de-Silanes, A. Shleifer and R. Vishny (1999), *The Quality of Government,* Oxford: Oxford University Press.

Lee J. (2000), Changes in the source of China's regional inequality, *China Economic Review* 11(3), 232-245.

Lee K., M.H. Pesaran and R. Smith (1997), Growth and convergence in a multi-country empirical stochastic Solow model, *Journal of Applied Econometrics* 12, 357-392.

Lee W. and J.E. Roemer (1999), Inequality and redistribution revisited, *Economics Letters* 65, 339-346.

Lehmann H. and J. Wadsworth (2001), Wage arrears and the distribution of earnings in Russia, IZA Working Paper 2001:410.

Lehman H., Wadsworth J. and A. Aquisti (1999), Crime and punishment: job security and wage arrears in the Russian Federation, *Journal of Comparative Economics* 27, 595-617.

Lerman R.I. and S. Yitzhaki (1985), Income inequality effects by income source: a new approach and applications to the United States, *Review of Economics and Statistics* 67(1), 151-156.

Lerman R.I. and S. Yitzhaki (1989), Improving the accuracy of estimates of Gini coefficients, *Journal of Econometrics* 42(1), 43-47.

Li H., Squire L. and H. Zou (1998), Explaining international and intertemporal variations in income inequality, *Economic Journal* 108(466), 26-43.

Li S. (2001), Changes in poverty profile in China, WIDER Discussion Paper 2001/21, Helsinki: UNU/WIDER.

Liebbrandt M. and I. Woolard (2001), The labour market and household income inequality in South Africa: existing evidence and new panel data, *Journal of International Development* 13, 671-689.

Liebbrandt M., C. Woolard and I. Woolard (2000), The contribution of income components to income inequality in the rural former homelands of South Africa: a decomposable Gini analysis, *Journal of African Economies* 9(1), 79-99.

Lindert P.H. and J.G. Williamson (2001), Does globalization make the World more unequal?, NBER Working Paper 2001:8228.

Lloyd T., O. Morrissey and R. Osei (2001), Problems with pooling in panel data analysis for developing countries: the case of aid and trade relationships, CREDIT Research Paper 2001:14.

Loewy M.B. and D.H. Papell (1996), Are US regional incomes converging? Some further evidence, *Journal of Monetary Economics* 38, 587-598.

LondoNo J.L. and M. Szekely (2000), Persistent poverty and excess inequality: Latin America, 1970-1995, *Journal of Applied Economics* III(1), 93-134.

Lorenz M.O. (1905), Methods of measuring the concentration of wealth, Journal of the American Statistical Association 9, 209-219, reprinted in S. Subramanian (ed) *Measurement of inequality and poverty*, Oxford University Press, pp. 71-80.

Luttmer E.F.P. (2001), Measuring poverty dynamics and inequality in transition economies: disentangling real events from noisy data, The World Bank Policy Research Working Paper 2001:2549.

Maasoumi E. (1996), On mobility, in D. Giles and A. Ullah (eds) *Handbook of Applied Economic Statistics,* Marcel Dekker.

Maasoumi E. (1997), Empirical analysis of inequality and welfare, Chapter 5 in Handbook of Applied Econometrics Volume II: Microeconomics, Pesaran M.H. and P. Schmidt (eds), *Blackwell Handbooks in Economics,* pp.202-245.

Maasoumi E., Diamond C., Nieswiadomy M., and D.J. Slottje (1994), *The effects of relative price changes and cost of living adjustments on some welfare indices, in Measurement of welfare and inequality,* in W. Eichhorn (ed), Springer Verlag.

Maasoumi E. and A. Heshmati (2000), Stochastic dominance amongst Swedish income distributions, *Econometric Reviews* 19(3), 287-320.

Maasoumi E. and A. Heshmati (2003), Evaluating dominance ranking of PSID incomes by various household characteristics, Unpublished manuscript.

Maasoumi E. and J-H. Jeong (1985), The trend and the measurement of world inequality over extended periods of accounting, *Economics Letters* 19, 295-301.

Maddison A. (2001), *The world economy: A millennial perspective, Development Centre Studies,* Paris: OECD.

Mahler V.A. (2001), Economic globalization, domestic politics and income inequality in the developed countries: a cross-national analysis, Luxembourg Income Study Working Paper 273, Luxembourg.

Mankiw N.G., D. Romer and D.H. Weil (1992), A contribution to the empirics of economics growth, *The Quarterly Journal of Economics* 107, 407-438.

Mayshar J. and S. Yitzhaki (1995), Dalton-improving indirect tax-reform, *American Economic Review* 85, 793-807.

Mayshar J. and S. Yitzhaki (1996), Dalton-improving tax reform: When households differ in ability and needs, *Journal of Public Economics* 62, 399-412.

McDonald J.B. and Y.J. Xu (1995), A generalization of the beta distribution with applications, *Journal of Econometrics* 66, 133-152.

McGulloch N., B. Baukh and M. Cherel-Robson (2003), Poverty, inequality and growth in Zambia during the 1990s, In: van der Hoeven R. and A. Shorrocks, Perspectives on Growth and Poverty United Nations University Press.

Mellor J.M. and J. Milyo (2001), Income inequality and health, *Journal of Health Politics, Policy and Law* 26(3), 487- 522.

Milanovic B. (1998), Income, inequality, and poverty during the transition from planned to market economy, Washington, DC: The World Bank.

Milanovic B. (2000), The median-voter hypothesis, income inequality, and income redistribution: an empirical test with the required data, *European Journal of Political Economy* 16, 367-410.

Milanovic B. (2001), World income inequality in the second half of the 20th century, World Bank, Development Research Group.

Milanovic B. (2002a), True world income distribution, 1988 and 1993: First calculation based on household surveys alone, *Economic Journal* 112(476), 51-92.

Milanovic B. (2002b), Can we discern the effect of globalization on income distribution? Evidence from household budget surveys, World Bank Policy Research Paper 2876, Washington DC: World Bank.

Milanovic B. and S. Yitzhaki (2001), Decomposing world income distribution: does the world have a middle class?, WB 2001:2562.

Mills A.M. and S. Zandvakili (1997), Statistical inference via bootstrapping for measures of inequality, *Journal of Applied Econometrics* 12, 133-150.

Mishra P. and A. Parikh (1997), Distributional inequality in Indian states, *Journal of Income Distribution* 7(1), 89-108.

Moffitt R.A. and P. Gottschalk (2002), Trends in the transitory variance of earnings in the United States, *The Economic Journal* 112, March C68-C73.

Mookherjee D. and A. Shorrocks (1982), A decomposition analysis of the trends in UK income inequality, *The Economic Journal* 92(368), 886-902.

Morduch J. and T. Sicular (2002), Rethinking inequality decomposition, with evidence from rural China, *Economic Journal* 112(476), 93-106.

Morrisson C. (2000), Historical perspectives on income distribution: the case of Europe, in Atkinson A.B. and Bourguignon F. (Eds), *Handbook of Income Distribution*, Volume 1, North Holland, chapter 4, pp.217-260.

Nerlove M. (2000), Growth rate convergence, fact or artifact? An essay on panel data econometrics, in J. Krishnakumar and E. Ronchetti, eds., *Panel Data Econometrics: Future Directions*, pp. 3-34, Amsterdam: North Holland.

Ng Y-K. (1996), Happiness survey: Some comparability issues and an explanatory survey based on just perceivable increments, *Social indicator research* 18, 127-xxx.

Noorbakhsh F. (1998), The human development index: some technical issues and alternative indices, Journal of International Development 10, 589-605.

Ogwang T. (2000), A convenient method of computing the Gini index and its standard error, *Oxford Bulletin of Economics and Statistics* 62(1), 123-129.

Ogwang T. and U.L.G. Rao (2000), Hybrid models of the Lorenz curve, *Economics Letters* 69, 39-44.

Ok E.A. and P. Lambert (1999), On evaluating social welfare by sequential generalized Lorenz dominance, *Economics Letters* 63, 45-53.

O'Rourke K.H. (2001), Globalization and inequality: historical trends, NBER Working Paper 8339, Cambridge MA: NBER.

O'Rourke K.H. and J.G. Williamson (2000), Globalization and history: the evolution of a nineteenth-century Atlantic economy, Cambridge MA: MIT Press (see Review Essay by A.G. Frank (2002), *Journal of World-Systems Research* 8(2), 276-290).

Pannenberg M. and J. Schwarze (2000), Wage dynamics and unemployment in Germany: evidence from regional panel data, *Labour* 14(4), 645-665.

Paraje G. (2002), Inequality, welfare and polarisation in the Greater Buenos Aires, 1986-1999. Unpublished manuscript presented at the International Workshop on Income Distribution and Welfare, Bocconi May 30 to June 2, 2002.

Parikh A. (2002), Interregional labour mobility, inequality and wage convergence, Unpublished manuscript.

Park D. (2001), Recent trends in the global distribution of income, *Journal of Policy Modeling* 23, 497-501.

Park A., S. Wang and G. Wu (2002), Regional poverty targeting in China, *Journal of Public Economics* 86, 123-153.

Parker S.C. and S. Gardner (2002), International income mobility, *Economics Letters* 76, 179-187.

Parker S.C. and J. Rougier (2001), Measuring social mobility as unpredictability, *Economica* 68(269), 63-76.

Partridge M.D., D.S. Rickman and W. Levernier (1996), Trends in U.S. income inequality: evidence from a panel of states, *The Quarterly Review of Economics and Finance* 36(1), 17-37.

Pendakur K. (2002), Taking prices seriously in the measurement of inequality, *Journal of Public Economics* 86, 47-69.

Perron P. (1989), The great crash, the oil price shock and the unit root hypothesis, *Econometrica* 57(6), 1361-1401.

Persson T. and G. Tabellini (1994), Is inequality harmful for growth? *American economic Review* 84, 600-621.

Piketty T. and E. Saez (2003), Income inequality in the United States, 1913-1998, *Quarterly Journal of Economics CXVIII*(1), 1-39.

Podder N. and S. Chatterjee (2002), Sharing the national cake in post reform New Zealand: income inequality trends in terms of income sources, *Journal of Public Economics* 86, 1-27.

Pradhan M., D.E. Sahn and S.D. Younger (2003), Decomposing world health inequality, *Journal of Health Economics* 22, 271-293.

Preston S.H. (1975), The changing relation between mortality and level of economic development, *Population Studies* 29, 231-248.

Pyatt G. (1976), On the interpretation and disaggrgation of Gini coefficient, *Economic Journal* 86(342), 243-255.

Quah D. (1993), Galton's fallacy and tests of the convergence hypothesis, *Scandinavian Journal of Economics* 95, 427-443.

Quah D. (1996a), Twin Peaks: growth and convergence in models of distribution dynamics, *The Economic Journal* 106(437), 1045-1055.

Quah D. (1996b), Regional convergence clusters across Europe, *European Economic Review* 40, 951-958.

Quah D. (1996c), Empirics for economic growth and convergence, *European Economic Review* 40, 1353-1375.

Quah D. (1996d), Convergence empirics across economies with (some) capital mobility, *Journal of Economic Growth* 1, 95-124.

Quah D. (1997), Empirics for growth and distribution: stratification, polarisation, and convergence clubs, *Journal of Economic Growth* 2(1), 27-59.

Quah D. (1999), Some dynamics of global inequality and growth, London School of Economics, London School of Economics, mimeo.

Quah D. (2001), Some simple arithmetic on how income inequality and economic growth matter, Paper presented at WIDER conference on Growth and Poverty, 25-26 May 2001, Helsinki.

Quah D. (2002), One third of the world's growth and inequality, LSE, Economics Department, CEPR Discussion Paper 2002:3316.

Ram R. (1995), Economic development and income inequality: An overlooked regression constraint, *Economic Development and Cultural Change* 43(2), 425-434.

Ramos X. (2001), The dynamics of individual male earnings in Great Britain: 1991-1999; Universitat Autonoma de Barcelona, Spain.

Ravallion M. (1997), Good and bad growth: the human development reports, *World Development* 25(5), 631-638.

Ravallion M. (1998), Does aggregation hide the harmful effects of inequality on growth?, *Economics Letters* 61, 73-77.

Ravallion M. (2001), Growth, inequality and poverty: looking beyond averages, *World Development 29*(11), 1803-1815.

Ravallion M. (2003a), The debate on globalization, poverty and inequality: why measurement matters, *International Affairs* 79(4): 739-53.

Ravallion M. (2003b), Inequality convergence, *Economics Letters* 80, 351-356.

Ravallion M. and S. Chen (1999), When economic reform is faster than statistical reform: measuring and explaining income inequality in Rural China, *Oxford Bulletin of Economics and Statistics* 61, 33-56.

Ravallion M. and S. Chen (2003), Measuring pro-poor growth, *Economics Letters* 78, 93-99.

Ravallion M. and G. Datt (2000), When is growth pro-poor? Evidence from the diverse experience of Indian states, World Bank Policy Research, WP 2263

Ravallion M., G. Datt and van der Walle (1991), Quantifying absolute poverty in the developing world, *Review of Income and Wealth* 37(4), 345-361.

Riphahn R.T. (2001), Rational poverty of poor rationality? The take-up of social assistance benefits, *Review of Income and Wealth* 47(3), 379-398.

Ritakallio V-M. (2001), Trends of poverty and income inequality in cross-national comparison, Luxembourg Income Study Working Paper No. 272.

Rodriguez-Andres A. (2003), *Suicide rates in European countries: An empirical investigation,* University of Southern Denmark, Unpublished.

Ryu H.K. and D.J. Slottje (1996), Two flexible functional form approaches for approximating the Lorenz curve, *Journal of Econometrics* 72, 251-274.

Ryu H.K. and D.J. Slottje (1999), Parametric approximation of the Lorenz Curve, in S. Silber and A. Sen (eds), Handbook of Income Distribution, Chapter 10, 291-314, Kluwer Academic Press.

Sacks J. and A. Warner (1995), Economic reform and the process of global integration, Brookings Papers on Economic Activity 1:95.

Sahn D.E. and D.C. Stifel (2000), Poverty comparisons over time and across countries in Africa, *World Development* 28(12), 2123-2155.

Sahn D.E. and D.C. Stifel (2003), Progress towards the MDG in Africa, *World Development* 31(1), 23-52.

Sala-i-Martin X. (2002a), The disturbing "Rise" of global income inequality, NBER Working Paper Series 8904.

Sala-i-Martin X. (2002b), The world distribution of income (estimated from individual country distribution), NBER Working Paper 8933.

Salas R. (1998), Welfare-consistent inequality indices in changing populations: the marginal population replication axiom: a note, *Journal of Public Economics* 67, 145-150.

Sarabia J.M, Castillo E. and D.J. Slottje (1999), An ordered family of Lorenz curves, *Journal of Econometrics* 91, 43-60.

Schechtman E. and S. Yitzhaki (1999), On the proper bounds of the Gini correlation, *Economics Letters* 63, 133-138.

Schluter C. and M. Trede (2002), Statistical inference for inequality and poverty measurement with dependent data, *International Economic Review* 43(2), 493-508.

Schmidt A. (2002), Statistical measurement of income polarisation: a cross-national comparison, Paper presented at the Berlin 10th International conference on panel data.

Schultz T.P. (1998), Inequality in distribution of personal income in the world: how is it changing and why?, *Journal of Population Economics* 11(3), 307-344.

Seligon M. and J. Passe-Smith (2003), Eds, Development and Underdevelopment: The Political Economy of Global Inequality, 3rd edition, Boulder, CO: Lynne Reinner Publishers.

Shi L. (2001), Changes in poverty profile in China, WIDER Discussion Paper 2001/21, Helsinki: UNU/WIDER.

Shorrocks A.F. (1978a), The measurement of mobility, *Econometrica* 46(5), 1013-1024.

Shorrocks A.F. (1978b), Income inequality and income mobility, *Journal of Economic Theory* XIX, 376-393

Shorrocks A.F. (1980), The class of additively decomposable inequality, *Econometrica* 48(3), 613-625.

Shorrocks A.F. (1982), Inequality decomposition by factor components, *Econometrica* 50(1), 193-211.

Shorrocks A.F. (1983), The impact of income components on the distribution of family incomes, *Quarterly Journal of Economics* 98(2), 311-326.

Shorrocks (1984), Inequality decomposition by population subgroups, *Econometrica* 52(6), 1369-1385.

Shorrocks A. and S. Kolenikov (2001), Poverty trends in Russia during the transition, Unpublished manuscript.

Shorrocks A. and R. van der Hoeven (2005), Eds., Growth, inequality, and poverty: Prospects for pro-poor economic development, Oxford University Press.

Shorrocks A. and G. Wan (2004), Spatial decomposition of inequality, Unpublished manuscript.

Sibley C.W. and P.P. Walsh (2002), Earnings inequality and transition: a regional analysis of Poland, IZA Discussion Paper No. 2002:441.

Silber J. (1999), Eds, Handbook of Inequality Measurement, Kluwer Academic Publishers.

Singh S.K. and G.S. Maddala (1976), A function for size distribution of incomes, *Econometrica* 44(5), 963-970.

Solimano A. (2001), The evolution of world income inequality: assessing the impact of globalization, Unpublished manuscript, ECLAC, CEPAL – Serie Macroeconomica del desarrollo No. 11, Santiago, Chile.

Stiglitz J.E. (1998), More instruments and broader goals: moving towards the Post-Washington consensus, WIDER Annual Lecture 2, Helsinki: UNU/WIDER.

Stiglitz J.E. and A. Weiss (1981), Credit rationing in markets with imperfect information, *American Economic Review* 71(3), 393-410.

Subramanian S. (1997a), (ed.), Measurement of inequality and poverty, Readers in Economics, Oxford University Press.

Subramanian S. (1997b), Introduction: the measurement of inequality and poverty, in S. Subramanian (ed), *Measurement of inequality and poverty, Readers in Economics,* Oxford University Press, pp. 1-53.

Summers R. and A. Heston (1991), The Penn World Table (Mark 5): an expanded set of international comparisons, 1950-1988, *Quarterly Journal of Economics* 106, 327-368.

Svedbery P. (2002), Income distribution across countries: how is it measured and what do the results show?, IIES Seminar Papers, SWoPEc 2002:698.

Sylwester K. (2000), Income inequality, education expenditures, and growth, *Journal of Development Economics* 63, 379-398.

Tsui K-Y. (1993), Decomposition of China's regional inequalities, *Journal of Comparative Economics 17*(3), 600-627.

Tsui K-Y. and Y. Wang (1998), Polarisation ordering and new classes of polarisation indices, memo, The Chinese University of Hong Kong.

UNDP (2003), Human Development Report 2003, United Nations Development Program.

Van de gaer D. Funnell N. and T. McCarthy (1999), Statistical inference for two measures of inequality when incomes are correlated, Economics Letters 64, 295-300.

Van der Hoeven R. and A. Shorrocks (2003), Eds., Perspectives on growth and poverty, United Nationa University Press, Tokyo, Japan.

Van Doorslaer E., A. Wagstaff, H. Bleichrodt, S. Calonge, U-G. Gerdtham, M. Gerfin, J. Geurts, L. Gross, U. Häkkinen, R.E. Leu, O. O'Donnell, C. Propper, F. Puffer, M. Rodriquez, G. Sundberg and O. Winkelhake (1997), Income-related inequalities in health: some international comparisons, *Journal of Health Economics* 16, 93-112.

van Praag B. and A. Ferrer-i-Carbonell (2004), *Happiness Quantified: A Satisfaction Calculus Approach,* Oxford University Press.

Wade R.H. (2001a), The rising inequality of world income distribution, *Finance and Development* 38(4), December.

Wade R.H. (2001b), Global inequality: Winners and losers, *The Economist,* April 28.

Wan G.H. (2001), Changes in regional inequality in rural china: decomposing the Gini index of income sources, *The Australian Journal of Agricultural and Resource Economics* 45(3), 361-381.

Wan G.H. (2002a), Regression-based inequality decomposition: Pitfalls and a solution procedure, WIDER Discussion Paper 2002/101, Helsinki: UNU/WIDER.

Wan G.H. (2002b), Income inequality and growth in transition economies: are nonlinear models needed?, WIDER Discussion Paper 2002/104, Helsinki: UNU/WIDER.

Warr P. (2001), Poverty in Thailand: a regional perspective, including comments by S. Jayasuriya, *Regional Development Dialogue* 22(2), 142-159.

Whiteford A. and D. van Seventer (2000), South Africa's changing income distribution in the 1990s, *Studies in Economics and Econometrics* 24(3), 7-30.

Wilkinson R.G. (2005). The Impact of Inequality: how to make sick societies healthier. New Press, N.Y.; and Routledge, London.

Williamson J.G. (1996), Globalization and inequality then and now: the late 19th and 20th centuries, NBER Paper 5491, Cambridge MA: NBER.

Williamson J.G. (2002), Winners and losers over two centuries of globalization, WIDER Annual Lecture 6, Helsinki: UNU/WIDER.

Winkelmann L. and R. Winkelmann (1998), Why are the unemployed so unhappy? Evidence from panel data, *Economica* 65, 1-15.

Wolfson M.C. (1994), Conceptual issues in normative measurement: when inequalities diverge, *American Economic Review* 84(2), 353-358.

Wood A. (1997), Openness and wage inequality in developing countries: the Latin American challenge to East Asian continental wisdom, *World Bank Economic Review* 11(1), 33-57.

Wood A. and C. Ridao-Cano (1999), Skill, trade, and international inequality, *Oxford Economic Papers* 51, 89-119.

Xu K. (2000), Inference for generalized Gini indices using iterated-bootstrap method, *Journal of Business and Economic Statistics* 18, 223-227.

Xu L.C. and H-F. Zou (2000), Explaining the changes of income distribution in China, *China Economic Review* 11, 149-170.

Yemtsov R. (2002), Quo Vadis: inequality and poverty dynamics across Russian regions in 1992-2000, Paper prepared for WIDER project meeting Microsimulation of Tax Benefit Reform in Russia, 2-3 August 2002, Helsinki.

Yitzhaki S. (1983), On an extension of the Gini inequality index, *International Economic Review* 24(3), 617-628.

Yitzhaki S. (1991), Calculating Jackknife variance estimator for parameters of the Gini method, *Journal of Business and Economic Statistics* 9, 235-239.

Yitzhaki S. (1994), Economic distance and overlapping of distributions, *Journal of Econometrics* 61(1), 147-159.

Yitzhaki S. (2002), Do we need a separate poverty measurement?, *European Journal of Political Economy* 18, 61-85.

You I. (1998), Income distribution and growth in East Asia, *Journal of Development Studies* 34(6), 37-65.

Zandvakili S. (1999), Income inequality among female heads of households: racial inequality reconsidered, *Economica* 66, 119-133.

Zandvakili S. (2000), Dynamics of earnings inequality among female-headed households in the United States, *Journal of Socio-Economics* 29, 73-89.

Zandvakili S. (2002), Trends in earnings inequality among young adults, *Review of Social Economy* 60(1), 93-107.

Zandvakili S. and J.A. Mills (2001), The distributional implications of tax and transfer programs in US, *The Quarterly Review of Economics and Finance* 41, 167-181.

Zhang X. and R. Kanbur (2001), What difference do polarisation measures make? An application to China, *Journal of Development Studies* 37(3), 85-98.

Zhang Z., A. Liu and S. Yao (2001), Convergence of China's regional incomes, 1952-1997, *China Economic Review* 12(2/3), 243-258.

Zheng B. and B.J. Cushing (2001), Statistical inference for testing inequality indices with dependent samples, *Journal of Econometrics* 101, 315-335.

Zitikis R. and J.L. Gastwirth (2002), The asymptotic distribution of the S-Gini index, *Australian & New Zealand Journal of Statistics* 44, 439-446.

INDEX

F

I

T